International Criminal Evidence Law

Studies in International Criminal Law

VOLUME 8

The titles published in this series are listed at *brill.com/sicl*

International Criminal Evidence Law

Legal Traditions in Conflict: Common and Continental Law at the ICC

By

Demetra Sorvatzioti

BRILL | NIJHOFF

LEIDEN | BOSTON

Some parts of the book have been published in Sorvatzioti, Demetra Fr. “Free Evaluation of Evidence: Does the ICC Need a Law of Evidence?” *International Criminal Law Review* 22, nos. 5–6 (2021): 895–919 and Sorvatzioti, Demetra Fr. “Proportionality and Moral Blameworthiness in Ongwen’s ICC Sentencing Decision.” *International Criminal Law Review* 23, nos. 5–6 (2023): 755–781.

Cover illustration: Untitled watercolour, 2011, Edward Matwijkiw (1937–2012), reproduced with kind permission of the family.

Library of Congress Cataloging-in-Publication Data

Names: Sorvatzioti, Demetra Fr. author
Title: International criminal evidence law : legal traditions in conflict : common and continental law at the ICC / by Demetra Sorvatzioti.
Description: Leiden ; Boston : Brill Academic Publishers, Inc, 2026. | Series: Studies in International Criminal Law ; volume 8 | Includes bibliographical references and index.
Identifiers: LCCN 2025037929 | ISBN 9789004741003 hardback | ISBN 9789004741010 epub
Subjects: LCSH: Evidence, Criminal (International law) | International Criminal Court | LCGFT: Law materials
Classification: LCC KZ7422 .S67 2026 | DDC 345/.06--dc23/eng/20250814
LC record available at https://lccn.loc.gov/2025037929

Typeface for the Latin, Greek, and Cyrillic scripts: “Brill”. See and download: brill.com/brill-typeface.

ISSN 2666-903X
ISBN 978-90-04-74100-3 (hardback)
ISBN 978-90-04-74101-0 (e-book)
DOI 10.1163/9789004741010

This book is printed on acid-free paper and produced in a sustainable manner.

Only the dead will know the end of the War

PLATO

Contents

CHAPTER 1

Introduction

1 Decoding the Project

1.1 *Overview*

This book delves into the impact of continental and common law traditions and their dynamic interplay within the International Criminal Court's (ICC) framework. It focuses specifically on evidence law rather than rules and procedures, a crucial distinction to make. While evidence rules govern the admissibility of evidence at trial, they do not constitute evidence law themselves. Evidence law is derived from the aggregation of principles and rules. It is created and evolved through case law. Ultimately, it safeguards the right to a fair trial, encompassing the prosecutorial burden of proof and ensuring the presumption of innocence.

1.2 *The Legal Framework of the ICC Is Hybrid*

By incorporating features from both common law and continental legal traditions, the ICC attempts to create an amalgam. Three features coexist at trial: the free evaluation of evidence, the court's truth-seeking mandate, and the prosecutorial burden of proof. However, the coexistence of the prosecutorial burden of proof beyond a reasonable doubt with the free evaluation of evidence (*l'intime conviction*) creates a disjunction rather than a seamless amalgam. The definition of the free evaluation of evidence is clear in the German delegation's proposal made on August 23, 1996, during the negotiations for the Rome Statute at the United Nations Diplomatic Conference of Plenipotentiaries (held in Rome from June 15 to July 17, 1998). The principle of free evaluation means that the court is neither bound by evidence submitted by the prosecution and the defence nor by a guilty plea or evidence rules. The decisive element for a decision is the conviction of the court.

While both free evaluation and prosecutorial burden have a role in the ICC trial, when trying to coexist simultaneously, free evaluation tends to overlook the necessary evidence assessment against the prosecutorial burden. This suggests a flaw not in the legal framework itself but in its application. The preparatory discussions, detailed later in the book, support this view.

While the legal framework may seem unchangeable, it is proposed to focus on improving the understanding and application of the common law and continental elements to secure a fair trial. This approach aims to bridge the gap

 | DOI:10.1163/9789004741010_002

created by the differing legal traditions and ensure a more cohesive judicial process within the ICC.

Chapter 2 delves into the evolution of legal traditions. The classic continental system's approach to advancing *l'intime conviction* and precluding a prosecutorial burden of proof is deeply rooted in the 1808 Napoleonic Code of Criminal Procedure and has remained essentially unchanged. In contrast, with its exclusionary rules, the common law system developed a principled evidence law that addresses complex evidence issues. This evolution places significant emphasis on the prosecutorial burden of proof, the presumption of innocence, and the principles of a fair trial.

The interpretation of the ICC's evidence rules revolves around two significant elements: the free evaluation of evidence, which allows judges to assess the credibility and reliability of evidence based on their judgment; and the prosecutorial burden of proof beyond a reasonable doubt. Both elements are intertwined with the judges' mandate to seek the truth. However, these elements are often in fierce conflict during ICC trials. When applied by judges from a classic continental background, the truth-seeking mandate tends to overshadow the prosecutorial burden. Consequently, when the evaluation of evidence for admissibility and weight is conducted in a truth-seeking manner for atrocities, it often feels like navigating a primitive boat in windy, open seas. This will become clear in the case analyses that follow. Nonetheless, confidence remains a virtue, and continental judges seem assured they are doing the right thing, as they have successfully done for years. This confidence is quite reasonable, given their extensive experience.

For research purposes, I analyse three cases that have attracted significant criticism and academic interest: the ICC decisions in the *Bemba*, *Gbagbo and Blé Goudé*, and *Ongwen* cases. These cases include nearly as many separate decisions as there are judges on the panels. As the analysis will demonstrate, there is a distinct divergence between judicial reasoning rooted in the classic continental tradition versus common law, leading to antithetical decisions on the same issues.

The analysis maintains a neutral stance, refraining from passing judgment on the correctness of the final decisions or the guilt of the accused. It focuses solely on the evidence problems of the cases, ensuring an impartial and objective analysis. The underlying context of all three situations is atrocities resulting in countless victims, usually committed by both sides of the conflicting parties. At times, the ICC prosecutor has focused on one side of the disaster, influenced by political history, which falls outside the scope of this book.

The analysis includes brief historical-political backgrounds explaining the events leading to the ICC arrest warrants. However, in the case of *Ongwen*, a more extensive analysis of the Acholi people's history, to which Dominic Ongwen belongs, is provided. This context is crucial for understanding the affirmative defences raised, the expert evidence examined, and the sentencing decision. This is the only case where the sentencing trial is reviewed, as the other cases resulted in acquittals.

Each of the three cases highlights evidence problems, some recurring. The different judicial opinions reveal the legal traditions familiar to the judges. Consequently, the Court's majority analysis at times reflects a continental approach to evidence evaluation, while at other times it reflects a common law approach. When unanimity is achieved, the influence of a particular tradition becomes clear again. Nevertheless, the Court has attracted criticism whenever the judges' views are diametrically antithetical. This is discussed in detail in the last chapter, in light of the *Independent Expert Review of the International Criminal Court and the Rome Statute System* in 2020. The research is comprehensive, covering a wide range of evidence issues and judicial opinions to provide a thorough understanding of the challenges the ICC faces.

I concentrate on one particular legal adversarial system to address evidence law issues: the Canadian system. The choice of an adversarial, rather than an inquisitorial, system is due to the fact that the Rome Statute provides for an adversarial trial. My familiarity with the Canadian system and extensive study of Canadian case law informs this choice. Over the years, I have observed that its principled approach allows jurisprudence to evolve despite persistent evidence problems, resulting in a refined judicial reasoning process. This does not imply that other common law jurisdictions have not yet achieved similar advancements. However, my comparative research in U.K. and U.S. case law leads me to prioritize the Canadian approach. Canadian evidence law is particularly adept at navigating complex evidence issues due to its principled and evolving nature, as will be evident in Chapters 3, 4, and 5.

One fundamental aspect of Canadian evidence law is its emphasis on balancing the rights of the accused with the need for effective prosecution. This balance is maintained through rigorous adherence to the principles of fairness, relevance, and reliability. For example, Canadian courts have developed a nuanced approach to circumstantial evidence, ensuring that such evidence is meticulously scrutinized to prevent wrongful convictions. This meticulousness can be highly relevant to the ICC, where evidence is often circumstantial and derived from conflict zones.

More importantly, Canadian jurisprudence provides clarity through a structured path for judicial thinking. Canadian principled evidence law does not reflect a mere practical application of evidence rules but a robust thought process resulting from experience, evolution, and respect for fair trial rights. This approach can serve as an intellectual paradigm for the ICC.

Throughout the entire research and analysis, Canadian evidence law emerges in every chapter to demonstrate its evolved functional nature. Canadian law provides clear guidelines on a principled approach to the admissibility of evidence, which can help the ICC establish a more consistent approach to admissibility issues. Canadian courts, for example, employ a principled approach to hearsay, allowing it under specific, justified circumstances. The ICC can refine its hearsay admissibility process to enhance the reliability of evidence without compromising fairness. Furthermore, the stringent scrutiny of expert evidence in Canadian courts ensures that only reliable, relevant expert testimony is admitted – a practice that can benefit the ICC, where expert evidence plays a crucial role in complex cases.

However, as explained in Chapter 2, I neither advocate for legal transplants for the ICC nor argue that one legal tradition should dominate the other or that the two traditions should remain in perpetual conflict. Instead, I contend that the long-standing stereotypical legal misunderstandings from one side of the Atlantic about the other are outdated and no longer relevant. Legal systems in modern legal civilization have undergone substantial evolution for good reasons. Contemporary evidence law has significantly progressed to ensure greater fairness and justice. Stereotypes narrow perspectives and hinder the evolution of legal understanding. They act as blinders, limiting our perspective to a single direction. Just as blinders prevent a horse from seeing anything except what is directly in front of it, legal stereotypes narrow our perception, causing us to see only a limited and often incorrect view of legal traditions with which we are unfamiliar.

This project advocates for a bespoke evidence law tailored explicitly to address the evidence problems of the Rome Statute's crimes and provide consistency. Such a customized approach will undoubtedly enhance the Court's effectiveness and fairness, providing a solid foundation for the future of international criminal evidence law.

1.3 *Brief Legal Background*

Chapter 2 discusses in detail the ICC's legal framework and the two incorporated legal traditions to help readers understand the analysis that will follow. The ICC was established to prosecute individuals for the most serious offences of international concern, such as genocide, war crimes, crimes against humanity, and the crime of aggression. Its hybrid legal framework, including its rules of evidence and procedure, was designed to accommodate the common law and continental law systems.

In a nutshell, common law systems rely heavily on case law and precedents. They have detailed rules of evidence and have developed a distinct path of law known as evidence law. The prosecution's burden of proof is to establish guilt beyond a reasonable doubt. The adversarial system involves active roles for defence and prosecution, with judges acting as neutral arbitrators. Conversely, continental law systems are based on legal codes without evidence rules or laws. Judges in these systems play an active role in investigating the facts of the case to find the truth. The principle of free evaluation of evidence (*l'intime conviction*) allows judges to freely evaluate evidence according to their conscience without a formal burden of proof on the prosecution.

Understanding these foundational differences (Chapter 2) sets the stage for examining the problems that arise from trying to merge these two distinct legal traditions within the ICC trial.

1.4 *Problemata*

The ICC's attempts to merge the two distinct legal traditions of continental and common law have led to significant challenges. As demonstrated, the common law prosecutorial burden of proof beyond a reasonable doubt is the antithesis of the continental principle of *l'intime conviction*, where judges can independently evaluate the evidence without a formal burden on the prosecution. The philosophy of the principle of free evaluation does not recognize barriers such as the burden of proof, considering judicial freedom paramount to facilitate the investigation of truth. Conflict often arises in ICC trials where these two elements need to coexist because they are fundamentally incompatible. The result is the inconsistent and sometimes contradictory application of the prosecutorial burden of proof when evaluating evidence for weight reasons. The ICC's reliance on a hybrid system often seems to produce confusion among judges, who may have different understandings and interpretations of evidence rules based on their legal backgrounds.

To address these problems, beyond explaining and understanding where and how the two elements work in an adversarial ICC trial, there is a compelling argument for the ICC to develop its evidence law designed to fit the unique context of international criminal evidence. The ICC's evidence law should be derived from something other than theoretical discourse; it should be the outcome of its case law which will resolve evidence problems in a principled approach. Clear and consistent application of evidence law for the admissibility of evidence and weight evaluation is essential. Ensuring ICC judges are trained to recognize and mutually understand evidence problems and solutions can provide consistency across cases. By drawing on evolved evidence law paradigms, the ICC can create a robust and fair evidence law within its framework.

1.5 *Methodological Framework*

1.5.1 How the Methodological Framework (Doctrinal, Comparative, Case Law) Works in Practice

The methodological framework combines doctrinal analysis, comparative analysis, and case law examination to comprehensively understand evidence law at the ICC.

Doctrinal analysis thoroughly examines the legal texts governing evidence at the ICC, such as the Rome Statute, the Rules of Procedure and Evidence, and relevant ICC case law. This method helps clarify the legal standards and evidence rules governing ICC trials by identifying and interpreting foundational principles.

The comparative legal analysis method is structured around two primary pillars. First, it contrasts the legal reasoning and practices of common law and civil law systems. Second, it compares them with a specific jurisdiction like Canada, highlighting differences and similarities that can inform improvements in the ICC's evidence law.

The ICC case law analysis focuses on three landmark cases: *Bemba*, *Gbagbo and Blé Goudé*, and *Ongwen*. It examines trial, appeal, and interlocutory decisions to identify critical issues related to the burden of proof, evidence admissibility, and evaluation of evidence. This analysis reveals how theoretical principles are applied in practice by scrutinizing judicial decisions. It further explores whether judges' reasoning reflects a continental or common law approach and assesses its impact on the fairness of proceedings.

1.5.2 The Relationship Between Theoretical Analysis and ICC Decisions

The theoretical analysis provides the foundational understanding of legal principles and evidence rules, essential for identifying potential issues conflicting with fair trial rights. On the other hand, the ICC case study demonstrates how the principles and rules are implemented in real-world scenarios. By examining these cases, the research can identify inconsistencies, challenges, and areas for improvement in the ICC's application of evidence rules.

For example, theoretical analysis might highlight that evidence must be relevant and reliable. Case study analysis then examines specific instances where ICC judges applied or misapplied this principle, leading to fair or unfair outcomes. This interplay between theory and practice allows for a more nuanced understanding of how evidence law operates at the ICC and provides a basis for understanding the need for principled evidence law.

The forthcoming analysis reviews principles of admissibility and examines evidence evaluation within the context of the prosecutorial burden of proof and the presumption of innocence. It delves into specific evidence issues, such as circumstantial evidence, similar facts evidence, and hearsay, to identify the roots of antithetical judicial reasoning. It further examines how similar evidence problems have been addressed through the Canadian principled approach.

The findings from the doctrinal, comparative, and case law analyses are thoroughly discussed and synthesized. The final chapter addresses the outcomes, which are more positive than negative. By identifying the areas of misunderstanding, the ICC is suggested to gradually develop and refine its evidence law to ensure the effective and consistent application of its evidence rules. This proactive approach will help harmonize the divergent legal traditions and enhance the overall efficacy of the ICC's judicial processes.

2 Critical Case Studies: *Bemba*, *Gbagbo and Blé Goudé*, and *Ongwen*

Each case is examined in a separate chapter, beginning with a brief historical and political background. The chapters then present the decisions where evidence problems have led the Court to conflicting rulings or opinions. Due to the nature of these evidence issues, each chapter's structure varies, following each case's unique progression, which enhances readability. When an evidence problem reappears in a case, the related decisions are traced and analysed across different stages (pre-trial, trial, and appeal).

The focus is on how judicial reasoning is formed and whether it demonstrates familiarity with applying the prosecutorial burden of proof or the free evaluation of evidence. This familiarity is disclosed through the judges' legal arguments and whether they exhibit confusion or vagueness regarding admissibility rulings and evidence evaluation. Extensive experience with the free evaluation of evidence in civil law systems often fails to identify evidence problems that common law has addressed and resolved. This will become apparent in the subsequent chapters. The example of Canadian evidence law is illustrated through its case law, integrated into each case analysis to provide clarity and demonstrate a robust judicial thinking process.

The first case, *The Prosecutor v. Jean-Pierre Bemba Gombo* (ICC-01/05-01/08), is examined in Chapter 3. Bemba was the President and Commander-in-Chief of the Movement for the Liberation of Congo (MLC) at the time of the warrant. He was arrested in Europe in 2008. He was charged with crimes against humanity and war crimes allegedly committed between 2002 and

2003 in the Central African Republic (CAR). Although the Trial Court found him guilty, the Appeal Court acquitted him. The trial decisions highlight significant disputes over evidence admissibility and the evaluation of evidence weight with respect to the prosecutorial burden of proof. Key issues included the admissibility of hearsay evidence, the weight given to witness testimonies, and the assessment of circumstantial evidence. The Prosecution faced challenges in proving Bemba's direct command responsibility for crimes committed by his troops. The judges' varying backgrounds influenced their assessment of the evidence. Before his acquittal, Bemba spent ten years in prison.

The second case, discussed in Chapter 4, is *The Prosecutor v. Laurent Gbagbo and Charles Blé Goudé* (ICC-02/11-01/15). The warrant for arrest was issued in 2011. Gbagbo is the former President of Côte d'Ivoire who faced charges of crimes against humanity committed during a post-election civil war in 2010–2011. Gbagbo's trial involved complex evidentiary issues, including evaluating witness testimonies and documentary evidence. The case highlights the role of massive circumstantial evidence that failed to prove Gbagbo's criminal responsibility beyond a reasonable doubt. The Prosecution argued for a holistic evaluation of the case's "system of evidence". The Court decided there was no case to answer (2019), and both accused were acquitted. The Appeals Court affirmed the trial decision. Gbagbo was in prison for almost seven years and Blé Goudé for five.

The third case, discussed in Chapter 5, is *The Prosecutor v. Dominic Ongwen* (ICC-02/04-01/15). This is the only case among the three where the accused was convicted unanimously, and the Appeals Court upheld the decision. Ongwen, a former child soldier and later a commander in the Lord's Resistance Army (LRA), was prosecuted for war crimes and crimes against humanity in Uganda. Ongwen's background, including his early abduction and forced conscription into the LRA, added layers of complexity to the case. Ongwen's defence raised affirmative defences of duress and mental incapacity, which the Court addressed for the first time since its inception and rejected. The discussion of the burden and the standard of proof was crucial during the trial stage. However, Ongwen's social background was essential in his sentencing trial. The Defence requested the Court to consider the duress and mental incapacity defences for sentencing purposes, but the Court rejected this request, while issues with the burden of proof reappeared. Cultural disputes regarding a Westernised view of expert evidence evaluation emerged in the decision. Although some suggested a life sentence, Ongwen was sentenced to thirty years.

All three cases discuss and expose the deep-seated misconceptions within the continental tradition concerning standards of proof, evidence admissibility, and evidence weight assessment. Each case reveals a troubling reliance on the myths of professional continental judges' infallibility and the rigid technicality of common law rules. These myths have ossified into crippling stereotypes. The stark, often antagonistic language of judges expressing their antithetical views on evidence admissibility and evaluation is overstriking. Equally revealing are the probing questions about the burden of proof posed by the parties and the Court's responses. The judges' inherent antagonism and blatant misinterpretation of each other's principles creates a palpable tension. The overpowering influence of the judges' entrenched legal traditions on their reasoning is glaringly evident.

3 Assessing the Boundaries and Impact of This Research: Limitations and Significance

3.1 *Complexity of Comparative Legal Analysis*

Comparing evidence law across different legal traditions, such as common law and continental law, involves navigating differing legal cultures, terminologies, and procedural nuances. Procedural nuances refer to the subtle, often complex differences and specific details in the procedures followed by different legal systems. These nuances can include variations in how evidence is gathered, presented, and evaluated; the roles and responsibilities of judges, lawyers, and juries; and the specific steps and rules that govern legal proceedings. Understanding these procedural nuances is crucial for accurately comparing and contrasting different legal traditions.

This inherent complexity can make the analysis challenging for readers who are not well-versed in comparative law. Such comparisons require careful consideration of each system's unique characteristics and historical development. However, I have endeavoured to present each tradition's elements within the Rome Statute framework, making it easier for the reader to understand its functionality and identify where the problems lie in the ICC trial. By highlighting the distinct features and procedural nuances of common law and continental law systems, I aim to locate areas of misunderstanding and their roots to help towards the development of ICC evidence law.

3.2 *Case-Specific Focus and Generalizability*

The book focuses on specific ICC cases (*Bemba, Gbagbo and Blé Goudé, Ongwen*), providing an in-depth analysis of their decisions in evidence matters. However, this focus may limit the generalizability of the conclusions to other cases or contexts within international criminal law. While these cases offer valuable insights into evidence problems, the findings may not apply to future ICC cases, but I hope they will to validate this research.

3.3 *Mitigating Bias*

To reduce the perception of bias and ensure a balanced perspective, this book addresses all the decisions issued either in favour of or against one legal tradition. The analysis examines specific evidence issues and demonstrates how the two traditions, as reflected in the judges' antithetical decisions, address them. Since the prosecutorial burden of proof beyond a reasonable doubt is the standard against which evidence should be measured, I identify which decisions discuss this burden and how it affects evidence evaluation. The discussions in the chapters on the three cases include the most crucial issues at trial, relevant academic literature, and case law. This approach aims to provide a comprehensive and objective analysis, acknowledging the strengths and limitations of each legal tradition.

3.4 *Evolution of ICC Case Law*

International criminal law is continuously evolving, incorporating new case law and addressing emerging evidence challenges, such as digital evidence. Consequently, the analysis presented here may need updating. However, its primary role serves as a stepping stone for the ICC's development. I hope the findings and recommendations of this research and analysis will eventually become outdated due to the development of a comprehensive ICC evidence law. I offer this with aspiration, rather than egotism, that this work contributes to the ICC's progress.

3.5 *Subjectivity in Judicial Thinking*

Critiquing the continental system's reliance on *l'intime conviction* versus the common law's evidence law underscores significant differences in evidence evaluation methodologies. However, judicial cognitive processes are inherently subjective and can exhibit substantial variation even within the same legal tradition, complicating the analysis. Acknowledging this subjectivity is essential for accurately assessing the findings' applicability and mitigating the risk of overgeneralization.

3.6 *Practical Implementation Challenges*

Advocating for the ICC to develop its evidence law inspired by evolved, principled evidence law systems and existing paradigms is theoretically sound. However, practical implementation within the ICC's unique framework and constraints presents substantial challenges. The practicalities of creating and enforcing a unified evidence law at the ICC must be meticulously addressed. This includes managing the massive volume of evidence following atrocities, evaluating different types of evidence, and assessing their respective frailties for relevance, necessity, and reliability. Since the first ICC case's evidence until today, we already know where the problems are. Addressing these issues now will help ensure effective prosecutions in the future.

3.7 *Significance of the Research*

This project aims to enhance mutual understanding of the two legal traditions under the Rome Statute (common law and continental law) to stimulate legal dialogue towards evolution within the ICC. Given the ICC's pivotal role in international criminal justice, understanding how national traditions can be unified under a collective norm is essential, particularly in developing a cohesive approach to evidence law.

From a practical perspective, this book could benefit the ICC directly in prosecuting atrocities and ensuring fairness and consistency within its trials regarding evidence issues. It is crucial to recognize that when the ICC administers justice, its decisions should reflect transparent, concise, and precise reasoning accessible to the public. Enhancing trust in the ICC will strengthen its universally demanding role. While procedural fairness is fundamental, it alone cannot ensure the right to a fair trial. Fair trial rights must be practical and effective, not merely theoretical. Thus, the need for the ICC to develop a tailored evidence law is manifest.

The significance of this research lies in its potential to contribute to the understanding and application of evidence law within the ICC. By critically analysing the differences between common law and continental law traditions and identifying misunderstandings and misconceptions, this book highlights the necessity for the ICC to establish its own distinct evidence law framework. It aims to advocate for a paradigm shift transcending traditional legal boundaries to enhance the fairness and effectiveness of the ICC's trials. Additionally, the findings might inform other international criminal tribunals and national jurisdictions, promoting a more unified approach to complex evidence issues. Ultimately, this could potentially influence future policy and judicial practice, ensuring more effective and just prosecutions of atrocities.

4 Findings and Proposals

The ICC faces profound challenges in evidence law because it does not adjudicate ordinary crimes but large-scale atrocities. National legal systems, whether common law or civil law, are fundamentally designed to prosecute individual crimes. These trials revolve around discrete acts committed by identifiable offenders relying on documentary, testimonial, and forensic evidence to establish guilt.

In contrast, the ICC adjudicates systemic, large-scale crimes that often occur within hierarchical command structures or bureaucratic networks. Unlike domestic trials, where direct evidence typically may link a defendant to a specific criminal act, international crimes necessitate proof of responsibility within a collective system. This presents three primary evidentiary difficulties:

- Absence of direct evidence: ICC trials seldom yield a singular, conclusive piece of proof ("smoking gun") that connects an accused individual to the crime. Instead, liability is inferred through patterns of conduct, organizational structures, and extensive circumstantial evidence.
- Proving intent (*mens rea*): Perpetrators of mass atrocities rarely give explicit orders to commit crimes. Instead, they operate through policy decisions, indirect actions, encouragement, or passive acquiescence.
- Complexity of causation: Unlike domestic trials, where causation is relatively straightforward, international crimes involve layers of command responsibility and systemic coordination, requiring a different approach to evidentiary analysis.

Hannah Arendt's *Eichmann in Jerusalem* underscores the problem of bureaucratic criminality, which affects evidentiary reasoning in international trials. Arendt observed that modern mass atrocities are rarely committed by sadistic criminals acting alone but by bureaucratic functionaries working within state structures. The ICC encounters similar challenges in establishing command responsibility, especially when defendants claim they were merely part of a larger system and did not directly commit crimes.

4.1 *Complementarity and the Case for a Bespoke ICC Evidence Law*

According to Article 1 of the Rome Statute, the ICC exercises complementary jurisdiction, meaning it steps in only when national courts are unwilling or unable to prosecute international crimes. A counterargument against the need for a bespoke ICC evidence law could be based on complementarity, asserting that national courts are already equipped to handle war crimes, crimes against humanity, genocide, and the crime of aggression, thereby making a distinct ICC evidence law unnecessary. If a national judge can adjudicate war crimes in a domestic system, the argument follows that the same judge can do so at the ICC without additional legal adaptation.

However, this argument overlooks a fundamental distinction: Domestic trials always align with the legal traditions of the national system conducting them. Regardless of the severity of atrocities or the quality of evidence gathered, national courts apply their own legal doctrines to international crimes. This reality fundamentally differentiates national trials from ICC trials and emphasizes the need for a specialized ICC evidentiary framework.

4.2 *Domestic Courts and Their National Legal Mindset*

When international crimes are prosecuted within domestic legal systems, judges and legal practitioners naturally apply their national legal traditions. The legal culture of the system adjudicating the case inevitably shapes how:

- evidence is admitted and assessed (e.g., judicial discretion vs. strict evidentiary rules);
- witness testimony is evaluated (e.g., adversarial cross-examination vs. judge-led questioning);
- the burden of proof is applied (e.g., beyond a reasonable doubt vs. free judicial evaluation).

Even when domestic courts handle mass atrocities, they still operate within their own procedural frameworks. This means that even in cases of extreme international crimes, national courts fundamentally remain national in their evidentiary reasoning.

Example: If a legal system does not require the prosecution to prove guilt beyond a reasonable doubt, then the trial proceeds without this requirement, even in war crimes cases.

4.3 *The ICC's Unique Compromise: Judges of Conflicting Legal Mindsets*

The ICC, however, operates under an entirely hybrid system. It is a sui generis court, requiring judges trained in opposing legal traditions to function within one hybrid legal framework designed specifically for atrocity crimes.

Unlike national judges, who remain firmly within their domestic legal systems, ICC judges must:

1. adapt to a legal system that is neither fully common law nor fully civil law;
2. apply evidentiary rules that often contradict their legal training;
3. interpret case law differently based on their legal backgrounds.

This creates inconsistencies within the same court, as some judges:

- apply free evaluation of evidence (civil law) in ways that overshadow the prosecutorial burden of proof (common law);
- favour broad judicial discretion (civil law), while others insist on adversarial party-led proceedings (common law);
- use indirect inferences to establish guilt (civil law), while others demand direct evidence of criminal intent (common law).

This unique legal compromise at the ICC – where judges from antithetical legal backgrounds must interpret the same evidence – proves that a simple "fusion" of legal traditions is unsustainable.

4.4 *Why Complementarity Strengthens the Argument for a Bespoke ICC Evidence Law*

Since national courts always align with their own legal traditions, and ICC judges must navigate conflicting evidentiary mindsets, complementarity actually reinforces the need for a bespoke ICC evidence law rather than negating it.

A specialized ICC evidentiary framework is necessary for the following reasons:

1. National courts do not encounter the ICC's unique hybrid legal conflicts.
2. ICC judges come from opposing legal traditions, leading to inconsistencies not present in domestic courts.
3. The ICC requires clear, unified evidentiary standards that transcend national traditions to ensure consistency.

Without a dedicated ICC evidence law, trials will continue to suffer from:

- unpredictable judicial reasoning, as judges apply their own legal training rather than a uniform ICC doctrine;
- fragmented evidentiary rulings, making ICC case law incoherent and unreliable as precedent.

Thus, far from negating the need for an ICC-specific evidentiary model, complementarity reinforces it. Since national courts can always apply their own legal traditions, it is even more critical for the ICC to move beyond legal tradition conflicts and establish an independent evidentiary law tailored to its own reality.

4.5 *The Preparatory Works Reveal Fundamental Misunderstandings*

The final chapter of this book revisits the preparatory works to clarify continental misunderstandings in the ICC's application of evidence law. It examines the distinction between admissibility rulings based on free evaluation – a flexible continental tool – and evidence weight evaluation at the determination stage within a prosecutorial burden-of-proof trial context.

The ICC trial is adversarial, meaning continental judicial features, such as broad judicial discretion in evaluating evidence, cannot play a decisive role in determining guilt. Although the ICC legal framework does not mandate otherwise, case law suggests frequent misinterpretations. This chapter addresses the apparent misunderstandings through the examined case law, explaining how they stem from the legal backgrounds of ICC judges rather than from structural deficiencies in the Court's evidentiary framework.

The book exposes a significant flaw in the ICC's evidentiary reasoning. However, there remains a silver lining: the ICC has the capacity to create and gradually refine its evidence law, resolve legal uncertainties, and develop a coherent approach. Since its establishment in 2002, the ICC has reached a critical crossroads. The ICC needs to choose to evolve, grow wiser, and diminish criticism. The ICC must shun narrow-minded adherence to familiar traditions to survive and thrive globally. Such one-sided views stifle its global impact, despite its extraordinary dynamics.

The ICC's hybrid legal framework, a forced symbiosis of continental and common law traditions, needs to provide consistency through case law to safeguard fair trial rights. While both legal traditions offer unique strengths that could complement each other, ICC case law exposes the significant challenges in balancing the continental judicial discretion with the common law prosecutorial burden of proof and stringent evidence rules. Thus, a tailored ICC evidence law is imperative to address the grave challenges of gathering evidence in the aftermath of atrocities.

4.6 *The Urgent Need for Judicial Training and Legal Consistency*

Implementing comprehensive judicial training programmes is essential to fostering mutual understanding and ensuring the consistent application of modern, principled evidence law.

Even though some evidentiary issues remain unresolved, primarily due to individual ICC judges' approaches, the potential for a coherent ICC-specific evidence law exists as the Court matures. This evolution requires understanding that:

1. Evidence law transcends mere evidence rules, encompassing the broader principles, judicial thinking processes, and philosophies that guide how evidence should be evaluated and used to pursue justice.
2. Professional continental judges are not divine creatures. Their legal training shapes their evidentiary mindset, often in ways unsuited to an adversarial trial model.

3. Free evaluation is valuable for admissibility but should not replace rigorous evidence assessment against the burden of proof; otherwise, legal inconsistency prevails.
4. Judicial discretion is essential, but it must not be used to disregard either the burden of proof or ICC case law without a well-founded rationale.
5. Judicial training and adherence to stare decisis are crucial for the ICC's long-term sustainability.

This book boldly invites engagement with the intellectual rigour of Canadian evidence law, illustrating how evidence law, when it evolves, can become functional for fair trial reasons. However, this evolution requires a solid backbone of fair trial principles, which the ICC's legal framework has secured. More importantly, it demands the willingness of ICC judges, parties, and participants to commit to a functional, principled evidence law.

Only through this commitment can the ICC survive, thrive, and effectively deliver justice on the international stage.

CHAPTER 2

The Forced Marriage: Meet the Unlikely Couple

1 The ICC and the Legal Traditions of Common and Continental Systems

The establishment of the International Criminal Court (ICC) through the Rome Statute merges two distinct legal traditions – common law and continental law – into a hybrid system.[1] This chapter presents the core elements of the traditions within the ICC framework and raises questions about the effectiveness and coherence of their union.

The Rome Statute's (hereinafter the Statute) Preparatory Works show that a compromise legal model would be the only way to resolve structural and procedural disagreements among the parties. The discussions among the parties were related to significant characteristics of the continental and common law systems. For example, the continental principle of free evaluation of evidence would provide "flexibility".[2] The prosecutorial burden of proof would satisfy the common law countries. The amalgamation of the two legal traditions should provide a hybrid court with flexibility for judges and prosecutors to investigate and efficiently try genocide, war crimes, crimes against humanity, and the included crime of aggression.[3]

Not all States welcomed or signed the Statute. The Statute's Preparatory Works and subsequent negotiations were prolonged and contentious.[4] The Statute, the foundational treaty of the ICC, was adopted on July 17, 1998, and

---

1 The legal traditions of common and continental law are two of the four principal systems, which include Socialist Law and the systems that are based on principles related to religion and philosophy (Muslim, Hindu, Chinese, Japanese, and African), *see* Rene David & John EC Brierley, *Major Legal Systems in the World Today: An Introduction to the Comparative Study of Law* (New York, NY: Simon and Schuster, 1978).

2 Donald K. Piragoff, "Evidence", in Otto Triffterer, ed., *Commentary on the Rome Statute of the International Criminal Court* (München: C.H. Beck Hart Nomos, 2008) 1306, 1322, 1317.

3 The crime of aggression was included in the Rome Statute on June 11, 2010. The ICC's jurisdiction over the crime of aggression was activated on July 17, 2018. ICC, Crime of Aggression – Amendments Ratification, online: https://asp.icc-cpi.int/crime-of-aggression; *See* the history of the crime of aggression: Crime of Aggression Info. *The Global Campaign for Ratification and Implementation of the Kampala Amendments on the Crime of Aggression.* https://crimeofaggression.info/history/.

4 Roy S. K. Lee & Håkan Friman, eds, *The International Criminal Court: Elements of Crimes and Rules of Procedure and Evidence* (Ardsley, NY: Transnational Pub Inc, 2001). pp. iv–ixv.

 | DOI:10.1163/9789004741010_003

came into force in 2002.[5] The Statute and the entire legal framework should serve the rule of law in the context of international criminal justice.

The legal framework of the Court, as provided by the Statute and the Rules of Procedure and Evidence, brings together three pivotal elements from common law and continental traditions. These are: (a) the prosecutorial burden of proof, a common law characteristic which requires the prosecution to prove guilt beyond a reasonable doubt; (b) the free evaluation of evidence, a continental principle empowering judges to assess and interpret evidence based on their conceptual understanding freely; and (c) the active truth-seeking role of the judge, another continental feature wherein judges actively engage in investigating and uncovering the truth through inquiries, witness questioning, and evidence gathering. These foundational elements shape ICC trials.

However, when the prosecutorial burden of proof functions along with the free evaluation of evidence, it creates complex and often antithetical dynamics. The prosecutorial burden of proof demands a stringent standard where the prosecution must prove beyond a reasonable doubt the defendant's guilt. In contrast, the free evaluation of evidence grants judges considerable latitude to evaluate evidence based on their internal beliefs and conceptual understanding, potentially leading to subjective assessments. This antithesis can create tension within the judicial process, as the strict requirements of proof beyond a reasonable doubt must coexist with the judge's broad discretion in evaluating evidence.

To appreciate the distinctive characteristics of these traditions as embedded in the Rome Statute, we will examine the continental and common law legal systems through a macroanalysis (See Table 2.1). This will set the stage for a deeper exploration of how these contrasting elements interact in ICC proceedings, often challenging the balance between objective legal standards and subjective judicial discretion. First, we will look at the continental legal system.

Outlining the key characteristics, the role of the continental judge is to seek the truth; his investigative role is provided by national criminal procedure law, and he is the dominant figure in the trial.[6] The prosecutor is not considered a

5 Rome Statute of the International Criminal Court, United Nations, Treaty Series, vol. 2187, No. 38544, Depositary: Secretary-General of the United Nations, http://treaties.un.org.

6 *See* Mirjan Damaška, "Structures of Authority and Comparative Criminal Procedure" (1975) 84:3 Yale L. J. 480–544, where he discusses the hierarchical model of the continental law system, pp. 487–498. *See also* Kai Ambos, "International Criminal Procedure: 'Adversarial', 'Inquisitorial' or Mixed?" (2003) 3:1 Int. Crim. L. Rev. 1–37, at 4 and his reference to the dominant role of the ICC and the presiding judge and the preparatory discussions between the common law and civil law supporters.

TABLE 2.1 Basic characteristics of continental, common law, and ICC trials

Feature	Continental law system	Common law system	ICC trials
Judge's role	Seeks the truth Investigative role Dominant figure in trial	Does not investigate the truth, No dominant figure	Hybrid system seeking both truth and procedural fairness Judges have an investigative role but within an adversarial framework
Prosecutor's role	Not a party to the trial No burden of proof beyond a reasonable doubt	Party to the trial Burden of proof beyond a reasonable doubt	Independent office, party to the trial Burden of proof beyond a reasonable doubt
Evidence rules	No evidence rules All evidence admitted except the unlawful Free evaluation of evidence applies	Evidence rules Not all evidence admitted Admissibility is guided by the evidence rules and evidence law	Admissibility guided by rules, but free evaluation is applicable
Guilty plea	Does not prevent trial hearing for conviction	Prevents trial hearing for conviction	Does not prevent trial hearing Confession must be corroborated by other evidence
Precedent	No binding precedent	Binding precedent	No binding precedent, but prior decisions are influential
Trial mode	Continuous mode One trial hearing session	Multiple trial hearings Separate mode	Combination of continuous and separate trial modes depending on case complexity Sentencing is a separate hearing
Sentencing	No separate sentencing hearing All evidence adduced during conviction hearing All is admitted Evidence rules do not apply Free evaluation of evidence applies	Separate sentencing trial hearing Evidence for sentencing reasons adduced during sentencing trial Evidence rules apply Only admitted evidence evaluated	Separate sentencing trial hearing Evidence submitted at the sentencing trial hearing Free evaluation and burden of proof coexist
Decision delivery	Delivered orally immediately after hearing, detailed written judgement follows	Decisions delivered in written form, publicly accessible, not immediately after the trial	Decisions delivered in written form, publicly accessible, not immediately after the trial.

party to the trial and has no prosecutorial burden of proof beyond a reasonable doubt. The prosecution should also investigate in favour of the accused.[7] A guilty plea does not prevent a trial hearing on conviction because it is insufficient. The court must find the truth on its own. For this reason, even in cases where the prosecution proposes acquittal, the court may decide to convict the accused. There are no evidence rules regarding admissibility. Only some vague evidence provisions are included in the criminal procedure code.[8] The court evaluates all the evidence according to the principle of free evaluation (*l'intime conviction*) except for that which was unlawfully gathered. Sentencing does not happen in a separate trial. All sentencing evidence, no matter its prejudicial nature (i.e., bad character evidence), is adduced during the hearing on conviction. The continental trial runs continuously, so the case is tried in one hearing session. The accused always has the right to speak after the prosecutor and at the end of the hearing before the Court's decision. The decisions on conviction and sentencing are delivered orally right after the end of the hearing but written later (continuous trial mode). There is no binding precedent in criminal law.[9]

---

7 *See*, for example, the legal overview of Germany and Austria overview of the prosecutor's role and the Court's free evaluation of evidence in 2021: "In the German criminal justice system, the public prosecutor's office is not a party. Thus, the prosecution is obliged not only to unilaterally collect evidence of the suspect's guilt, but it must also investigate in favour of the accused person, section 160 (1), (2) Code of Criminal Procedure (StPO). The court investigates the facts of the case ex officio and thus tries to find out what truly happened, section 244 (2) Code of Criminal Procedure (StPO). The trial follows the principle of free judicial assessment of evidence, section 261 Code of Criminal Procedure (StPO)". Social Fieldwork Research (FRANET), "Presumption of Innocence: Procedural Rights in Criminal Proceedings", Country: Germany (May 27, 2020: Revised version: August 20, 2020; second revision: August 28, 2020) 38–39, online: https://fra.europa.eu/sites/default/files/fra_uploads/germany-2021-country-research-presumption-innocence_en.pdf. The Austrian legal overview: "There is no rule on the burden of proof formally anchored in the Criminal Procedure Act. The criminal police, the prosecution and the court are obliged by §3 Criminal Procedure Act to investigate the truth objectively. There are no relevant cases, nor there are relevant legal discussions on §3 Criminal Procedure Act to be reported. In that respect, the burden of proof is closely linked to the obligation to conduct investigations in a spirit of objectivity". Social Fieldwork Research (FRANET), "Presumption of Innocence: Procedural Rights in Criminal Proceedings", Country: Austria (May 2020), 37, online: https://fra.europa.eu/sites/default/files/fra_uploads/austria-2021-country-research-presumption-innocence_en.pdf.

8 Richard May & Marieke Wierda, *International Criminal Evidence* (New York, NY: Transnational Publishers, 2002) 335.

9 Regarding an analysis between the American common law and the European continental systems, *see* Mirjan Damaska, "Evidentiary Barriers to Conviction and Two Models of Criminal Procedure: A Comparative Study" (1973) 121:3 U Pa L Rev 506.

The core elements of the common law system are the following: The prosecutor is a party to the trial and has the burden of proof beyond a reasonable doubt. The judge does not seek the truth as in the continental system; he does not investigate the truth. The parties marshal the evidence. Only some of the submitted evidence is admitted. Evidence rules guide the admission of evidence and apply both during the conviction hearing and the separate sentencing trial. The court evaluates the totality of the admitted evidence to determine whether guilt has been proven beyond a reasonable doubt. If the accused enters an informed guilty plea, the court decides on conviction and sets the sentencing hearing. Trial hearings and sentencing hearings are distinct and separate (separate trial mode). The precedent is binding but can be refined to shape the evolution of common law.[10]

Understanding the fundamental differences between the common law and continental systems, we can now explore how these distinct traditions have been integrated into the ICC's hybrid legal framework.

The ICC follows a hybrid system where evidence rules and principles of relevance and fairness guide evidence admissibility. This means that the Court will determine whether the evidence is relevant to the case and whether its admission would be fair, considering both the rights of the accused and the interests of justice. Admissibility, however, may be determined later, after the parties have closed their cases. Similar to the continental system, the ICC employs the principle of free evaluation of evidence. This allows the judges to assess the evidence based on their inner conviction and understanding without being strictly bound by rigid rules of admissibility, as seen in common law systems. A guilty plea or confession does not automatically prevent a trial hearing. The ICC requires that confessions be corroborated by other evidence to ensure reliability and fairness in the judicial process. The Court may exercise its discretion in a truth-seeking manner and can accept submitted evidence within a free evaluation spectrum. However, at the ICC, guilt must be proven by the prosecutor beyond any reasonable doubt.

In the ICC, evidence relevant to sentencing can be introduced during a separate sentencing phase. It is evaluated by balancing free evaluation and the burden of proof requirements. Although there is no binding precedent, previous decisions of the ICC are influential. This means that while judges

10 The distinction between common law and continental systems is limited here only to the elements the Rome Statute has incorporated. The reference to the way the two systems work is macro-comparative. However, in this research, the evidence law analysis and how it happens in Canada and the ICC is micro-comparative. Jürgen Basedow, "Comparative Law and Its Clients" (2014) 62: 4 Am. J. Comp. L. 830.

are not strictly bound to follow precedents, these decisions can guide and influence their evaluation and interpretation of evidence.[11]

This hybrid approach aimed to merge the flexibility of the continental system with the procedural safeguards of the adversarial trial of the common law system, ensuring that the evidence considered in ICC trials is both relevant and fairly assessed. The overarching goal of international criminal justice should be to find the truth of war crimes, crimes against humanity, genocide, and the crime of aggression and bring the alleged culprits to justice. However, this is not the ultimate goal of the international criminal trial.[12] The International Criminal Court has to apply international justice through a fully reasoned decision according to the high international standards established by its unique legal framework.

The history of the discussions on evidence before the ICC reveals a debate between the common law evidence rules, which were considered technical, and the continental free evaluation of evidence, which was considered flexible.[13] The winner was the flexibility of free evaluation, but within an adversarial trial where guilt must be proved beyond a reasonable doubt. An esoteric contradiction was concealed within the ICC's legal compromise.

2 The Awkward Introduction of the Burden of Proof to the European Continentals

When the Rome Statute was signed in 1998, classic continental legal systems did not impose a burden of proof on the prosecution in criminal trials. This

11 Article 64–67, 69,76, Rome Statute.

12 Regarding the overarching goal of the ICC to end impunity and establish truth, *see* Mark Klamberg, "What Are the Objectives of International Criminal Procedure – Reflections on the Fragmentation of a Legal Regime" (2010) 79: 2 Nord. J. Intl. L. 290, 301–302, which refers to Robert Cryer et al., eds.. *An Introduction to International Criminal Law and Procedure*, 3rd ed. (Cambridge, UK: Cambridge University Press, 2007) 350, regarding the help the inquisitorial system can provide the international criminal proceedings' aim to create "an accurate historical record" of the situations; *Ibid* at 25 for the importance of establishing truth in serious crimes, *ibid* 27 for the role of the criminal trials, which is not to "ensure a full discussion of history". *See also* Theodor Meron, *Standing up for Justice: The Challenges of Trying Atrocity Crimes* (Oxford: Oxford University Press, 2021) 34–38. Meron discusses that judges from the civil law tradition may consider the search for the truth as highly significant for international criminal justice. However, he clarified: "The core mandate of an international criminal court is to try individuals within a governing framework". *Ibid* at 36.

13 Piragoff, *supra* note 2 at 1306, 1317.

gap persisted when the Statute came into force in 2002 and remained for the EU's continental systems until at least 2018, as discussed below. This context is crucial because ICC judges favouring the classic European continental tradition struggle to correctly apply the prosecutorial burden of proof when evaluating evidence at the determination stage. Here and for research purposes, the term "classic" continental system is used to distinguish between the majority of continental legal systems in which the prosecution does not have a burden of proof beyond a reasonable doubt and a few modern continental systems that later adopted some common law features.[14]

To fully grasp the implications of inexperience in applying the prosecutorial burden of proof beyond a reasonable doubt, it is essential to recognize that the classic continental systems of the European Union were only recently mandated to incorporate the prosecutorial burden in their national legislations. This significant change was introduced in 2016 with Directive 2016/343, which required the European Union States to ensure that the prosecution bears the burden of proof for establishing guilt, marking a pivotal moment in the European continental legal history.[15] The Directive's implementation deadline was April 2018. More importantly, the same Directive mandated the presumption of innocence. The Directive recognized that in some states, judges are seeking the truth, and the burden is not applicable as in common law:

> In various Member States not only the prosecution, but also *judges and competent courts are charged with seeking both inculpatory and exculpatory evidence*. Member States which do not have an adversarial system should be able to maintain their current system *provided that it complies*

14 About the Italian system, *see* Alessandro Corda, "Sentencing and Penal Policies in Italy, 1985 to 2015: The Tale of a Troubled Country", M. Tonry, ed., *Sentencing Policies and Practices in Western Countries* (Chicago: University of Chicago Press, 2016) 128–130. The term *classic* is also used by Chief Justice Eboe-Osuji in his Concurring Separate Opinion of Judge Eboe-Osuji, ICC01/05-01/08-3636-Anx3, June 14, 2018 in the case *The Prosecution v. Jean Pierre Bemba Gombo.* No. ICC-01/05-01/08.

15 Directive (EU) 2016/343, Article 6. Burden of proof: 1, Member States shall ensure that the burden of proof for establishing the guilt of suspects and accused persons is on the prosecution. This shall be without prejudice to any obligation on the judge or the competent court to seek both inculpatory and exculpatory evidence, and to the right of the defence to submit evidence in accordance with the applicable national law. Directive (EU) 2016/343 of the European Parliament and of the Council of March 9, 2016 on the strengthening of certain aspects of the presumption of innocence and of the right to be present at the trial in criminal proceedings, online: https://eur-lex.europa.eu/legal-content/EN/TXT/PDF/?uri=CELEX:32016L0343.

> *with this Directive* and other relevant provisions of Union and international law.[16] [emphasis added]

For comparative purposes and to gain a conceptual understanding of how continental systems interpret reasonable doubt and the prosecutorial burden of proof, we refer to Directive Article 6(2):

> Member States shall ensure that any doubt as to the question of guilt is to benefit the suspect or accused person, including where the court assesses whether the person concerned should be acquitted. [emphasis added]

The provision uses the term "any doubt" instead of "reasonable doubt". Steven Cras and Anže Erbežnik provide further insights into the discussions surrounding the Directive's provisions, which might now unsettle common law thinkers:[17]

> All parties agreed that *any doubt as to guilt* should benefit the suspects or accused persons. The question arose as to what the consequences of such doubt should be. [emphasis added]
>
> The European Parliament considered that when there is *"doubt"* as to the guilt of a suspect, the accused person should be acquitted. [emphasis added]
>
> The Council felt that this reasoning would be too simple, since *100% certainty is rare*. [emphasis added]
>
> *Would any doubt, even the slightest one*, have as a consequence that the person concerned should be acquitted? [emphasis added]
>
> Moreover, the Council had the more principal objection that the *European legislator should not impose any concrete instructions on courts and judges* as to what to decide in a criminal case. [emphasis added]

---

16 *Ibid* Preamble at para 23.

17 Steven Cras & Anže Erbežnik, "The Directive on the Presumption of Innocence and the Right to be Present at Trial: Genesis and Description of the New EU-Measure", (2016) 1 Eucrim 31.

> In the end, a solution was found by stating, in Art. 6(2), that Member States should ensure *that any doubt* as to the question of guilt is to benefit the suspect or accused person, "including where the court assesses whether the person concerned should be acquitted". [emphasis added]

After extensive debates regarding the meaning and weight of doubt, the final decision was to include the prosecutorial burden of proof in member states' legislation. However, the Directive's implementation leaves room for European member states to choose the form and method of change.[18] Unsurprisingly, European continentals did not exactly embrace the burden requirement with open arms. Spotting the burden in the Directive, they decided to carry on as usual, dodging it in court. After all, no continental ever rushed to a Court claiming unfair trials or a breached presumption of innocence due to the lack of this burden. Besides, you must first understand how it works to complain about the prosecutorial burden. That day, it seems, has yet to dawn.[19]

Consequently, the classic European continentals never found themselves in the legal quandary of having to discuss the relationship between the prosecutorial burden and the presumption of innocence as their common law peers did way back in 1935 with *Woolmington*.[20] This landmark case emphatically

18 Treaty of the Functioning of the European Union, art. 288, online: https://eur-lex.europa.eu/legal-content/EN/TXT/PDF/?uri=CELEX:12012E/TXT&from=EN, states that the EU operates through various forms of legal acts: "[T]he institutions shall adopt regulations, directives, decisions, recommendations and opinions. [...] A directive shall be binding, as to the result to be achieved, upon each Member State to which it is addressed, but shall leave to the national authorities the choice of form and methods". *See also* Paul Craig & Gráinne De Búrca, *EU Law: Text, Cases, and Materials* (Oxford: Oxford University Press, 2008) 85.

19 Especially for Directive 343/2016, the 2021 Commission's Report said that Member States had different approaches to its implementation. Additionally, the States responded that they had "existing measures" in their system. The Report mentioned that "broadly", the existing legislation could be considered in line with the Directive, European Parliament and of the Council, Report from the Commission to the European Parliament and the Council on the Implementation of Directive (EU) 2016/343 of the of March 9, 2016 on the strengthening of certain aspects of the presumption of innocence and of the right to be present at the trial in criminal proceedings, COM/2021/144 final, online: https://eur-lex.europa.eu/legal-content/EN/TXT/?uri=COM:2021:144:FIN, at para 4 (Conclusion).

20 *Woolmington* v. *D.P.P.* [1935] AC 462. This case is known for the so-called "golden thread" rule as Lord Sankey called the prosecutorial burden: "Throughout the web of the English Criminal Law one golden thread is always to be seen, that it is the duty of the prosecution to prove the prisoner's guilt subject to what I have already said as to the defence of insanity and subject also to any statutory exception. If, at the end of and on the whole of the case, there is a reasonable doubt, created by the evidence given by either the prosecution or the prisoner, as to whether the prisoner killed the deceased with a malicious

clarified that the prosecution's burden to prove guilt beyond a reasonable doubt always rests on the prosecution throughout the entire trial, and the defendant doesn't have to prove his innocence. Meanwhile, in 2016, the continentals were still puzzling over what a "doubt" is and how much doubt is needed for an acquittal, something *Lifchus* had already unequivocally spelled out in 1997:[21]

1. The standard of proof beyond a reasonable doubt is inextricably intertwined with that principle fundamental to all criminal trials: the presumption of innocence.
2. The burden of proof rests on the prosecution throughout the trial and never shifts to the accused.
3. A reasonable doubt is not a doubt based on sympathy or prejudice.
4. It is based on reason and common sense.
5. It is logically connected to the evidence or absence of evidence.
6. It does not involve proof to an absolute certainty; it is not proof beyond any doubt nor is it an imaginary or frivolous doubt.
7. *More is required than proof that the accused is probably guilty* – a jury which concludes only that the accused is probably guilty must acquit. [emphasis added]

Without continental landmark case law such as *Woolmington* and *Lifchus*, European classic continentals have never clarified the interplay between "any doubt" and the prosecutorial burden of proof. This ambiguity persists, especially in a trial where the judge is responsible for investigating the truth through free evaluation of evidence. However, several ICC decisions, including *Bemba*, *Gbagbo and Blé Goudé*, and *Ongwen*, highlight significant conceptual difficulties, particularly concerning the burden of proof. These decisions reveal contradictory reasoning that exposes the fundamental differences between the two legal traditions. They also reflect the judges' varying experiences in addressing evidentiary issues related to the prosecutorial burden and the presumption of innocence.

However, the continentals' behaviour was entirely predictable once one grasps the concept of free evaluation of evidence. After all, it is the holy grail

intention, the prosecution has not made out the case and the prisoner is entitled to an acquittal. No matter what the charge or where the trial, the principle that the prosecution must prove the guilt of the prisoner is part of the common law of England and no attempt to whittle it down can be entertained". Online: http://www.bailii.org/uk/cases/UKHL/1935/1.html.

21 *R.* v. *Lifchus*, [1997] 3 S.C.R. 320, at para 36.

of their legal world. And so, we delve deeper into this sacrosanct principle and its magnificent qualities.

3 Free Evaluation of Evidence: The Continentals' Holy Grail

The principle of free evaluation of evidence, or *l'intime conviction*,[22] and the judge's truth-seeking mission were introduced into the Napoleonic Code of Criminal Procedure in 1808 following the French Revolution.[23] Historical evidence suggests that the jury trial and the principle of *l'intime conviction* were adopted from the English jury system in the late eighteenth century.[24,25] However, in France, jury trials operated under a mixed model, allowing both juries and judges to apply the principle of *l'intime conviction*.[26]

During the ancient legal regime, trials often relied on ordeals and God's intervention, deeply rooted in religious-based approaches to justice. A guilty plea, following ordeals or two prosecutorial witnesses (usually fabricated), secured a conviction according to the evidence rules of the time.[27] However, the democratic ideals that emerged after the French Revolution marked a

22 The free evaluation of evidence and *l'intime conviction* are originally the same principles. The French principle was adopted by the Continent. *L'intime conviction* provides broad judicial discretion and pairs with the truth-seeking mission of the Judge. *See* Demetra Sorvatzioti & Allan Manson, "Burden of Proof and L'intime conviction: Is the Continental Criminal Trial Moving to the Common Law?" (2018) 23:1 Can Crim L Rev 114, 115, fn 46. *See also* Mireille Delmas-Marty & J. R. Spencer, eds., *European Criminal Procedures* (Cambridge: Cambridge University Press, 2006) 309–310. Free evaluation of evidence is a common principle for German and French procedures. However, it is argued that the German system applies the rule "in a form more rational and less subjective", *ibid* at 328.

23 See James M. Donovan, *Juries and the Transformation of Criminal Justice in France in the Nineteenth & Twentieth Centuries* (Chapel Hill, University of North Carolina Press, 2010) 41–45.

24 *See* the historical analysis of the principle in Sorvatzioti & Manson, *supra* note 22 at 109–113.

25 Regarding the jury trial transferring to France from England and the mixed model of trials *see* Damaška, *supra* note 6 at 492–493; William Roumier, *L'Avenir du Jury Criminel* (Paris: LDGJ, 2003) 3–9.

26 In Europe, the court can be a jury, a mixed jury of professional judges and lay judges, or a judge alone. See the explanation in *Taxquet* v. *Belgium*, [2010] ECHR 926/05 at paras 43–60.

27 Usually, ordeals included hot iron or dropping into cold water, where the accused's death or survival (according to God's will) would determine guilt or innocence. Regarding the ancient regime, *see* John Langbein, "Torture and Plea Bargaining" (1978) 46 U Chi L Rev 3–8.

clear departure from ordeals and fabricated evidence.[28] Central to this transformation was establishing a statutory truth-seeking mission for judges. This mission empowered courts to go beyond mere prosecutorial evidence and consider acquitting the accused based on a principle of free evaluation of evidence. This flexible approach allowed judges to disregard prosecutorial evidence without reasoned justification. Even a guilty plea was considered insufficient for conviction without a formal trial under this principle.[29]

This shift granted judges broad discretion to affirm innocence by disregarding inculpatory evidence, protecting the (newly adopted) presumption of innocence.[30] In this regime, the burden of proof on the prosecution was unnecessary and catastrophic. It would limit the judge's freedom.

Since 1808, continental judges have conducted criminal trials guided by the sacred principle of free evaluation of evidence. However, free evaluation is neither holy nor does it guide how to evaluate criminal evidence. Moreover, the original rationale for its adoption by judges has become obsolete. Modern continental systems strictly prohibit torture, ordeals, and the use of fabricated or unlawfully gathered evidence, ensuring robust protections for the right to a fair trial.[31]

The principle of free evaluation grants judges significant latitude. Crucially, all evidence is admissible, and its assessment occurs within the judge's mind, an opaque process. The principle encompasses ambiguous evidence assessments, which are neither clear nor principled. This is hugely problematic because no prosecutorial burden of proof is applied in the classic continental system.

After more than two centuries, the ancestral features of free evaluation and the truth-seeking mission, the most sacred historical components of the continental system, are found in the Rome Statute. We know the reason why free evaluation was transplanted from the continental system: its flexibility. How-

---

28 For a detailed description of the trials and the role of the judge in France according to the Code d' Instruction Criminelle, *see* James Fitzjames Stephen, *A History of the Criminal Law of England*, Vol. 1 (London: Macmillan, 1883) (digitally reprinted version Cambridge University Press, 2014) 535–549.

29 According to the Ancient Regime, judges convicted based on either the evidence of two witnesses or a confession, even if it was obtained by torture. For the abolition of the old regime and transformation of the French criminal justice system *see* Donovan, *supra* note 23 at 29–33.

30 French Declaration of the Rights of Man and of the Citizen (1789), Article 9.

31 Article 3 European Convention of Human Rights. *See also* Prohibition of Torture: Landmark Judgments, online: https://www.coe.int/en/web/human-rights-convention/torture1.

ever, how much flexibility can the ICC's evidence evaluation be afforded when the prosecutorial burden of proof is mandatory?

4 The Mantra "Evidence Rules Are Technical and Not for Professional Judges"

The rules of evidence began to appear in the common law system in England before the eighteenth century.[32] The burden of proof on the prosecution emerged by the nineteenth century.[33] Today, evidence rules do not apply identically in jurisdictions with common law systems. However, they share the quality of being developed based on principles that promote the interests of justice. In many modern common law systems, such as Canada, the rules have evolved to serve fair trial rights. Canadian evidence law has shifted to a purposive approach regarding the admission of evidence, increasing admissibility, fostering the development of an "overarching exclusionary discretion", and embracing technological advancements.[34]

In the discussions preceding the Rome Statute, evidence rules were perceived as technical, with no focus on the broader context of evidence law.[35] However, the term "technical" is inaccurate. It is limited to the exclusionary nature of the evidence rules' genesis and does not capture the richness and complexity of the evidence law that underpins these rules.

Moreover, the term "technical" has a long history. In searching the legal history of common law, Sir James Fitzjames Stephen's speech on evidence rules in India in 1871 provides an explanation of why the rules were perceived as technicalities at the time and why he disagreed:[36]

---

32 For example, the rule against hearsay crystallized in the seventeenth century, and it was rationalized in the 1700s, *see* Kenneth S. Broun et al., eds., *McCormick on Evidence*, 6th ed. (St. Paul, MN, USA: Thomson/West Publishing, 1999) 420–421. John Langbein, *The Origins of Adversary Criminal Trial* (Oxford: Oxford University Press, 2003), 261–266. Rupert Cross, *Evidence* (London: Butterworth, 1958) 178–180.

33 Langbein, *ibid* at 113.

34 David Paciocco, Palma Paciocco & Lee Stuesser, *The Law of Evidence*, 8th ed. (Concord, Canada: Irwin Law, 2020) 11.

35 *See* the discussion about the term "technical rule" in Piragoff, *supra* note 2 at 96–97.

36 The quotation is found in Peter Murphy, "No Free Lunch, No Free Proof: The Indiscriminate Admission of Evidence is a Serious Flaw in International Criminal Trials", (2010) 8:2 JICJ 549, https://doi.org/10.1093/jicj/mqq029.

> There is, in short, in the lay world, including in the expression the majority of Indian civilians, *an impression that rules of evidence are technicalities* invented by lawyers principally for what Bentham called fee-fathering purposes, and of no real value in the investigation of truth. I cannot admit that this impression is in any degree correct. I believe that *rules of evidence are of very great value* in all enquiries into matters of fact, and in particular in enquiries for judicial purposes; and that it is practically impossible to investigate difficult subjects without regard to them. [emphasis added]

> The practical effect of the English rules of evidence in those cases was to shorten the proceedings enormously, and at the same time to consolidate and strengthen them, *keeping out nothing that a reasonable person would have wished to have before him as material for his judgement.* [emphasis added]

The term "technical" still survives. Many continental legal scholars and practitioners defend the absence of evidence rules in their respective systems, arguing that such rules are primarily designed for common law jury trials. However, it is essential to note that common law trials are not exclusively jury trials. Except for the United States, many jurisdictions conduct more judge-alone trials than jury trials.[37] The thought that evidence rules are made for juries frequently appears in the cases discussed here and is a common assertion, even found in the decisions of ad hoc international tribunals.[38] This suggests that professionally trained continental judges do not require evidence

---

37 Regarding the inaccurate argument that evidence rules are the product of jury trials, *see also* Peter Murphy and Lina Baddour, "International Criminal Law and Common Law Rules of Evidence", in Karim Khan et al., eds., *Principles of Evidence in International Criminal Justice* (Oxford: Oxford University Press, 2012), 101–103.

38 *Prosecutor* v. *Jejnil Delalic and Others* January 18, 1998 (Decision on the Motion of the Prosecution for the Admissibility of Evidence), para 20: "While the importance of the rules on admissibility in common law follows from the effect which the admission of a certain piece of evidence might have on a group of lay jurors, the trials before the International Tribunal are conducted before professional judges *who by virtue of their training and experience are able to consider each piece of evidence which has been admitted and determine its appropriate weight*", and adds that for this reason they *"are further capable of disregarding purely prejudicial material"* [emphasis added]. Judge May (of the International Criminal Tribunal for the former Yugoslavia) discussed some evidentiary issues related to technical evidence rules and the "liberal approach" of civil law. He stated that the "liberal approach must be seen against the background of the rules relating to the burden and standard of proof". Richard May, "Evidence before the Inter-

rules. However, the following analysis will demonstrate that this notion is not merely an implication but a firmly held belief by the ICC judges who favour the continental tradition.

The old argument that rules are not for professional judges implies that continental judges are well-equipped to address evidence problems competently upon completing judges' school. Admission to judges' schools usually requires passing a highly competitive entrance exam. The training programme includes extensive professional theoretical and practical legal training. However, continental or common law judges do not instantly gain wisdom simply by assuming their judicial roles.[39] Unlike common law judges, who meticulously evaluate the evidence against the prosecutorial burden of proof, classic continental judges do not engage in this evaluative process. This divergence does not arise from a mere lack of rigorous training in their respective judges' schools. It stems from an absence of specialized knowledge of evidence law and inexperience in assessing evidence for admissibility and weight reasons.

The stages of evidence evaluation in common law are two. In the admissibility phase, the focus is on determining whether the evidence meets specific admissibility criteria for the trial. Only relevant, reliable, and non-prejudicial evidence can be presented in court. The judge plays a gatekeeping role, ensuring that the evidence admitted complies with these standards. At the deliberation phase, the court (either judge or jury) reviews and weighs all the admitted evidence to assess its credibility and significance. The court then applies the findings of fact derived from the admitted evidence to the relevant rules of substantive law. This process ultimately leads to a decision regarding the matter at hand.[40]

It is important to remember that continental law schools do not include evidence law as a core or elective course in their curriculum. This area of law is entirely absent from their educational programmes. Similarly, professional judges' schools in these systems do not cover evidence law in the curriculum. As a result, there is a profound and systemic ignorance of evidence law, its role, and its significance within the classic continental legal tradition.[41]

---

national Criminal Tribunal for the Former Yugoslavia: An Overview" (1999) 1 Int L F D Int 198.

39 *See* Murphy, *supra note* 36 at 551 on the "mystical power" of the "judicial robe".

40 Paciocco, *supra* note 34 at 10.

41 *See* the comparative discussion on judges' training in France and the United States in Richard S. Frase, "Comparative Criminal Justice as a Guide to American Law Reform: How Do the French Do It, How Can We Find Out, and Why Should We Care?", (1990) 78 *CLR* 539–684, 566–567. Frase acknowledges that the American judges are not trained in a judges' school, but they follow training sessions on trial advocacy after appointment. He

In classic continental courts, evidence problems are addressed through the judge's free evaluation of evidence because this is what the law provides. On the other hand when encountering an evidence problem in common law courts, a judge will refer to case law developed over the years, providing a logical analysis leading to solutions for many evidence issues.

To further understand the differences in judicial approaches between these systems, it's helpful to consider Mirjan Damaška's models of judicial authority.[42] Damaška discusses the hierarchical and coordinated models of authority shaping judicial processes. The hierarchical model centralizes judicial power in continental legal systems, emphasizing the search for material truth through proactive judicial investigation. Judges are deeply involved in probing cases, reflecting the inquisitorial nature of continental tradition. According to Damaška, this active judicial role facilitates a meticulous and comprehensive examination of facts, potentially unearthing truths that might elude an adversarial system.[43]

In contrast, the coordinate model, prevalent in common law systems, diffuses power among the parties and prioritizes procedural fairness and adversarial contests to ascertain truth. Here, the judge functions as a neutral arbiter, overseeing the legal duel between prosecution and defence. The adversarial framework ensures vigorous case presentation by both sides, hinging heavily on the attorneys' skills, which can sometimes lead to disparities if one side is more competent or better resourced.[44]

These distinctions in judicial roles and authority models highlight two contrasting approaches: the judge's role in applying evidence rules within a coordinate model and the judge's role in the free evaluation of evidence within a hierarchical model. The functioning of the two systems differs significantly. The coordinate model emphasizes adherence to evidence rules in a principled approach and judicial neutrality, while the hierarchical model allows judges broad discretion in evaluating evidence. Each system operates effectively within its respective national context, ensuring fairness and justice according to local legal traditions. However, challenges arise when hierarchical and coordinate systems converge at the ICC. Integrating diverse judicial practices

---

suggests that "French judges need to be better trained given their active role at trial and during pretrial investigation". *See also* Damaška, *supra* note 6 at 491–497, 521–522, where he discusses the professional adjudicators and their origin along the absence of stare decisis.

42 Damaška, *supra* note 6 at 480.

43 *Ibid* at 487, 525–527.

44 *Ibid* at p. 524, 526–529.

and reconciling different evidentiary standards can complicate proceedings and affect the consistency of international criminal justice.

How do the hierarchical and coordinated models of authority finally converge to shape the ICC's judicial processes? Moreover, what ramifications do these models have on ensuring fair trial rights within this unique hybrid international criminal court? These questions are pivotal in understanding how the ICC navigates its complex mandate to deliver justice while respecting the diverse legal traditions of the continental and common law.

5 Is the ICC's Legal Framework a Mosaic of Transplanted Legal Provisions?

The ICC's legal framework integrates common law and continental systems' an apostrophe provisions. This blend of legal traditions raises intriguing questions about the potential implications and effects. How does this mosaic influence the consistency of judicial decisions? What is the root of the judges' unharmonized and antithetical views on evidence law within this amalgamated system? The answers might lie in the theory of legal transplants.

However, the theory of legal transplants is under debate. Outlining it, one side (the positive view) believes that legal transplants can succeed if cultural and contextual differences are adequately managed. The opposing side argues that legal transplants are impractical or impossible due to fundamental differences in legal traditions and systems. At the heart of the debate is examining how legal systems can either adapt to or resist new elements while maintaining their core principles. Understanding the natural environment of national legal elements and their cultural, historical, and systemic dynamics is essential for conceptualizing their transfer within a similar or different legal tradition.[45]

The term "legal transplant" was introduced by legal historian Alan Watson in 1974, who represents the positive view. He refers to the adaptation and adoption of legal norms, principles, and practices from one jurisdiction to another. Watson argues that legal transplants are common and play a crucial role in legal development, often leading to significant innovations and improvements in the receiving legal systems. Law is autonomous of social

---

45 Nina Kršljanin, "Legal Transplants", in Mortimer Sellers & Stephan Kirste, eds., *Encyclopedia of the Philosophy of Law and Social Philosophy* (Dordrecht: Springer, 2023) 2085–2086, https://doi.org/10.1007/978-94-007-6519-1_1120. Regarding the origin of the term "transplant", see 2085–2086.

structures and, therefore, capable of transplantation. Despite being a proponent of legal transplants, he acknowledges that their success depends on how well the transplanted norms are adapted to fit the new legal environment. Misapplications can occur if the receiving jurisdiction fails to modify the norms according to traditions and needs.[46] He gradually developed thirteen criteria for a transplant to succeed.[47]

Several examples illustrate that legal transplants have shaped the ICC's legal framework. The prosecutorial burden of proof is one such example. The ICC adopted the common law principle that the prosecution bears the burden of proof beyond a reasonable doubt. This ensures rigorous standards for proving guilt and protecting the accused's rights. However, balancing this standard with the continental system's free evaluation of evidence can create tension in applying consistent proof standards.

Another example is the principle of free evaluation of evidence, adopted from the continental system. This allows judges to freely evaluate all evidence without strict admissibility rules, providing flexibility to consider all relevant information for their comprehensive understanding of cases. The challenge, however, lies in integrating this with common law's prosecutorial burden of proof and evidence rules, some of which are also included in the ICC's legal framework and can lead to inconsistencies in evidence handling.

In terms of precedent, the ICC uses previous decisions as influential but not binding, unlike common law, which relies on binding precedent. This approach is perceived as allowing flexibility, which is mainly characteristic of a continental system. However, the lack of binding precedent can lead to varied interpretations and potential inconsistencies in judicial decisions, especially regarding the ICC's evidence evaluation.

Watson's theory on legal transplants was vehemently opposed.[48] In 1997, Pierre Legrand (the negative view) challenged the concept of legal transplants, arguing in "The Impossibility of 'Legal Transplants'" that they are impossible due to the inherent cultural and contextual differences between legal systems.[49] Legrand posits that laws are deeply embedded in the specific cultural, historical, and social contexts of their origin, and when transplanted, they lose

46 Alan Watson, *Legal Transplants: An Approach to Comparative Law* (Athens, GA: University of Georgia Press, 1974). *See also* Anna Dolidze, "Bridging Comparative and International Law: *Amicus Curiae* Participation as a Vertical Legal Transplant" (2015) 26:4 *EJIL* 857, https://doi.org/10.1093/ejil/chv059.

47 Watson, *ibid* at 95–101.

48 Kršljanin, *supra* note 45 at 2085–2092.

49 Pierre Legrand, "The Impossibility of 'Legal Transplants'" (1997) 4:2 *MJ* 111–124.

their meaning and efficacy. He suggests that what is transferred is merely a form without substance, as the cultural and contextual essence of the law cannot be replicated in a different environment. Legrand's critique is centred on the idea that legal norms and practices are not just technical rules but are deeply intertwined with the societies that produced them. When these norms are moved to a different context, they might not function as intended, leading to misunderstandings and misapplications. For example, the adversarial nature of common law, which depends heavily on the skills of the lawyers and the judge's role as a neutral arbiter, might not translate well into a system where judges have an investigative role. According to Legrand, the cultural context includes the historical development, legal philosophy, societal values, and institutional structures that shape the functioning of the law. When a legal norm is transplanted without contextual background, it may lose effectiveness and be misinterpreted or misapplied in the new environment.[50]

The ICC created a legal framework by transplanting features from continental and common law systems. However, this transplantation occurred within a "newly made" culture, representing internationalism.[51] The newly made international culture of the ICC is distinct from pre-existing legal cultures due to its unique hybridity, which intentionally integrates elements from both common law and continental law traditions. This framework was designed to function beyond national boundaries, with a mandate to address international crimes like genocide, crimes against humanity, war crimes, and aggression.

---

50 Other scholars have also critiqued legal transplants from various perspectives. Gunther Teubner, "Legal Irritants: Good Faith in British Law or How Unifying Law Ends Up in New Divergences" (1998) 61:1 *MLR*, argues that legal transplants often fail due to cultural and functional discrepancies between legal systems. He suggests that legal norms and institutions are products of specific social, economic, and political conditions, and when transplanted without adaptation, they may become dysfunctional. Daniel Berkowitz, Katharina Pistor & Jean-Francois Richard, "The Transplant Effect" (2003) 51:1 Am.J. Comp.L. 163–203, suggest that the success of legal transplants is influenced by the origin of the legal system, with similar origins leading to more successful transplants. Ann Seidman & Robert Seidman, *State and Law in the Development Process: Problem-Solving and Institutional Change in the Third World* (London: Palgrave Macmillan, 1994), emphasize the importance of understanding local contexts, arguing that successful transplants require tailoring norms to fit specific social, economic, and political conditions. William Twining, *Globalisation and Legal Theory* (Cambridge: Cambridge University Press, 2000), criticizes the oversimplification of legal transplants, arguing that the process involves more than just transferring rules and includes the underlying principles, practices, and institutional structures.

51 Dolidze, *supra* note 47 at 853, 856, about the process of vertical diffusion where a legal transplant becomes internationalized.

The ICC's legal culture is shaped by its diverse composition of judges and legal practitioners from various legal backgrounds, reflecting its global focus. It operates under the Rome Statute, drawing on international treaties and norms rather than national laws, and emphasizes flexibility and adaptability to evolving legal challenges. This "new" legal culture does not adhere to any single national tradition, making it a truly international legal entity. This new context may suggest that Pierre Legrand's theory, which argues against the effectiveness of legal transplants due to cultural and contextual differences, is not entirely applicable here.

When Legrand discussed the incompatibility between common law and continental law traditions, he found their integration impossible. His 1996 discussion focused on European common law and the potential for a unified European legal identity. He emphasized that each legal culture's inherent characteristics and legal *mentalité* create pragmatic obstacles to uniformity and harmonization under the then-European Community's legal framework. He stated:

> There exist in Europe irreducibly distinctive modes of legal perception and thinking, that the ambition of a European concordantia is (and must be) a chimera, that European legal systems are not converging.[52]

However, the ICC's legal framework brought together some core components of common law and continental traditions, incorporated them into the Rome Statute, and mandated their integration at trial. Legrand's discussion about common European law and identity is about transforming a national mentality into a European one, a significant leap. Ideally, a European should be both a citizen of a specific state's legal order and a European citizen. The European legal system has not merely added different legal tools or merged them to provide European law, it has created a unified legal order for all member states while allowing them to manage their national legal systems independently.[53] What Legrand actually said is how the then-European Community could func-

52 Pierre Legrand, "European legal systems are not converging" (1996) 45:1 ICLQ 81. About the legal mentalité concept, *see* 60–64.

53 "The European Union is based on the rule of law. This means that every action taken by the EU is founded on treaties that have been approved democratically by its members. EU laws help to achieve the objectives of the EU treaties and put EU policies into practice. There are two main types of EU law– primary and secondary." European Commission, "Types of EU Law", online: https://commission.europa.eu/law/law-making-process/types-eu-law_en.

tion as a cohesive entity despite the distinct, deep differences between the civil and common law traditions.

6 The ICC's Legal Transplants and the Judges' Mandate to Adapt

The Rome Statute has adopted core elements of the continental and common law legal traditions in their pure original format. Internationalizing the isolated elements of continental criminal procedure (free evaluation of evidence and truth-seeking mandate) and common law criminal evidence law (prosecutorial burden and evidence rules) presents an impressively complex challenge.

These elements are not standalone laws but integral parts of their traditional legal systems. Given the antithetical views of the judges in their written opinions in the ICC cases that follow, the question is whether these elements can function effectively without their roots found in continental criminal procedure or common law evidence law or without their legal history. They have evolved within the traditional systems and mindsets of the judges who apply them. This raises a critical question: What happens when judges are required to use both elements in a trial but are trained and experienced in only one of the two legal traditions? The elements have evolved within their own systems, and judges perceive them as integral parts of their national legal systems. Familiarity is crucial, yet national judges are naturally unfamiliar with other legal systems. When they become international judges, is it assumed they inherit the required legal conceptual understanding of both traditions?

When Legrand discussed the incompatibility of the two traditions under the European Community entity, he addressed their fundamental differences, including legal reasoning, systematization, the character of rules, the role of facts, the meaning of rights, and the role of legal precedent. He emphasized that prior understanding must exist, what he called "cognitive commensurability". He stated that the two systems do have shared epistemological premises. In expressing these differences, Legrand seemed to favour the continental system more.

The ICC's hybrid system did not incorporate foreign elements into a pre-existing cultural and legal order. Instead, it selectively chose elements from other legal systems to create its own new legal order. As a result, there were no pre-existing norms to contradict the newly adopted features. But what about the judges who run the Court? Here, Legrand's critique becomes highly relevant in practice. Judges bring their ingrained legal and cultural backgrounds with them. What happens when the continental judges meet their common law peers? Do they end up in harmonized symbiosis or do their decisions show otherwise?

This book shows that judges familiar with one or the other legal system interpret and apply evidence rules and the burden of proof differently, resulting in case law inconsistencies. The influence of judges' original legal cultures validates Legrand's concerns.

This is the difficulty of the ICC legal transplants and the challenges of harmonizing a unified legal system. This analysis indicates that judges stayed within their own legal cultures. When the burden of proof meets free evaluation, continental judges easily apply the principle of free evaluation. Conversely, common law judges, accustomed to stability in evidence law, maintain the burden of proof principles with ease.

Through case law analysis, I have concluded that continental judges have conceptually misunderstood evidence evaluation in an adversarial trial. The ICC trial incorporates both adversarial and continental features. However, the prosecutorial burden would vanish if the trial were purely continental. Interestingly, however, the legal framework of the ICC has put antithetical elements as the prosecutorial burden of proof and the free evaluation of evidence in an adversarial setting. The prosecutorial burden prevails as it is genuinely compatible with the presumption of innocence.

The ICC evidence law transplants are deeply embedded in their original cultural contexts. When transplanted, they created a new legal regime. However, the significance is judges from the transplants' cultural backgrounds participate in the ICC. The discussed case law seems to support the observation that the diverse legal backgrounds of its judges create friction and inconsistency. The ICC's attempt to blend these systems has not fully bridged the cultural and procedural gaps, leading to the observed divergences that follow later in this book.

While the theory of legal transplants provides a framework for understanding how and if antithetical legal transplants can be integrated, it is crucial to consider the practical challenges ICC judges face in applying the transplanted elements within the ICC's regime. To ensure the Court's effective functioning, it is not enough to merely combine elements from different legal systems; there must also be a concerted effort to foster a unified legal culture and understanding among its judges and practitioners. The cases of *Bemba*, *Gbagbo*, and *Ongwen* highlight the challenges of integrating different legal traditions.

Recognizing the ICC's hybridity as a living reality, I firmly believe that the need for shared understanding in legal traditions should be viewed as the target, not the obstacle, for advancing international criminal justice. This is where our focus should be, and this book identifies the points of misunderstanding to address them effectively.

7 Is the Canadian Paradigm a Transplant Proposal?

Historically speaking, during the Rome Conference, the Canadian delegation was instrumental in negotiating critical aspects of the ICC's foundation, including its jurisdiction, definition of crimes, and procedural principles. Known for bridging divides and creatively addressing concerns, Canada helped preserve the core principles necessary for a robust ICC. Despite weeks of extensive negotiations resolving many technical issues, significant divisions remained on critical points like the Court's jurisdiction and independence. Philippe Kirsch, chairing the Committee of the Whole, with the support of coordinators, drafted a final, balanced proposal. This draft reflected the majority's desire for a strong and independent ICC while constructively addressing minority views. On the conference's final day, the proposal crafted under Canada's leadership gained widespread approval.[54]

While this book's proposal is not directly related to this history, it acknowledges Canada's legal sophistication and international influence as a common law country.[55] However, although Canada is generally considered a common law country, the legal system in the Province of Quebec is unique. The Quebec Act of 1774, passed by the British Parliament, restored French civil law in Quebec. Consequently, private law in Quebec is governed by the Civil Code of Quebec, which has its roots in French and Napoleonic traditions. However,

54 The Rome Statute of the International Criminal Court was ultimately adopted by a notable vote of 120 in favour, 7 against, and 21 abstentions, marking a significant achievement for international justice. Government of Canada, Canada and the International Criminal Court. Available at https://www.international.gc.ca/world-monde/international_relations-relations_internationales/icc-cpi/index.aspx?lang=eng.

55 *See* Ran Hirschl, *Comparative Matters: The Renaissance of Comparative Constitutional Law* (Oxford: Oxford University Press, 2014) 30–31, for insights on the Supreme Court of Canada to new approaches, especially regarding universal concepts. *See also* Peter McCormick, "Waiting for Globalization: An Empirical Study of the McLachlin Court's Foreign Judicial Citations" (2009) 41:2 Ottawa L Rev 209–243, about the non-Canadian citations by the Supreme Court of Canada in supporting law globalization. This practice of citing foreign judicial decisions is seen as a way to support and contribute to the globalization of law. It reflects the Court's openness to integrating international perspectives and aligning Canadian legal standards with broader, global legal principles.

public law, including criminal law and procedure, follows the common law system, consistent with the rest of Canada.

Canada's evolving legal history demonstrates a profound respect for social, political, and cultural norms. Given the complexity of merging these two legal traditions, the next step is identifying practical models to guide this integration. The Canadian legal system, known for its principled approach to evidence law, offers valuable insights. More importantly, the Supreme Court of Canada has issued landmark decisions informed by global legal practices and philosophies, consistently avoiding chauvinism and reflecting a commitment to universal principles of justice.[56] Moreover, the American model typically represents the adversarial system in comparative legal studies, while the German model exemplifies the continental approach. However, Canada's model has uniquely influenced many jurisdictions, mainly through its "model of proof in human rights procedures", fostering a deeper legal understanding with its theoretical discussions. This influence underscores Canada's role in shaping international jurisprudence.[57]

This book suggests considering the Canadian judicial thinking process on evidence law as a model for the ICC. This is not a proposal to transplant Canada's evidence law into the ICC's legal framework. Instead, it recommends that the ICC develop its evidence law, drawing inspiration from the Canadian principled approach to handling complex evidence issues. The ICC could benefit from integrating best practices from various legal systems. However, the crucial point is ensuring the ICC judges are not left struggling alone to adapt their national legal experience to the unique demands of the ICC's international legal order. Without proper support, conflicts in their written opinions are inevitable.

Adopting legal transplants within the ICC, given the diverse legal traditions of its judges, without providing them advanced training can only result in case law inconsistency. As Judge Meron emphasized, the use of precedents by judges should prioritize certainty while also allowing for evolution in the

56 *See*, for example, the case *Carter* v. *Canada (Attorney General)*, 2015 SCC 5, [2015]. In discussing the issue of euthanasia, particularly assisted suicide, the Canadian Supreme Court noted that the legislative landscape on physician-assisted death has evolved significantly since the precedent set in Rodriguez in 1993. At that time, no Western democracy permitted assistance in dying. By 2010, however, eight jurisdictions allowed some form of assisted dying: the Netherlands, Belgium, Luxembourg, Switzerland, Columbia, Oregon, Washington, and Montana, at para 8.

57 Moshe Cohen, "The Burden of Proof in Comparative and International Human Rights Law: Civil and Common Law Approaches with Special Reference to the American and German Legal Systems" (1999) 93: 2 AJIL 557–558.

interest of justice.[58] This balanced approach ensures that while the legal system remains stable and predictable, it can also adapt to new circumstances and evolving interpretations to better serve justice.

This research focuses on evidence law, a field distinct from mere procedural codification. In modern common law systems, evidence law transcends the simple listing of rules and procedures. It is a dynamic, ever-evolving discipline shaped by case law to address complex evidence issues. It involves a deeper understanding of the purpose and function of evidence within the judicial system, focusing on fair and just decision-making rather than merely following procedural rules. It embodies a principled approach to evidence, continuously refining how evidence is treated to uphold fair trial rights. This is precisely the transformative power that the ICC needs: a bespoke, adaptive body of evidence law that evolves with its unique challenges and steadfastly serves the cause of justice.

To address challenges, it's crucial to acknowledge the inherent differences in legal reasoning among ICC judges. The ICC can achieve greater consistency and mitigate differences and critiques by developing its own evidence law tailored to its unique and complex cases.[59] Canadian evidence law, with its thorough case law analysis of evidence principles, can serve as an exemplary model that can help bridge continental tradition with common law, fostering a unified legal culture within the ICC.

---

58 Theodor Meron, *supra* note 12 at 34.

59 *See Independent Expert Review of the International Criminal Court and the Rome Statute System Final Report* September 30, 2020, online https://asp.icc-cpi.int/Review-Court. *See also* the difficulties of "old evidence" collection and evaluation in Morten Bergamo, Cheah Wui Ling & Antonio Angotti, eds., *Old Evidence and Core International Crimes* (Brussels: Torkel Opsahl Academic EPublisher, 2024).

CHAPTER 3

The Case of Jean-Pierre Bemba Gombo

Look, I've got scars on my body from the Bemba militia

•••

"We saw Bemba arrive by helicopter, ransack our homes, leave with our belongings, and give orders here," declared PK12 and Damara victims, who were taken aback when FIDH explained the reasons for the acquittal.

•••

What hurts the most, is, that in the eyes of the world, we don't exist anymore.

•••

How did it happen that Bemba was not found guilty?

•••

The ICC did not do its work properly[1]

1 International Federation of Human Rights (FIDH), The Bemba Case: Heavily Criticized, The ICC Must Maintain Victims' Legal Representation as the Establishment of Assistance Programs for Victims Is Awaited, press release, online: https://www.fidh.org/en/region/Africa/central-african-republic/the-bemba-case-heavily-criticised-the-icc-must-maintain-victims-legal.

 | DOI:10.1163/9789004741010_004

1 The Situation of the Central African Republic (2002–2003)

On 2016 the ICC Trial Chamber convicted Mr. Jean Pierre Bemba.[2] The accused was a national of the Democratic Republic of Congo (DRC). Mr. Bemba was considered a powerful, educated politician and served as one of the four vice presidents of the Democratic Republic of Congo. In 1998 he founded the Mouvement de libération du Congo (MLC) to overthrow the government in Kinshasa. This movement gradually became a political party and in 1999 adopted its own statute. The four organs of the political party were the President, the Political Military Council, the General Secretariat, and the Armée de libération du Congo (ALC), its military branch. The army's structure was similar to the army of the Democratic Republic of Congo and other armies and comprised approximately 20,000 soldiers.[3] From 1998 and throughout the time of the alleged crimes in the Central African Republic (CAR), Bemba was the President of the Mouvement de libération du Congo, the leader of the political party, and the Commander-in-Chief of the ALC. He also held the military rank of Divisional General.[4]

In the neighbouring Central African Republic, Ange-Félix Patassé was the first President elected twice through a democratic process in the CAR. In 2001, General François Bozizé was behind an attempted coup d'état against Patassé. The President dismissed him by presidential decree from being the Chief of the Forces Armées Centrafricaines (FACA), and an arrest warrant was issued against him. Bozizé did not comply with the arrest warrant and started an armed resistance trying to overthrow Patassé.[5] On October 25, 2002, his rebels arrived in Bangui. Patassé called Bemba for help.

Bemba deployed ALC troops from the Democratic Republic of Congo to the Central Africa Republic "to intervene in support of President Patassé".[6] The Trial Chamber's decision confirms that, in addition to his friendship with the President, Bemba also had strategic military and logistical reasons related to having a "rear base" in the area. The MLC troops in the CAR consisted of about

2 ICC, *The Prosecution* v. *Jean Pierre Bemba Gombo*, No. ICC- 01/05-01/08, Judgment pursuant to Article 74 of the Statute, ICC, March 21, 2016.

3 *Ibid* at para 390, for the details of the ALC structure. *Ibid* at paras 391–393, for the soldiers' training and their code of conduct.

4 *Ibid* at para 384.

5 International Federation of Human Rights, Report of the FIDH Legal Action Group (LAG) FIDH and the situation in the Central African Republic before the International Criminal Court The case of Jean-Pierre Bemba, 4, online: https://www.fidh.org/IMG/pdf/CPIaffbemba502ang2008.pdf.

6 ICC-01/05-01/08, March 21, 2016, *supra* note 2 at paras 380, 382, 453.

1500 men (three battalions).[7] They arrived in the CAR on October 26, 2002 and, alongside other forces aligned with President Patassé, commenced operations no later than October 27, 2002. The last rebels of General Bozizé withdrew from Bangui on October 30, 2002. However, counterattacks followed for months. The MLC troops maintained their presence throughout Bangui, committing acts of rape, murder, and pillaging against civilians.[8]

Wondering why that happened, we find some answers in the Trial Chamber's decision:

> As for the motivations behind the soldiers' conduct, there is evidence that MLC soldiers sought to punish civilians in the CAR, for example, for MLC losses or as suspected enemies or enemy sympathizers.

Some MLC soldiers considered victims to be "war booty" and/or sought to destabilize, humiliate, and punish suspected rebels and rebel sympathizers. MLC soldiers killed or threatened to kill those who resisted acts of pillaging and rape.[9]

The civil population of the CAR reported murders, rapes, and pillaging committed by the MLC troops. The victims' descriptions revealed horrific violence.[10] Bemba, after receiving the reports, ordered the *Mondonga Inquiry* and arrests, which were executed. In November 2002 Bemba travelled to the CAR and met President Patassé. He also addressed the MLC troops. Some witnesses said that his speech resulted in a reduction of crimes but others did not agree. Regardless of this dispute, the ICC Trial Chamber decided that the crimes continued after Bemba's speech.[11] As per the *Mondonga Inquiry*, it did not address responsibility for murders and rapes but only for pillaging. Finally, only seven soldiers were arrested and tried by an MLC court-martial on December 5, 2002. The trial took place in the DRC, and the soldiers were convicted for pillaging and sentenced to three to twenty-four months of detention. Bemba sent the court-martial report to the UN representative on January 4, 2003. He also referred the report to the FIDH President in February.[12] Bemba took more measures to find what happened, but nothing

7 *Ibid* at para 410.
8 *Ibid* at paras 456, 458, 460, 461.
9 *Ibid* at paras 565, 567.
10 *Ibid* at paras 462–523. *See also* FIDHA report, *supra* note 5.
11 ICC-01/05-01/08, March 21, 2016 *supra* note 2 at paras 590–591, 593–594, 596.
12 *Ibid* at paras 582–583, 586, 589, 597, 599–600.

helped to bring the culprits before the court, and his measures did not stop crimes.[13]

As the Central African Republic ratified the Rome Statute in 2001, the Government could refer to the ICC crimes, defined by the Rome Statute, which occurred in its territory. On December 21, 2004, the Government referred the case to the ICC. In June 2005, the ICC Prosecutor received documents about the crimes committed in the territory in 2002–2003, along with the records of the related unsuccessful judicial proceedings in Bangui.[14] The President of the CAR at that time was François Bozizé.

When the ICC Prosecutor examined the information received, she decided to open an investigation (May 10, 2007). The Rome Statute requirements were satisfied. A public announcement followed on May 27, 2007. One year later, an arrest warrant against Jean Pierre Bemba was issued, and Mr. Bemba was arrested on May 24, 2008 in Belgium.[15]

The charges were that he was responsible as a military commander (Article 28a of the Rome Statute) for the crimes committed by MLC troops in the CAR under his effective command. His MLC troops had committed crimes against humanity of murder (Article 7(1)(g)), and the war crimes of murder (Article 8(2)(c)(i)), rape (Article 8(2)(e)(vi)), and pillaging (Article 8(2)(e)(v)) against the civilian population.[16] The freezing and seizure of Mr. Bemba's property and assets followed soon after his arrest.

On July 4, 2008, Mr. Bemba appeared for the first time before the ICC. On January 15, 2009, Pre-Trial Chamber II considered that "there was sufficient evidence to establish substantial grounds to believe that Mr. Bemba is criminally responsible for having effectively acted as a military commander within the meaning of Article 28(a) of the Statute, for war crimes (murder, rape, and pillaging) and crimes against humanity (murder and rape)".[17]

Mr. Bemba's trial started one year later (November 2010). According to the case information, throughout the proceedings, the Chamber: (a) issued 1219 written decisions, orders, notifications, and cooperation requests, as well as 277 oral decisions and orders; (b) admitted a total of 733 items of

---

13 *Ibid*, the Zongo Commission, Bemba's Correspondence with General Cissé, and the Sibut Mission, paras 601–606, 612–620.

14 International Criminal Court, *Case information sheet: Situation in the Central African Republic*, online: https://www.icc-cpi.int/CaseInformationSheets/bembaEng.pdf.

15 *See also* Noah Weisbord, *The Crime of Aggression* (Princeton, NJ, USA: Princeton University Press, 2019) 154.

16 ICC-01/05-01/08, March 21, 2016, *supra* note 2 at para 380.

17 ICC, Case information sheet, *supra* note 14.

evidence, including 5724 pages of documents; (c) sat for 330 working days and heard 77 witnesses, including 40 witnesses called by the Prosecution, 34 called by the Defence, two witnesses called by the Legal Representative of Victims and one witness called by the Chamber, and also permitted three victims to directly present their views and concerns; and (d) granted 5229 persons the status of victims authorized to participate in the proceedings.[18] The trial lasted four years. The parties' last day of their closing arguments was November 13, 2014.

On March 21, 2016, Trial Chamber III, in a unanimous decision, declared Jean Pierre Bemba guilty beyond any reasonable doubt of two counts of crimes against humanity (murder and rape) and three counts of war crimes (murder, rape, and pillaging). The Court decided that the measures Bemba took when he learned about the committed crimes in the CAR by his troops "were limited in mandate, execution and /or results". His response was considered "grossly inadequate", politically motivated, and "directly related to the negotiation of the Sun City agreements".[19]

The sentence of 18 years in prison was announced on June 21, 2016.

Three appeals followed, one by Mr. Bemba against his conviction and two by both Mr. Bemba and the Prosecutor against the sentence. In January 2018, the appeal was heard by the Appeals Chamber. On June 8, 2018, Mr. Bemba was acquitted by a majority decision.

Reuters reported:

> A crowd of hundreds of supporters cheered outside Bemba's party headquarters in the Congo capital Kinshasa, shouting: *Our president is free! Jean Pierre Bemba is our candidate!*[20] [emphasis added]

Mr. Bemba had remained in custody for ten years. Soon, he was released from prison. The victims of the MLC troops' atrocities in the CAR operation were shocked.

---

18 *Ibid.*

19 *Ibid* at paras 720, 727, 730. *See also* ICC, Case information sheet, *supra* note 14.

20 Stephanie Van Den Berg, "Congolese ex-Vice President Bemba acquitted of war crimes on appeal", Reuters June 8, 2018, online: https://www.reuters.com/article/us-warcrimes-congo-bemba-idUSKCN1J42GN; Africa News.com., "Jean Pierre Bemba's return to DRC [The Morning Call]" (August 2, 2018), online: https://www.africanews.com/2018/08/02/jean-pierre-bemba-s-return-to-drc-the-morning-call/.

2 Defining the Central Legal Question of This Case

No one ever denied that horrible crimes happened in the Central African Republic between October 27, 2002 and March 15, 2003. The legal question, however, for the ICC is whether the Prosecutor proved that Mr. Bemba was guilty beyond a reasonable doubt for the crimes committed by his MLC troops according to the Rome Statute. While the Rome Statute encompasses two legal traditions, free evaluation must operate within an adversarial trial according to the standard of proof beyond a reasonable doubt.

The Trial Court and the Appeal Court issued dissimilar decisions. However, the issue here is neither whether Bemba was guilty or innocent nor the proper role of appellate review.[21] The question is why the Trial and the Appeal decisions reveal important contradictory views on evidence assessment for admissibility and weight reasons. Does this indicate an important problem for the ICC?

The chapter discusses a few interlocutory decisions on evidence matters issued between 2010 and 2012 and the appeal from one of them. It then discusses the Trial decision in 2016 and the Appeal Chamber decision in 2018, which reversed it.

3 Evidence Admissibility by the ICC

The legal framework of the ICC gives discretion to the Court in respect of rulings on evidence admission and evaluation. Article 74(2) of the Statute provides that "the Court may base its decision only on evidence submitted and discussed before it at the trial". Relevance and admissibility are raised when evidence is submitted before a Chamber.[22] However, Article 69(4) states:

> The Court *may* rule on the relevance or admissibility of any evidence, taking into account, inter alia, the probative value of the evidence and any prejudice that such evidence may cause to a fair trial or to a fair evaluation of the testimony of a witness, in accordance with the Rules of Procedure and Evidence. [emphasis added]

---

21 See ICC, *Independent Expert Review of the International Criminal Court and the Rome Statute System, Final Report*, September 30, 2020, paras 608–613, online: https://asp.icc-cpi.int/iccdocs/asp_docs/ASP19/IER-Final-Report-ENG.pdf.

22 ICC, Rules of Procedures and Evidence, Rule 4.

The use of "may" has been interpreted broadly to mean that the Trial Chamber can deal with evidence admissibility either when submitted or later at the end of the trial when evaluating the totality of the evidence.[23] Moreover, Rule 63(2) provides that the Court can "assess freely all evidence submitted" to determine relevance or admissibility. Also, the Trial Chamber may request the submission of evidence if it is considered "necessary for the determination of the truth".[24] Here, it is clear that free evaluation applies for "relevance or admissibility" reasons only. However, it is not clear why the Statute uses "or" instead of "and". Relevance is attached to admissibility reasons.

The Court may rule on the relevance and admissibility of any evidence, taking into account, *inter alia*, the probative value of the considered evidence and whether it outweighs prejudice. Prejudice is assessed narrowly in regard only to fair trial concerns or fair evaluation of witness testimony.[25] The Court must give reasons for any evidence ruling,[26] and it shall not admit evidence illegally obtained by means of a violation of the "Statute or internationally recognized human rights".[27] Irrelevant or inadmissible evidence shall not be considered by the Court.[28] Finally, and most importantly, Article 66 guarantees that the accused is presumed innocent, and the prosecution has the burden of proving guilt beyond reasonable doubt.

The legal framework provides the authority for the model of free assessment of judicial thinking when the Court deals with the admission of evidence. Traditionally, the continental free assessment of evidence goes along with the truth-seeking mission of the Court. Here, the ICC can call for more evidence for truth-seeking reasons. However, to the extent that the ICC Chambers can investigate the truth, this should not prevail over the prosecutor's duty to prove guilt beyond reasonable doubt. The Court's ultimate role should be to ensure a fair trial which safeguards the presumption of innocence.

Article 74(2) requires the Trial Chamber to decide "based on its evaluation of the evidence and the entire proceedings". Here the Statute does not use the term "free" because free evaluation is not applicable when the prosecutorial burden applies. The decision must "contain a full and reasoned statement of the Trial Chamber's findings on the evidence and conclusions".[29] It is manda-

23 Donald K. Piragoff, "Evidence", in Otto Triffterer, ed., *Commentary on the Rome Statute of the International Criminal Court* (München, C.H. Beck Hart Nomos, 2008) 1322.

24 Article 69(3).

25 Article 69(4).

26 Article 64(2).

27 Article 69(7).

28 Rule 64(3).

29 Article 74(5).

tory to issue a reasoned judgement explaining why and how guilt is proven. The decision should explain the treatment of both inculpatory and exculpatory evidence. Judicial review is secured through clear and justified arguments. The first outcome is that the Statute's free evaluation applies only at the time of admissibility decisions. However, free evaluation on admission is governed by relevance, probative value, and prejudice.

3.1 *Relevance, Probative Value, and Prejudice in the* Bemba *Interlocutory Decisions*

In the *Bemba* case, we will first examine some interlocutory Court decisions related to the admissibility of evidence. This will show the Court's conceptual understanding of evidence law.

In 2010, the Trial Court decided on the admission into evidence of materials contained in the prosecution's evidence list. The Majority's decision introduced the term "*prima facie* admissibility".[30] According to this decision, a "*prima facie* assessment" on evidence admission is related to what is "*a priori* relevant to the case".[31] This phase was distinguished by the Court from the determination phase on probative value and weight to be given at the final judgement of the case. It was also clarified that probative value "refers *inter alia* to the reliability and weight" of the evidence.[32] The Majority also referred to the drafting history of the Rome Statute and the adoption of civil law "flexibility" instead of the common law "technical formalities".[33] The *prima facie* assessment was considered "significant" in terms of time-saving, which favoured an expeditious trial that respected fair trial rights.[34]

The dissenting decision of Judge Ozaki argued that the legal framework of the ICC never provided an "intermediate stage" of admissibility.[35] Therefore, "*prima facie* admissibility" was not permitted. Evidence should be admitted or not before the end of the trial in a piece-by-piece process, not in a "wholesale admission". Here, the Court seems to have invented one more stage for evidence evaluation: two for admissibility reasons and one for weight assessment. There is also some confusion or lack of clarity regarding the specific role of

30 ICC-01/05-01/08, November 19, 2010 at para 9.

31 *Ibid* at para 10.

32 *Ibid* at para 9.

33 *Ibid* at para 17, with reference to Donald K. Piragoff, "Evidence", in Roy S. Lee & Håkan Friman, ed., *The International Criminal Court. Elements of Crimes and Rules of Procedure and Evidence* (New York, NY: Transnational Publishers, 2001) 349–401, and Piragoff, *supra* note 23 at 1317.

34 *Ibid* at paras 23, 24.

35 ICC-01/05-01/08, November 23, 2010.

probative value when it is considered alongside other factors such as reliability, weight, and prejudice in legal proceedings. The court has stated that probative value includes or pertains to the reliability and weight of the evidence, but how it interacts with or is distinguished from these other factors (reliability, weight, and prejudice) remains unclear.

Moreover, Judge Ozaki discussed the risks of hearsay evidence admission in this case. She said that although hearsay evidence is not excluded according to the Statute, it does not have the same probative value as direct evidence.[36] This decision focused on the potential violation of accused rights when evidence, especially hearsay, is admitted as a whole, and explained the hearsay perils against the fair trial right. As per the role of professional judges, she stated:[37]

> While professional judges are, unlike a jury, capable of evaluating the probative value that may be granted to hearsay evidence, this should not serve as a justification for the automatic introduction into evidence of statements which may be, given their nature, prejudicial to the fair conduct of the proceedings or to a fair evaluation of the in-court testimony of a witness.

The Appeal Court in 2011, with a unanimous decision,[38] clarified that no such term or process as "*prima facie* admissibility" is provided by the Statute or the Rules of Procedure and Evidence. Therefore, the Trial Court had acted outside the required legal framework. This Appeal decision stated that the Trial Court should have given the parties the opportunity to raise arguments on relevance and admissibility according to Rule 64(1).[39] A wholesale admission showed little if no consideration for each piece of evidence,[40] and it resulted in an improper exercise of judicial discretion.[41] While expeditiousness is a fair trial component, it cannot justify statutory deviations.[42] Therefore, the Trial Court had to consider relevance, probative value, and potential prejudice for each piece of evidence at some point, either when the evidence was submitted or at the end of the trial.[43] Timing is not a statutory concern according to Article 67

36 *Ibid* at paras 10, 11, 12.

37 *Ibid* at para 10.

38 ICC-01/05-01/08 OA 5 OA 6, May 3, 2011.

39 *Ibid* at para 50.

40 *Ibid* at para 52.

41 *Ibid* at para 79.

42 *Ibid* at para 55.

43 ICC-01/05-01/08, *supra* note 38, para 37.

(1)(a), which clarifies the right of the accused to be promptly informed in detail of the nature, cause, and content of the charge as part of his right of evidence disclosure.[44]

Regarding hearsay evidence, the Court found its admission incompatible with the principle of orality.[45] This principle safeguards the right of the accused to confront evidence against him.[46] The Appeal decision distinguished between direct and hearsay evidence and clearly stated the restrictions set by Rule 68 for the admission of prior recorded testimonies. Moreover, it clarified that, according to Articles 68(5) and 69(2), any deviation from the general rule of in-court personal testimony should not be prejudicial and should take into account the rights of the accused and the fairness of the entire process. The Court noted the factors to consider when admitting hearsay evidence of a prior recorded witness testimony.[47]

In another 2011 decision, the Trial Court's Majority decided in favour of the "submission into evidence of the entirety of the witnesses' statement(s) (…) when considered necessary for the determination of the truth" as provided by Article 69(3).[48] Judge Ozaki dissented.[49] The Court stated that it would consider the admissibility of each piece of evidence if the parties raised objections.[50] Furthermore, the Majority ruled that despite the absence of evidence submitted by a party, the Court may request a submission of evidence to determine the truth.[51]

In 2012,[52] the Trial Court ruled on the admissibility of evidence item-by-item with respect to the Prosecution's and Defence's requests for evidence

---

44 *Ibid* at para 63.

45 This Appeal Court interlocutory majority decision does not refer to the term "hearsay evidence". It refers to the term of "prior witnesses' " written statements. The Court seems to prefer describing the evidence than characterizing the kind of evidence. The Trial Chamber Judgment pursuant to Article 74 of the Statute names the evidence as hearsay evidence, ICC-01/05-01/08, March 21, 2016 at para 238.

46 ICC-01/05-01/08, *supra* note 38 at paras 74–78.

47 ICC Rules, *supra* note 22 at Rule 68 (2)(b)(i).

48 ICC-01/05-01/08, May 31, 2011 (Decision on the order of the procedure to the submission of evidence).

49 *Ibid* Judge Ozaki, in her dissenting opinion, disagreed with paras 11 and 12 of the Majority decision. She said that the decision was not in accordance with the provision of Rule 68 (2) and there was an *expressed preference* by the Court *for the admission of these statements in their entirety*.

50 *Ibid* at para 11.

51 *Ibid* at para 12.

52 ICC-01/05-01/08, February 09, 2012, Decision on prosecution and defence requests for Admission of Evidence, dated December 15, 2011.

admission. The Court stated that applying the principle of free evaluation to assess whether the submitted evidence is relevant and admissible will follow a three-part test. The test will examine whether the submitted evidence is relevant to the trial, whether it has probative value and whether the evidence is sufficiently relevant and probative to outweigh prejudice.[53]

With respect to prejudice, the Court ruled that even if prejudice may exist, the question is whether the probative value and relevance outweigh it. If so, the evidence will be admitted regardless of prejudice. Conversely, the evidence will not be admitted if potential prejudice is so great as to outweigh probative value and relevance. However, these assessments on relevance, probative value, and prejudice were only "preliminary in nature".[54] The Court would assess the entire evidence and determine the weight to be given to each piece of evidence at the end of the trial.

The Court explained the three parts of the test. First, the submitted evidence is relevant when it can logically make a fact more or less probable and, therefore, can help the Court resolve the case. Relevance is assessed either in isolation or in relation to other evidence. Secondly, probative value is considered "through a fact-specific inquiry", looking at indicia of reliability, trustworthiness, accuracy, voluntariness, related circumstances to the evidence, authentication, and whether the item is what it purports to be. Thirdly, evidence is considered prejudicial when it unfairly prejudices the presentation of the parties' case. More importantly, the admission of the evidence should not affect the accused's rights and the fairness of the procedure.[55] However, this is a very narrow view of prejudice which concentrates on fairness and does not account for other potentially adverse consequences of admission. In the absence of parties' objections on admissibility, evidence was admitted by the Court as relevant,[56] even when the Defence abstained from giving reasons on admissibility.[57]

The three-part test seems accurate here. Later, we will understand whether and how the Court applied the test.

3.2 *The Hearsay Evidence in the* Bemba *Interlocutory Decisions*

Some forms of hearsay evidence were discussed by the Court in the 2012 decision. The majority (Judge Ozaki dissenting) admitted the hearsay evidence of

53 *Ibid* at paras 13–16.
54 *Ibid* at para 18.
55 *Ibid* at paras 14–16.
56 *See*, for example, *ibid* at paras 24, 31, 56, 79.
57 *See*, for example, *ibid* at paras 52, 73, 115.

prior witnesses' written testimonies since these witnesses had testified before the Court. The Court distinguished between those statements that are "complements" to the (same) witnesses' in-court testimonies and those which are "supplements". The decision stated that the principle of orality is not violated when the hearsay can be used as a "complement" to direct evidence. If the statements can help the Court to better evaluate the in-court testimony, it should be admissible.[58] Finally, the Majority admitted evidence of prior witnesses' testimonies in order "to be able to compare a witness" testimony against the entirety of his or her written statement and therefore to "properly discharge its statutory truth-finding prerogative".[59] Here, the Court was apparently serving the truth-finding regime to evaluate the credibility of an in-court testimony through the hearsay evidence of a prior written statement.

Another category of hearsay evidence submitted by the prosecution consisted of 203 *procès-verbaux* given to a CAR magistrate. Significantly, the Court accepted a wholesale admission of all items in this category. When the Court applied the three-part test of relevance, probative value, and prejudice, it took some steps that warrant comments. Both with respect to relevance and prejudice, the Court emphasized that the hearsay was offered not to prove the accused's criminal responsibility but only "contextual elements of the crimes charged".

The Court's understanding of prejudice was narrow. It did not include a consideration of the potential adverse consequences like how these items may mislead ultimate fact-finding and whether they created any moral prejudice to the accused.[60] Regarding probative value, the Court looked more intently at factors of authenticity than matters of frailty and the question of how strongly and cogently the items proved what they purported to prove.

4 The Trial Court's Final Assessment of Evidence

The Trial Chamber convicted Bemba. The Court, in this decision,[61] recognised that each element of the crime should be established beyond reasonable doubt and that the burden was on the Prosecution.[62] The Trial decision clari-

---

58 *Ibid* at para 143.

59 *Ibid.*

60 *See* the discussion on prejudice in *R.v. Handy*, [2002] 2 S.C.R. 908, 2002 SCC 56 at paras 41–42, 56–57, 71–74, 100–101.

61 ICC-01/05-01/08, March 21, 2016, Judgment pursuant to Article 74 of the Statute.

62 *Ibid* at para 215.

fied that the Court followed the earlier Appeal Court's decision to defer the ruling on evidence and admissibility under Article 69(4) until the end of the proceedings, "making it part of its assessment of the evidence when it is evaluating the guilt or innocence of the accused person".[63] It would make a final determination of the weight of each evidence item at the end of the case based on the totality of the evidence, performing a "holistic evaluation".[64]

Here, the Court seems to conflate the evaluation of the totality of admitted evidence with a holistic evaluation of the entire submitted evidence. In other words, the Court wrongly treats the process of considering all evidence together as equivalent to evaluating each piece of the admitted evidence within the context of the totality.

As per the truth-seeking mission, the Court said that establishing truth is a principal statutory objective according to Article 69(3), and, therefore, the Court should "actively contribute".[65] The decision said that the "statutory framework" provides the Court with "a considerable degree of flexibility in weighing the evidence brought before it" and, according to the ICC legal framework, there is no type of evidence inadmissible per se.[66]

The Court summarized its view of evidence assessment:[67]

> In performing its "holistic evaluation and weighing of all the evidence" it is under *no obligation* "to refer to the testimony of every witness or every piece of evidence on the trial record". [emphasis added]
>
> Where it "did not refer to the evidence given by a witness, even if it is in contradiction to the Trial Chamber's finding, *it is to be presumed* that the Trial Chamber assessed and weighed the evidence, but found that the evidence did not prevent it from arriving at its actual findings". [emphasis added]

More specifically for hearsay evidence the Court stated:[68]

63 ICC-01/05-01/08-OA 5 OA 6, May 3, 2011 at para 37.
64 ICC-01/05-01/08, *supra* note 61 at paras 222–223, 225.
65 *Ibid* at para 232, fn.528, with reference to *Ngudjolo* Appeal Judgment and subsequent quotation. *See also ibid* at para 232, fn. 529 with reference to *Lubanga* Appeal Judgement and subsequent quotation.
66 *Ibid* at para 235, fn. 533.
67 *Ibid* at para 227, with reference to the ICTY and ICTR jurisprudence.
68 *Ibid* at para 238.

> The Chamber took a cautious approach in assessing evidence originating from hearsay. It did not rule out such evidence *ab initio, instead assessing the weight to be accorded to it,* taking into account the context and conditions in which such evidence was obtained, and with due consideration of the impossibility of questioning the information source in court. [emphasis added]

Regarding the hearsay evidence of *procès-verbaux,* the decision said that the Court relied on them "to the extent that they corroborate other evidence related to the contextual elements of the crimes charged".[69]

For circumstantial evidence the Court stated:[70]

> Nothing in the statutory framework prevents the Chamber from relying on circumstantial evidence. When based on the evidence available, there is only one reasonable conclusion to be drawn therein, the Chamber has concluded that particular facts have been established beyond reasonable doubt. Further, in relation to the mental elements of crimes, the Chamber notes that, pursuant to paragraph 3 of the General introduction to the Elements of Crimes, "[e]xistence of intent and knowledge can be inferred from relevant facts and circumstances".

Regarding fourteen witnesses' testimonies about which the parties had expressed concerns of "serious unresolved issues",[71] the Court referred to its discretion and stated:[72]

> The Chamber has *full discretion* to analyse, consider, and evaluate the weight of any evidence in the record in its determination of the truth and bases its decision pursuant to Article 74(2) on its evaluation of the evidence and the entire proceedings. In this determination, the Chamber, guided by its duty to ensure the fairness of the trial and full respect for the rights of the Accused, has assessed and carefully weighed all the evidence before it. [emphasis added]

In this decision, the Trial Court never ruled on evidence admissibility, but it admitted the evidence at a preliminary stage. Then, at the deliberation stage,

---

69 *Ibid* at para 266.
70 *Ibid* at para 239.
71 *Ibid* at para 262.
72 *Ibid* at para 263.

it failed to explain which evidence was considered admissible and for which reasons. However, the Court did not feel that it had failed but rather that it was acting according to the "full" discretion the free evaluation of evidence permits.

Using a common law evidence lens, we observe that in the decisions above, the Court addressed prejudice through the defence's fair trial rights, specifically focusing on disclosure and confrontation. The admission of hearsay evidence was freely assessed for truth-seeking purposes, allowing broad judicial discretion. The Court used hearsay evidence to investigate witnesses' credibility while simultaneously weighing the overall evidence.

The Court embarked on an investigative, truth-seeking mission, using the flexible method of free evaluation. It also assumed the Prosecutor's role of proving guilt beyond a reasonable doubt. Confident in the efficacy of free evaluation within a truth-seeking process, the Court exercised its discretion to bypass rulings on evidence admissibility, focusing instead on weighing the evidence based on a broad and often vague analysis. This approach is characteristic of the classic continental system.

In classic continental legal systems, both the prosecutor and the court are engaged in a joint truth-seeking mission. In the absence of the prosecutorial burden of proof, the primary fair trial tool available is the *in dubio pro reo* principle. This maxim, which favours the defendant, generally applies to all elements of a crime, unlike the reasonable doubt standard in the common law tradition, which applies to the core elements alone. *In dubio pro reo*, a Latin term meaning "when in doubt, for the accused", dictates that any uncertainty should be resolved in favour of the defendant. However, this is not equivalent to the burden of proof beyond a reasonable doubt.[73]

Legal professionals trained in this environment naturally apply these principles. A critical aspect is that the doctrine of free evaluation of evidence does not obligate the Court to explicitly analyse or specify which evidence was preferred and the reasons for such preference. In *Bemba*, the Trial Court emphatically asserted that it had assessed all the evidence through a holistic evaluation, which does not mandate explicit justification. Therefore, it should be presumed that the evidence was appropriately weighed to arrive at its conviction.

73 Mirjan R. Damaška, "Atomistic and Holistic Evaluation of Evidence: A Comparative View", in D.S. Clark, ed., *Comparative and Private International Law, Essays in Honor of John Henry Merryman on His Seventieth Birthday* (Berlin: Duncker & Humblot, 1990) 97.

5 The Appeal Court Disagrees and Acquits Bemba

The Appeal Court's Majority disagreed with the Trial Court's findings and ultimately acquitted Bemba in 2018.[74] The Appeal decision highlighted several key issues with the Trial Court's approach, particularly in how the evidence was evaluated and the application of legal principles.

We will examine the two separate opinions of the Majority, as they both highlight problematic areas within the continental approach to evidence admission and evaluation.[75] Both decisions identify similar issues regarding the Trial Court's refusal to make individual rulings on the admissibility of evidence.[76] This led to the accumulation of weak and inferior evidence.[77] The Trial Chamber failed to explain why and how it selected only certain inculpatory evidence while disregarding exculpatory evidence. Additionally, it did not clarify why the accused was not afforded the benefit of the doubt when some evidence was in his favour.[78] The holistic approach to evidence evaluation lacked transparency, making it difficult for the Appeal Court to scrutinize the Trial Court's findings.[79]

5.1 *Hearsay Evidence in ICC and Common Law*

From the various decisions and comments about evidence in *Bemba*, we see two primary points about hearsay, both of which are legitimate concerns. The first is the principle of orality. Evidence should be adduced orally before the Court so that the judges can assess its relevance and probative value. By definition, a hearsay statement is an out-of-court statement offered for its truth without the opportunity of contemporaneous cross-examination.[80] Thus, any issue of hearsay violates the orality principle. However, all legal systems, including the ICC, have accepted that there is no absolute prohibition against the admission of hearsay. Instead, there are exceptions which have proven over time to be sufficiently reliable that they are admitted. These exceptions have two underlying principles: necessity and reliability.[81] Hearsay evidence

74 ICC-01/05-01/08 A, June 8, 2018.

75 Separate opinion of Judge Christine Van den Wyngaert and Judge Howard Morrison, ICC-01/05-01/08-3636-Anx2, 08-06-2018, and Concurring Separate Opinion of Judge Eboe-Osuji, ICC-01/05-01/08-3636-Anx3, June 14, 2018.

76 *Ibid* ICC-01/05-01/08-3636-Anx2, 08-06-2018 at para 17.

77 *Ibid* at para 18.

78 *Ibid* at para 49.

79 *Ibid* at para 68.

80 See *R. v. Khelawon*, [2006] S.C.J No 57 (S.C.C.), para 35.

81 *Ibid* at para 49.

must be necessary because, without it, the source evidentiary value would be entirely lost.[82] Reliability means that the hearsay evidence must show sufficient indicia of reliability to warrant consideration by the trial court.[83] These principles will be discussed in greater detail below.

The second observation is the general sense of suspicion that arises given the political and social contexts within which the examples of hearsay were generated. This is especially true in post-civil war situations or in situations where conflict is ongoing. These suspicions are another aspect of reliability which extends to questions of authenticity. It is correct for a court to raise suspicions, but it must consider how it will resolve these concerns. An all-in or all-out approach is rarely the right answer. So, again we need to discuss how to address the questions about admission and probative value in a principled way that can be applied and can be scrutinized on appeal.

Let us look in general terms at how an experienced professional court should deal with hearsay. The first point one needs to make is directly related to the principle of orality and the concept of necessity.[84] Is the out-of-court speaker available to give evidence before the court? If not, what is the explanation for the absence? Death, illness, and enormous travel costs may be sufficient reasons to consider that the hearsay evidence is necessary. Inconvenience is rarely enough. But, given a general concern about the expenditure of time and money, the court will have some latitude in determining necessity. All of this must be considered within the frame of what essential element or material fact the evidence is offered to prove and how important this is to the trial.

The next point is central to what have been considered exceptions to hearsay prohibitions: the indicia of reliability.[85] Here, we must start with a basic understanding of frailties. Hearsay usually presents these deficiencies: no oath, no cross-examination, and an inability to assess the speaker's demeanour. Hearsay also carries with it certain dangers in terms of questions that cannot be addressed because the speaker is absent: issues of memory, perception, sincerity, and communication (i.e., use of language and the meaning of the statement). Hearsay should only be admitted when it is considered sufficiently reliable for the court's consideration. The admissibility decision should

---

82 *Ibid.*

83 *Ibid.*

84 David Paciocco & Lee Stuesser, *The Law of Evidence*, 7th ed. (Toronto: Irwin Law, 2015) 130–134.

85 *Ibid* at 135–139.

look to see whether and to what extent these essential dangers and deficiencies have been mitigated in the context of the specific piece of evidence. For example, a videotaped statement complete with a warning about the need to tell the truth may, to some extent, address the absence of an oath, the inability to assess the demeanour of the speaker and, perhaps, issues of memory, perception, sincerity, and communication. By comparison, a written statement may not share these attributes. The discretion to admit hearsay must be guided by principle so that reasons for its admission or exclusion can be given.

The third point we need to make is that admission does not mean that, on the ultimate issue of guilt or innocence, the evidence will be considered acceptable or sufficient.[86] Admission is based on a conclusion that the hearsay evidence is sufficiently reliable in a threshold sense to warrant consideration by the court. The evidence can still be challenged on grounds of authenticity, lack of credibility, or lack of probative value. The parties must be aware that these avenues of challenge are available so that they can call evidence and submit arguments before the hearsay is weighed in the context of the totality of evidence.

The last point is transparency. A decision about the admission or exclusion of hearsay must be reasoned and transparent. This is necessary to ensure that the parties, the victim, and the public can understand why the court has made its ruling. An equally important facet of transparency is the ability of an appellate court to review what the trial court has decided. Only if an evidentiary decision is explained with reference to the reasons upon which admissibility or exclusion has been based can an appellate court understand the decision and the evidentiary basis upon which the trial court decided guilt or innocence. Transparency on evidence issues has the added advantage of providing both the parties and the courts in future cases with a framework for assessing evidence without having to entirely guess about admissibility.

To understand how the ICC has been dealing with hearsay, let us return to the Appeal decision of Judge Wyngaert and Judge Morrison in *Bemba*. Early in this decision, they provided a summary of their perspective by saying that it is the *duty* of "appellate judges to intervene if we identify significant problems with the manner in which a Trial Chamber has analysed the evidence or applied the standard of proof".[87] After commenting on the "opacity of the

86 *Ibid* at 134–135; and *Khelawon, supra* note 80 at *paras* 3, 50.

87 *See* Separate Opinion of Judge Eboe-Osuji *supra* note 75 at para 5.

Conviction Decision in terms of outlining the evidentiary basis for many of the findings",[88] specifically with respect to hearsay, they said:

> Whereas hearsay is not per se inadmissible before the Court, this does not mean that it is permissible to make findings beyond a reasonable doubt on this basis, especially when *the Trial Chamber does not seem to have tried to establish* the reliability of the source of the information. Although the Trial Chamber accepted the need to be cautious when relying on hearsay evidence, it appears that in practice it often threw its own caution to the wind.[89] [emphasis added]

A major concern for them was the use made of *procès-verbaux d'audition*, or unsworn statements made before a CAR magistrate. These were a series of a large number of short, undetailed, and generally uninformative statements. Although authenticated by the magistrate, there was, in Judge Wyngaert's and Judge Morrison's view, no "guarantee about the reliability of their content".[90] In other words, nothing in the record addressed any of the deficiencies or dangers of hearsay. Judge Wyngaert and Judge Morrison noted that:

> It is true that the evidence shows that a large number of crimes were reported, but this cannot, in our view, prove beyond reasonable doubt that they actually took place, let alone that the MLC was solely responsible for them.[91]

With respect to anonymous hearsay, they stated that it was "entirely impossible to evaluate their evidentiary weight".[92] Their conclusion was that it

---

88 Judge Christine Van den Wyngaert and Judge Howard Morrison decision, *supra* note 75 at para 6.

89 *Ibid* at para 8.

90 *Ibid* at para 9.

91 *Ibid* at para 10, fn 5, where Judge Christine Van den Wyngaert and Judge Howard Morrison state: "When the evidence is analysed properly, it is only possible to identify seven witnesses who speak directly about the number of criminal acts. The vast majority of this testimony is based on (anonymous) hearsay. The same applies to the documentary evidence the Trial Chamber relied upon. It is true that the evidence shows that a large number of crimes were reported, but this cannot, in our view, prove beyond reasonable doubt that they actually took place, let alone that the MLC was solely responsible for them".

92 *Ibid* at para 10.

would be "entirely inappropriate, in our view, to accept these claims as proof of their content".[93]

6 Circumstantial Evidence at the ICC and in Common Law

Circumstantial evidence refers to what is often called indirect evidence.[94] By comparison, direct evidence is testimony by which a witness recounts what he or she saw or heard that, by itself, offers some proof of an essential element or material fact. In other words, if the evidence is "I saw 'X' shoot 'Y' ", this is, subject to issues of credibility, direct proof that "X" shot "Y". Circumstantial evidence offers proof indirectly through an inference. For example, when "Y" is found dead in her home, the witness says, "I heard a gunshot and then saw 'X' run from 'Y's' home". This evidence can support an inference that "X" was in "Y's" home and shot her to death. Of course, there may be other explanations for the witness's testimony. Still, by itself, it is strong indirect evidence that inculpates "X".

Legal systems have learned that there are many situations where the court only has circumstantial evidence before it. This does not mean that the prosecution fails, but rather, it must show that the only reasonable inference from the circumstantial evidence is guilt.[95] If there are inferences consistent with innocence, then it would be unsafe to convict on this basis. Moreover, a reasonable inference is one that can be fully supported by the evidence. It is not speculative.[96] We see that circumstantial evidence can produce guilt, but courts have learned to exercise caution when evaluating it.[97]

But what did the Appeal Court in *Bemba* say about the way the Trial Court treated the issue of circumstantial evidence? The concurring opinion of Judge Eboe-Osuji in favour of acquittal explained the duty of the appellate court when reviewing a conviction:

> Consequently, the judgment of the Trial Chamber *must reveal*, in an *objectively verifiable and convincing way*, that no reasonable doubt was

93 *Ibid* at para 9.

94 Paccioco & Stuesser, *supra* note 84 at 31; *R.* v. *Villaroman*, [2016] S.C.J. No.33 (S.C.C.) para 23.

95 *Villaroman*, *ibid* at paras 19, 30.

96 *Ibid* at paras 37–38.

97 *Ibid* at paras 29–30.

> left in both the substance and the analysis of the evidence that resulted in the conviction of an accused person.[98] [emphasis added]

In other words, the reasoning of the Trial Court must show that it not only recognized the right legal principles but also applied them correctly when evaluating the evidence. Here, the treatment of circumstantial evidence is a key example of how the prosecution's burden of proof beyond a reasonable doubt affects the weighing of evidence. Judge Eboe-Osuji expressed in very strong terms the need to observe the strict criminal law rule about the scope of circumstantial evidence and how it relates to the burden of proof beyond a reasonable doubt:

> One way, but not the only one, in which the legal requirement of proof beyond reasonable doubt can be violated – indeed the alluring siren call of the idea of appellate deference to factual findings – is merely to say that the Trial Chamber based the conviction upon a "reasonable" interpretation of circumstantial evidence or upon a "reasonable" inculpatory inference from primary evidence.[99]

He makes it quite clear that the question is not whether one can characterize the Trial decision as "reasonable" but whether it has considered and rejected "other hypotheses that are also reasonable and consistent with innocence".[100] He concluded that the Trial Chamber failed to do so.

On the same issue of circumstantial evidence, Judge Wyngaert and Judge Morrison reached the same decision but offered a more precise analysis. They began with this important observation:

> Again, the Trial Chamber stated the correct principle that circumstantial evidence can only lead to findings beyond a reasonable doubt when the proposed inference *is the only plausible one*, but has often failed to adhere to this principle in its actual analysis.[101] [emphasis added]

98 *See* Separate Opinion of Judge Eboe-Osuji, *supra* note 75 at para 38.
99 *Ibid* at para 53.
100 *Ibid* at para 55.
101 *See* Judge Christine Van den Wyngaert and Judge Howard Morrison decision, *supra* note 75 at para 11.

Their complaint was not that the Trial Court did not know the right principle, but that they did not no know how to apply it. To support this view, they delved into the deep details of the Trial Court's decision by examining the "eight circumstantial factors that it considered *cumulatively* proved the existence of a policy to attack a civilian population"[102] [emphasis added]. They made it clear that the application of the burden of proof beyond a reasonable doubt requires a qualitative assessment of the evidence, not simply a quantitative one. They concluded, "if the factual basis of the circumstantial evidence is weak, the inferences drawn from it will be even weaker".[103] A large pile of weak evidence is still weak evidence. This is reminiscent of the caution issued years ago by former British Judge Murphy that the ICC approach to evidence attracted the collection and assessment of "evidential debris". Judge Murphy said:[104]

> The indiscriminate admission of any and all material the parties claim to be evidence, far from being the only means of promoting a successful search for the truth, buries the genuinely probative evidence in a vast accumulation of evidential debris, *frustrating rather than facilitating* the task of judges trying to establish the truth. [emphasis added]

As we have seen, the Trial Court in *Bemba* was devoted to determining the truth. Bemba was found guilty. He appealed the Trial judgement. The Appeal Court acquitted Bemba. At the end of the case, we cannot say that we know the truth about the accountability for the human tragedies that occurred in the Central African Republic. But we can say that justice has been done in terms of international criminal law according to the Rome Statute fair trial standard.

7 The Thinking Process of the *Bemba* Trial Court

Mixing two legal traditions to produce a new justice model can produce an intrinsic problem if judges are trained in only one of the two systems. A major aspect of each judge's experience is how they evaluate evidence. For trial purposes, this is the ultimate reasoning process. Thus, we find the central ques-

102 *Ibid* at para 12.
103 *Ibid* at para 12.
104 *See* Peter Murphy, "No Free Lunch, No Free Proof: The Indiscriminate Admission of Evidence is a Serious Flaw in International Criminal Trials", (2010) 8:2 J Int Crim Just 540.

tion: Is the free evaluation of evidence compatible with a burden of proof beyond a reasonable doubt?

James Fitzjames Stephen's observation was that evidence rules keep out aspects that are not material for a reasonable person's judgment.[105] However, a reasonable person should not decide based on speculation but rather on proven facts and justifiable inferences. This process of judicial thinking is exemplified by the Appeal Majority decisions in *Bemba* regarding the admissibility of circumstantial and hearsay evidence.[106]

The Rules of Procedure and Evidence of the ICC provide specific Rules of Evidence (Rules 63–75). Rule 68 (prior recorded testimony) provides exceptions for this kind of evidence to be admitted. I would suggest that this rule is an admissibility rule similar to common law rules. When the Trial Court in *Bemba,* in the interlocutory decision of 2012, dealt with circumstantial and hearsay evidence, it applied the three-part test for admissibility and referred to the Rules and the Statute.[107] During the deliberation phase, the Court evaluated and weighed the evidence simultaneously and found the accused guilty beyond a reasonable doubt.[108] However, the decision neither revealed the Court's syllogism on determining admissibility nor provided a transparent thinking process that established guilt beyond a reasonable doubt.

On appeal, Judge Wyngaert, Judge Morrison, and Chief Justice Eboe-Osuji explained why the evidence did not meet the standard of proof beyond a reasonable doubt. The burden of proof required a rigorous analysis that the Trial Court did not apply to the substantial body of evidence before it. In the *Bemba* case, the Trial Court adhered to its continental truth-seeking role, exercising free evaluation of evidence. This approach revealed a fundamental contradiction between the Court's truth-seeking mission during deliberation and the prosecutorial burden of proof. The core issue was the tension between the determination of guilt and the determination of truth. Ultimately, the Trial Court prioritized the quest for truth over the prosecutorial obligation to prove guilt beyond a reasonable doubt. This resulted in a verdict where the truth determination overshadowed the necessity for a rigorous analysis of whether the prosecution had met its burden of proof.

Firstly, we observe that when the free evaluation of evidence seeks to ascertain the truth, the burden of proof tends to dissipate. Secondly, the explicit provisions of the ICC's legal framework do not offer a clear path to judicial

105 *Ibid* at 550.

106 Majority opinion, *supra* note 45.

107 ICC-01/05-01/08, *supra* note 52 at paras 13–16.

108 ICC-01/05-01/08, *supra* note 61.

clarity akin to that provided by a robust evidence law. More critically, it is evident that judges in both legal systems have been trained over centuries to adhere to either the free evaluation approach or the prosecutorial burden of proof.[109] Classic continental judges, accustomed to adjudicating without the prosecutorial burden of proof, have not been required to develop a nuanced approach to handling issues of relevance, probative value, and the burden of proof.

8 Distinguishing Evidence Law from the ICC's Rules of Procedure and Evidence

Let us now discuss why evidence law serves as an indispensable tool for a rigorous judicial thinking process. Evidence law provides a system of thinking for understanding what evidence demonstrates and how it is linked to matter in issue, the inferences that can be drawn, and potential issues of prejudice or other frailties. Therefore, it guides judges in assessing evidence against the burden of proof. In contrast, the free evaluation of evidence lacks such a system, essentially providing, according to Wigmore, "no system at all".[110]

Wigmore highlighted two distinct aspects of evidence principles: the general concept of proof and the rules of admissibility. He asserted that the "pro-

109 *See* the discussion on the fundamental differences of the two systems especially in relation to how they treat in practice the presumption of innocence in Demetra Fr. Sorvatzioti & Allan Manson, "Burden of Proof and L'intime conviction: Is the Continental Criminal Trial Moving to the Common Law?" (2018) 23:1 Can Crim L Rev 108. *See also* John Jackson & Yassin M'Boge, "The Effect of Legal Culture on the Development of International Evidentiary Practice: From the Robbing Room to the Melting Pot" (2013) 26:4 LJIL 947–970; Yvonne McDermott, "Strengthening the Evaluation of Evidence in International Criminal Trials" (2017) 17:4 Int Crim Law Rev 682–702.

110 Wigmore referred to the continental system of proof and said: "In the early 1800s the ancient worn-out numerical system of 'legal proof' was abolished by fiat, and the so-called 'free-proof' namely, no system at all was substituted". John Henry Wigmore, *The Principles of Judicial Proof: Or, The Process of Proof as Given by Logic, Psychology, and General Experience and Illustrated in Judicial Trials*, 2nd ed. (London: Little, Brown, 1931) 4. *See also* James Bradley Thayer, *A Preliminary Treatise on Evidence at the Common Law* (London: Little, Brown, 1898) 270, where he states that the continent of Europe, did not develop "under the head of evidence" a "separate and systematised branch of law". For a comparative discussion of the free evaluation in France and the evidence rules in England *see* James Fitzjames Stephen, *A History of the Criminal Law of England* Vol. 1 (Cambridge: Cambridge University Press, 1883, reprinted 2014) 548–549, and his comment on the "technical and essentially foolish" French rules of evidence before the Revolution, which were replaced by "nothing" at 548.

cess of proof represents the objective in every judicial investigation".[111] Some may argue that logical reasoning and the ability to distinguish evidence are inherent qualities of any competent judge, making additional guidance from evidence law unnecessary for continental judges. However, as illustrated by the *Bemba* Trial decision, this assumption does not hold true.

To prove what evidence law can provide I will use the problem of similar fact evidence. Since the nineteenth century, common law courts have accepted the general principle that a person should not be convicted solely upon evidence of bad character. While this often leads to excluding bad character evidence, the evidence may have another purpose that permits its admission, notwithstanding its bad character nature. One of the seminal cases on similar fact evidence is *Makin*, an 1893 decision by the Privy Council about an Australian verdict.[112] A couple was charged with the murder of an infant, and there was an issue as to whether the child had been killed or died of natural causes. The police investigation revealed that, at three addresses where the couple had previously lived, the bodies of 12 dead infants were found buried. The court ruled that the evidence of the buried bodies was admissible to confront the argument of natural causes. However, recognizing the "bad character" nature of the evidence, Lord Herschell cautioned:

> It is undoubtedly *not competent for the prosecution to adduce evidence* tending to shew that the accused has been guilty of criminal acts other than those covered by the indictment, for *the purpose of leading to the conclusion that the accused is a person likely from his criminal conduct or character to have committed the offence for which he is being tried.*[113] [emphasis added]

Thus, evidence of previous similar acts can be admitted to show guilt but not if the evidence shows only that the accused is the kind of person who is likely to commit the offence. For over a century, common law courts struggled with the conundrum of when similar fact evidence goes to guilt beyond simply showing a propensity to commit the crime. This problem produced many controversies and many appeals. The House of Lords thought it had solved the problem in 1975 when it said that the test was whether the probative value

---

111 *See* Wigmore, *supra* note 110 at 3, where he distinguishes between the principles of proof and the artificial rules of procedure.

112 *Makin v. A.G. for New South Wales*, [1894] A.C. 57.

113 *Ibid* at para 65.

exceeded the bad character prejudice.[114] But how should a trial judge apply this vague pronouncement in the various situations that arise in criminal trials?

In Canada, appeals continued, and the Supreme Court continued to try to develop an analysis which would give sufficient guidance to the thinking process of trial judges when confronted by a prosecution offering evidence of previous crimes or bad conduct. Finally, in 2002, the Supreme Court in *Handy*[115] succeeded in providing a logical framework that responded to the needs of the criminal law context while still respecting the right of the accused to a fair trial. Starting with the *Boardman* principle that the test must be probative value versus prejudice, the Supreme Court provided and explained the steps of a thinking process which evaluate probative value and prejudice in the case of similar facts. I have summarized the essential steps as follows:[116]

(1) Probative value of evidence
  a. The potential of collusion
  b. The identification of "the issue in question"
  c. Similarities and dissimilarities between the facts charged and the similar fact evidence
    (I) Proximity in time of the similar acts
    (II) Extent to which the other acts are similar in detail to the charged conduct
    (III) Number of occurrences of the similar acts
    (IV) Circumstances surrounding or relating to the similar acts
    (V) Any distinctive feature(s) unifying the incidents
    (VI) Intervening events
  d. Strength of the evidence that the similar acts actually occurred
(2) Assessment of prejudice
  a. Moral prejudice
  b. Reasoning prejudice
(3) Weighing up probative value versus prejudice

The above steps are not codified in an exclusionary technical rule. They lay out and explain the thinking process of proof when one compares probative value and prejudice within the context of the burden of proof. As stated in *Handy*, "Justice includes society's interest in getting to the truth of the charges as well as the interest of both society and the accused in a fair process".[117]

114 *D.P.P.* v. *Boardman*, [1975] A.C. 421.

115 *R.*v. *Handy*, [2002] 2 S.C.R. 908, 2002 SCC 56.

116 *Ibid* at paras 99–152, where the steps are discussed and explained.

117 *Ibid* at para 150.

The analysis of syllogism in *Handy* is an example of how the evolution of the law of evidence can respond to commonly occurring problems in a way that enhances the judicial process of proof without removing judicial discretion. Instead, the decision guides trial judges through the reasoning steps which the specific problem presents. This does not imply that the common law judges are smarter. It merely shows that, sometimes, a lengthy process of experience after experience and refinement after refinement is necessary to make a significant advance that will assist in measuring the evidence offered against the burden of proof. It addresses the problem and provides a framework for the judicial thinking process.

9 Insights and Lessons from the *Bemba* Case

> It would be transparently naive to expect that Anglo-American and Continental evidentiary arrangements are pure versions of either an atomistic or holistic approach.[118]

According to the reviewed decisions, some judges struggled to properly assess evidence in two stages as required for the ICC's trial process. The first stage pertains to admissibility, and the second to the weight of the evidence. The ICC's legal framework allows admissibility assessments to be made at any point, including during the Court's deliberations. This assessment is mandatory, regardless of its timing. Therefore, the Court has the discretion to decide when to conduct these assessments, but not whether to conduct them.

The Court perceived the absence of separate admissibility rulings as a holistic assessment. However, I am concerned that the holistic evidence analysis is rather misunderstood in trial practice, potentially leading to further confusion regarding evidence assessments.[119]

Damaška clarified that "holistic" and "atomistic" are "two models of cognition" for evidence law and explained:

> The holistic system of proof entails "inner persuasion". The atomistic "refer to external yardsticks, such as the viewpoint of a reasonable person exposed to the same information".[120]

118 Damaška, *supra* note 73 at 92.

119 William Twining, *Rethinking Evidence: Exploratory Essays* (Cambridge: Cambridge University Press, 2006) 81–86.

120 Damaška, *supra* note 73 at 92.

He also explained the origins of these differing approaches. In the atomistic approach, common law judges assess evidence individually as it is presented by the parties. In contrast, continental judges, who have access to the entire dossier with all the gathered evidence, have no reason to rule on admissibility. As a result, admissibility has never been a central issue for continental judges.[121] However, he noted that in common law criminal trials, the holistic approach is more prominent than in civil trials.[122]

If we accept Damaška's view that continental jurisdictions adopt a more holistic approach to evidence while Anglo-American jurisdictions are more atomistic, it would be simplistic to label one strictly as atomistic and the other as holistic. However, after reviewing the Rome Statute and the Rules of Procedure and Evidence, we can draw our conclusion. A holistic approach to evidence admissibility at the ICC allows for a more flexible evaluation of offered evidence, aligning with the Court's truth-seeking mandate and the judge's investigative role. However, this flexibility does not imply that all admitted evidence inherently meets the legal standards necessary for a conviction. The ICC's legal framework mandates an assessment of relevance, probative value, and potential prejudice. The results of this assessment should determine which evidence is admitted and which is excluded, based on its quality. Otherwise, the ICC's evidence rules would become obsolete, which is logically untenable.

When the Court evaluates the weight of the admitted evidence, the sole uncompromising rule is that the prosecution, not the Court, must prove guilt beyond a reasonable doubt. This rule necessitates a straightforward calculation where the evidence of guilt must surpass any reasonable doubt.

For some ICC judges, the Rome Statute provides a mixed approach by combining both approaches. Thus they attempt to integrate the prosecutorial burden of proof (a common law principle) with the judges' free evaluation and truth-seeking mandate (a continental principle).

This mixed approach can cause confusion because it tries to balance two fundamentally different judicial philosophies. While common law relies heavily on the prosecution proving guilt beyond a reasonable doubt, the continental system emphasizes the judge's active role in seeking the truth. Combining these can blur the lines between the roles of the prosecution and the judge, potentially complicating the standards of proof and the evaluation process.

121 *Ibid* at 103.

122 *Ibid* at 101.

The problem, therefore, is what the ICC should do when some of its judges are trained in systems where both the prosecutor and the judge have a truth-seeking role.[123] These judges are accustomed to freely evaluating evidence. The challenge arises when they must evaluate evidence for admissibility and also weigh it against the burden of proof. While they can understand this dual requirement, the question remains: how will they effectively apply it without the necessary experience?

The reason I emphasize legal experience is that evidence law terminology lacks a social meaning and exists solely within a legal context. When a system has not evolved to clearly define concepts such as reliability and credibility, moral versus legal prejudice, or how bias is distinguished from prejudice in legal terms regarding fair trial rights, it is unrealistic to expect that the clarity common law courts have achieved over centuries will be automatically possessed by professional judges transitioning into the ICC.

We will further explore this issue in the *Ongwen* case, where professional judges' assumptions about automatic knowledge will be scrutinized.

10 Conclusion

The Rome Statute has embedded both the prosecutorial burden of proof beyond a reasonable doubt and the principle of free evaluation of evidence. However, the ICC's legal framework mandates that the burden of proof cannot be disregarded during the deliberation phase when assessing evidence weight. During deliberations, the burden of proof must precede the Court's truth-seeking mission and the free evaluation of evidence. The latter primarily applies to the Court's authority to admit evidence more liberally than common law courts or to mandate the submission of additional evidence.[124] Nevertheless, in deciding which admissible evidence can substantiate guilt beyond a reasonable doubt, free evaluation in the name of truth is not only wholly inadequate but also inapplicable. The Court must meticulously and transparently weigh the evidence against the burden of proof.

It is crucial to acknowledge that, while a common law court also aims to uncover the truth, it does not confer broad discretionary power on the trial

---

123 *See also* the analysis of the prosecutorial role in the continental German system in Kai Ambos et al., eds., *Core Concepts in Criminal Law and Criminal Justice: Anglo-German Dialogues*. Vol. 1. (Cambridge: Cambridge University Press, 2020) 346–347.

124 *See* Article 69(4) and Rule 63(2).

judge for free evaluation of evidence in an investigative capacity.[125] In the *Bemba* case, the traditional continental approach,[126] accustomed to truth-seeking through free evaluation,[127] persisted strongly but led to significant errors when faced with the adversarial requirement to apply the burden of proof on the prosecution. This resulted in an erroneous judgment and drew criticism regarding the ICC's decision-making process.[128]

Evidence law, as developed and refined in common law jurisdictions, particularly in Canada, provides a more coherent and systematic approach to the intricate reasoning necessary for producing robust, well-founded decisions that comply with international standards. By adopting a similar conceptual framework, the ICC can evolve its evidence law, thereby enhancing the rigour and clarity of its judicial processes.

---

125 *See* Ambos' discussion on procedural v. material truth, and on the *wide discretion* of the *flexible civil law* approach. Kai Ambos, "International Criminal Procedure: 'Adversarial', 'Inquisitorial' or 'Mixed'?" (2003) 3:1 Int Crim L Rev 1–37, 21–22. *See* also, Thomas Weigend, "Is the Criminal Process about Truth: A German Perspective" (2003) 26:1 Harv J L & Pub Pol'y 157–174.

126 *See* the discussion in atomistic and holistic approach in evidence evaluation in relation to the legal culture in Yvonne McDermott, "Strengthening the Evaluation of Evidence in International Criminal Trials" (2017) 17:4 Intl Crim. L. Rev. 687–692.

127 Although Ambos states that "at the level of international criminal procedure, the traditional common-civil law divide has been overcome", he discusses the ICC's legal framework as a new model that has incorporated some features from both legal traditions but not the way justice is applied in judicial practice. He acknowledges, though, that knowledge of both systems by the parties and the Court will provide "truly mixed sui generis procedure", Ambos, *supra* note 125 at 34, 37.

128 Regarding the *Bemba* Appeal Decision, *see* ICC, *Expert Report*, supra note 21 at paras 608–613. This chapter has been published: Sorvatzioti, Demetra Fr, "Free Evaluation of Evidence: Does the ICC need a Law of Evidence?" (2021) 1 International Criminal Law Review, 22(5–6), pp. 895–919.

CHAPTER 4

The Case of Laurent Gbagbo and Charles Blé Goudé

1 The Situation in the Republic of Côte d'Ivoire

The case of Laurent Koudou Gbagbo and Charles Blé Goudé is deeply intertwined with a pivotal moment in Côte d'Ivoire's history – the 2010 post-election civil war. Following the second round of the 2010 election, both Laurent Gbagbo, the incumbent president, and Alassane Ouattara, his opponent, claimed victory and held inauguration ceremonies. This dispute, as documented by Human Rights Watch, led to a civil war, with both sides committing crimes and atrocities against civilians.[1] The ICC later issued arrest warrants for Gbagbo, his wife Simone and Minister of Youth Blé Goudé, marking a significant turn in the country's political trajectory.[2] The election dispute culminated years of political tension and power struggles in Côte d'Ivoire.

Before discussing the 2010 election conflict, it is essential to understand the political background and Ouattara's long efforts to become President. This context is crucial to grasp the outcome of the post-election crisis. Gbagbo was labelled the "President of the Ivorian people", while Ouattara was labelled the "President recognized by the International Community".[3] It has been argued that Ouattara was the preferred candidate of the international community. In contrast, Gbagbo was chosen by the Ivorian people but was not favoured by France, the United States and the United Nations. The reason was his political aspirations. As a Socialist, Gbagbo was perceived to threaten French private interests in Côte d'Ivoire. There were concerns that he might nationalize key companies that had previously been state-owned but were

---

1 Human Rights Watch. "They Killed Them Like It Was Nothing: The Need for Justice for Côte d'Ivoire's Post-Election Crimes", Human Rights Watch (October 5, 2011), online: https://www.hrw.org/report/2011/10/05/they-killed-them-it-was-nothing/need-justice-cote-divoires-post-election-crimes; Human Rights Watch, "Côte d'Ivoire: Impartial Justice Poses Test for Ouattara, Serious Crimes by Both Sides Demand Swift Response", Human Rights Watch (October 6, 2011), online: https://www.hrw.org/news/2011/10/06/cote-divoire-impartial-justice-poses-test-ouattara.

2 ICC-02/11, Warrant of Arrest for Laurent Koudou Gbagbo, November 23, 2011; ICC-02/11-01/12, Warrant of Arrest for Simone Gbagbo, February 29, 2012; ICC-02/11-02/11, Warrant of Arrest for Charles Blé Goudé, December 21, 2011.

3 K. Martial Frindéthié, *From Lumumba to Gbagbo: Africa in the Eddy of the Euro-American Quest for Exceptionalism* (Jefferson, NC, USA: McFarland & Company, 2016) 130.

 | DOI:10.1163/9789004741010_005

transferred to French multinationals by his predecessors. This potential move could jeopardize French control and profitability in these strategic sectors. Additionally, Gbagbo's intention to issue state currency, which he attempted to do during the post-electoral crisis, raised further concerns among French and international stakeholders about his push for further decolonization and its implications for their economic and political influence in the region.[4]

The political history of Côte d'Ivoire shows that when French colonization ended (1960), the country was already divided between what the French called "the useful Côte d'Ivoire" (the cocoa forest-rich South) and the marginalized North. Félix Houphouët-Boigny became the first president of the independent Côte d'Ivoire. He provided stability for three decades and doubled the Ivorian economy between 1960 and 1980.[5]

Laurent Gbagbo, a history professor, was a vocal critic of Houphouët-Boigny's one-party state. In 1982, he founded the Ivorian Popular Front (IPF). Gbagbo and his wife Simone were jailed several times for their oppositional views and trade union activism.[6]

In 1993, President Houphouët-Boigny died. A significant power struggle unfolded over his succession. The President of the National Assembly, Henri Konan Bédié, a member of Houphouët-Boigny's Democratic Party of Côte d'Ivoire (PDCI), was the constitutional successor. However, Alassane Dramane Ouattara, an economist and then-Prime Minister, sought to assert his influence, and many saw as a potential leader. When Bédié quickly assumed the presidency, Ouattara resigned and became Deputy Managing Director of the International Monetary Fund, leaving for the United States.[7]

4 *Ibid* at 86, 135. *See also* Tom Mbakwe, Côte d'Ivoire: The Laurent Gbagbo Saga, New African Magazine (January 16, 2019), online: https://newafricanmagazine.com/17893/.

5 Thierno Mouctar Bah, "Addressing Côte d'Ivoire's Deeper Crisis", (2012) 19 *Africa Security Briefs* 3.

6 See, for example, the 1992 imprisonment: CÔTE D'IVOIRE @Silencing the opposition – 77 prisoners of conscience convicted, Amnesty International (July 2, 1992), online: https://www.amnesty.org/fr/wp-content/uploads/2021/06/afr310081992en.pdf. For his imprisonment for "subversive teaching", see also, Cyril K. Daddieh, *Historical Dictionary of Côte d'Ivoire (the Ivory Coast)* 3rd ed., Kindle file (New York: Rowman & Littlefield, 2016) 262. For Gbagbo's arrest by Prime Minister Alassane Ouattara in 1992 and his subsequent two-year imprisonment for participating in a student protest against the government in Abidjan, see *ibid* at 265. *See also*, Ségolène Allemandou & Stéphanie Trouillard, "Ivory Coast's Laurent Gbagbo: A political fighter who won't quit", *France 24* (June 17, 2021), online: https://www.france24.com/en/africa/20210617-ivory-coast-s-laurent-gbagbo-a-political-fighter-who-won-t-quit

7 Ouattara joined the International Monetary Fund (IMF) in Washington in 1968 and later joined the Central Bank of West African States (BCEAO), *see* Alassane Ouattara, President of

During this period, Bédié introduced the concept of *Ivoirité*, defining what it meant to be genuinely Ivorian. This policy, which was considered anti-immigrant and nationalistic, with Southerners considered "authentic" Ivoirians, significantly impacted the political landscape, casting a shadow of discrimination and exclusion over the country's political processes.[8] Ouattara returned in 1995 to participate in the elections, but the *Ivoirité* policy questioned Ouattara's nationality and eligibility to run for president. Additionally, the electoral law did not allow Ivorians who had resided abroad in the previous five years to run. Ouattara was a Northerner of mixed Burkinabe-Ivoirian descent and lived in the United States. He was easily excluded from the 1995 presidential election, and Bédié was re-elected.[9]

In 1999, Ouattara returned to Côte d'Ivoire with a certificate of his pure Ivorian descent. In October, an Ivorian court invalidated his nationality certificate. At the end of 1999, pro-Ouattara General Robert Guéï led a coup d'état in Côte d'Ivoire, and President Bédié was ousted. The Guéï administration issued national identity cards to citizens and resident permits to foreigners as a requirement for voter registration. However, new electoral legislation required not one but two Ivorian parents for someone to be eligible for electoral candidacy.[10]

As Ouattara was again excluded from the 2000 presidential election of October 22, Gbagbo emerged as a prominent opposition figure to Robert Guéï. Bédié, the incumbent president during the 1999 coup, was barred from running due to the military takeover. Initially, General Guéï claimed victory. However, widespread protests and accusations of electoral fraud led to significant public backlash. Under immense pressure, Guéï fled, and Laurent Gbagbo was declared the winner. In response to Gbagbo's claim of victory, Ouattara and the Rally of the Republicans (RDR) insisted that the election be held again, challenging the legitimacy of the initial results. The Supreme Court ratified Gbagbo's victory, and he assumed the presidency.[11]

In 2002, a failed coup while Gbagbo was in Europe marked the first Ivorian Civil War between the North and the South. General Guéï was killed under unknown circumstances. The conflict resulted in a divided country between

---

the Republic of Côte d'Ivoire, World Bank.org. (April 17, 2019), online: https://live.worldbank.org/en/experts/a/alassane-ouattara. *See also* Daddieh, *supra* note 6 at 239.

8 Nicolas Cook, *Cote d'Ivoire's Post-Election Crisis* (Washington, DC: Congressional Research Service, 2011).

9 *Ibid* at 41.

10 Ibid at 43.

11 Cook, *supra* note 8 at 8.

the rebel-controlled North and the government-controlled South (the loyalists). In the North, the rebels established a basic administrative state.[12]

Alassane Ouattara's repeated exclusion from presidential candidacy fuelled political discontent among northerners in Côte d'Ivoire. The northern rebels, even though claiming to fight for all Ivoirians, were driven by a sense of marginalization and continuous oppression. Ouattara's exclusion was a critical factor in the rebellion's persistence.[13]

During Gbagbo's presidency, several peace agreements, including the Linas-Marcoussis Agreement (2003), the Accra III Agreement (2004), the Pretoria Agreement (2005), and the Ouagadougou Political Agreement (2007) aimed at reunifying the country.[14]

While Gbagbo's electoral term ended in 2005, he remained in power under emergency constitutional powers supported by the international community due to the ongoing peace process and formation of a unity government. Due to political disputes, slow progress in elections, disarmament, and reunification, the elections took place in late 2010.

Ouattara was a presidential candidate in the 2010 elections. After the first round of electoral results, Gbagbo was in first place, with Ouattara in second and Bédié in third. Although Bédié questioned the results against Ouattara, Gbagbo did not address his concerns. Bédié then asked his followers to vote for Ouattara. Despite this, Gbagbo garnered substantial support from the west, east, and south regions, extending beyond his ethnic group. During the October 2010 presidential campaign, Ouattara controlled the north, preventing opponents from campaigning and suppressing their support. Despite significant fraud and voter intimidation in rebel areas, the results were Gbagbo at 38.04%, Ouattara at 32.07%, and Bédié at 25.24%. The international community, hoping irregularities would aid Ouattara's victory, was concerned by Gbagbo's strong performance, indicating he could likely win re-election with fair campaigning and no voter intimidation.[15]

The election results turned into a catalyst for further unrest. The Independent Electoral Commission (IEC) established under the Linas-Marcoussis Agreement declared Ouattara the winner with 54.1% of the vote.[16] However,

---

12 *Ibid*; Daddieh, *supra* note 6 at 266.

13 Cook, *supra* note 8 at 49.

14 *Ibid* at 8.

15 David Dossou Zounmenou and Abdul Rahman Lamin, "Côte d'Ivoire's Post-Electoral Crisis: Ouattara Rules but Can He Govern?" (2011) 10:2 *Journal of African Elections* 8–9. Other sources suggest that Bédié had made it clear before the first round that he would not support Gbagbo – Cook, *supra* note 8 at 34. *See also* Frindéthié, *supra* note 3 at 128.

16 Cook, *supra* note 8 at p.2.

on December 1st, five applications were filed by the Gbagbo campaign seeking the annulment of the second round of balloting in eight departments "because of serious irregularities in the integrity of the poll".[17] The report presented by Joseph Kokou, head of the African Union Observer Mission on the Presidential Election in Cote d'Ivoire, stated:[18]

> [It] is a fact that in the entire district of Korhogo, serious cases of murders, death threats, intimidation, confinements, and physical assaults were perpetrated against [Gbagbo's] activists and representatives by New Forces [rebels] and the RDR activists. For example, one of [Gbagbo's] supervisors, Mrs. Coulibaly Sita, was savagely beaten then illegally detained before being murdered after denouncing irregularities she recorded during the polling process in her area of duty.

Another report said that Gbagbo's representatives were coerced under violence and death threats to sign minutes that falsely reported the results of the vote counts. These tallies did not reflect the actual votes cast.[19]

On December 3rd, after invalidating the results of seven regions for fraud, the Ivorian Constitutional Council annulled the IEC's results and declared Gbagbo the winner, with 51.5% of the vote.[20] The following day, Gbagbo and Ouattara each took oaths of office in Abidjan. Gbagbo's ceremony was held before the Constitutional Council, whereas Ouattara submitted his oath through a letter to the Council.[21]

The resulting conflict saw both sides, Gbagbo's loyalists and Ouattara's supporters, committing atrocities. These included widespread and systematic attacks against the civilian population, as well as other war crimes and crimes against humanity. The conflict was marked by violence and human rights violations, further deepening the crisis.

---

17 *Ibid* at 39.

18 Frindéthié, *supra* note 3 at 129.

19 *Ibid*, "The fraud and ballot stuffing in the North were so flagrant that on some minutes the total vote counts largely exceeded the entire population of the areas and in many other areas candidate Gbagbo had not a single vote, not even the votes of his own representatives. These were violations so flagrant that in its own communique, the Economic Community of West African States (ECOWAS) recognized that serious irregularities prevented citizens from freely expressing their votes".

20 *Ibid* at 130. *See* also Cook, *supra* note 8 at 8.

21 UNOCI, United Nations Operation in Côte d'Ivoire, Post-Election Crisis, online: https://peacekeeping.un.org/en/mission/past/unoci/elections.shtml.

The U.S., the French government, and the United Nations supported Ouattara. Gbagbo was supported only by Gambia, South Africa, Uganda, and Angola.[22] The Ouattara forces, "backed by the United Nations and French Licorne forces", arrested Laurent Gbagbo on April 11, 2011.[23] A warrant of arrest against Gbagbo was issued by the ICC on November 23, 2011, for crimes committed by pro-Gbagbo forces between November 28, 2010, and May 2011 against civilians who supported Ouattara. According to the warrant, Gbagbo acted with the necessary criminal intent and knowledge for the committed crimes; the crimes were directed at specific ethnic and religious communities and were widespread and systematic, pursuant to an organizational policy. However, the Pre-Trial Court III noted that Gbagbo's suggested liability as an "indirect co-perpetrator" under Article 25(3)(a) of the Statute may need to be revisited with the parties and participants in due time.[24]

The director of the Ivorian Observatory of Human Rights in Abidjan, Eric-Aimé Semien, said:[25]

> All the observers noted that the different crimes were committed from both sides, and only one side is prosecuted. And from this point of view, the ICC is disappointing expectations. Because what people want is that the ICC pursue prosecutions against the two different sides.

The ICC also issued arrest warrants for Gbagbo's wife, Simone Gbagbo, a professor and Member of Parliament, and Blé Goudé, Minister of Youth. While Gbagbo was arrested and transferred to the ICC, his wife Simone was tried by Ivorian authorities. In 2015, she was found guilty of crimes separate from the ICC charges against her and sentenced to twenty years imprisonment, a verdict upheld by the Appeal Court in 2016. In May 2016, she appeared before the Ivorian Criminal Court for crimes against humanity.[26]

---

22 Cook, *supra* note 8 at 11 fn.33.

23 Daddieh, *supra* note 6 at 267; see also, UNOCI, *supra* note 21.

24 ICC-02/11, November 23, 2011, Warrant of Arrest for Laurent Koudou Gbagbo, at para 10.

25 Talking Justice: The Trial of Laurent Gbagbo, Open Society Foundations (January 26, 2016), online: https://www.opensocietyfoundations.org/podcasts/talking-justice-the-trial-of-laurent-gbagbo. For the lack of investigation and subsequent accountability of President Ouattara's forces regarding the 2010–2011 post-election crisis, *see* Kenneth Roth, *World Report: Côte d'Ivoire*, Human Rights Watch (2014), online: https://www.hrw.org/world-report/2014/country-chapters/cote-divoire.

26 Ephrem Rugiririza, "The Rise and Fall of Ivorian Ex-First Lady Simone Gbagbo", JusticeInfo.net (March 9, 2017), online: https://www.justiceinfo.net/en/32412-the-rise-and-fall-of-ivorian-ex-first-lady-simone-gbagbo.html.

When a judge questioned Simone Gbagbo at a hearing on June 2, 2016, he asked why she and her husband had not stepped down at the end of 2010 to give peace a chance, and she replied:[27]

> Choosing to give up and flee would have been all the more grave when they were bombing us. I would never have left my country in the hands of France and its allies. As long as I live, I will continue my fight against the colonial power. But if I die, the Ivorian people will continue the struggle. The aggression against us was international. The whole world conspired against Côte d'Ivoire.

Following the ICC acquittals of Gbagbo and Blé Goudé, the Ouattara government granted Simone Gbagbo amnesty, and she was released from prison after seven years of incarceration.[28] Upon her release she said: "He is a son of the country who has many supporters and is returning home. It is good for peace and social cohesion".[29]

2 The Arrest of Laurent Gbagbo

> On 17 March 2011, two weeks before the military offensive which contributed to his victory, President Ouattara created an army, the FRCI, which was supposed to bring together the Forces de défense et de sécurité (FDS Defence and Security Forces) loyal to Laurent Gbagbo and the Forces armées des Forces nouvelles (FAFN, Armed Forces of the New Forces) who ruled the northern half of the country since the armed uprising of September 2002. [...] in the weeks following its creation, the FRCI committed massive human rights violations constituting war crimes and crimes against humanity, in particular during killings committed as part of a widespread and systematic attack against the civilian population in and around the Duékoué region (west of the country).[30]

---

27 *Ibid.*

28 Agence France Press, "Ivory Coast Ex-First Lady Simone Gbagbo Freed After Amnesty", JusticeInfo (August 8, 2018), online: https://www.justiceinfo.net/en/38370-ivory-coast-ex-first-lady-simone-gbagbo-freed-after-amnesty.html.

29 Abraham Kouassi, "After Gbagbo's Return, Traditional Leaders Speak on Reconciliation", JusticeInfo (June 22, 2021), online: https://www.justiceinfo.net/en/78981-after-gbagbo-return-traditional-leaders-speak-on-reconciliation.html.

30 Amnesty International, Côte d'Ivoire: The Victor's Law: *The Human Rights Situation Two Years after the Post-Electoral Crisis* (February 26, 2013) AFR 31/001/2013, 14.

3 Defining the Central Legal Question of this Case

In the *Gbagbo* and *Blé Goudé* case, the Trial Court's decision was upheld by the Appeal Court. However, the final verdict concluded that there was no case to answer.

The discussion of this case is not about whether Gbagbo and Blé Goudé should be convicted or whether the prosecutorial evidence was sufficient. The discussion focuses on the antithetical views of the ICC judges regarding evidence admissibility and evaluation, especially when only circumstantial evidence is provided by the Prosecution. Another important element is the judges' views on the prosecutorial burden of proof for a no-case-to-answer decision.

The no-case-to-answer outcome, despite the extensive duration of the proceedings – from Gbagbo's arrest in 2011, the confirmation of charges in 2013, the Trial decision in 2019, to the Appeal decision in 2021 – suggests that the evidence presented was insufficient. Over these ten years, what influenced the judges' perspectives, and how did their views shape the prolonged trial process? It is evident that there were contrasting opinions in the evaluation of evidence. From where do these opposing views originate? Are they found solely in the minority and majority decisions, or even among judges who agree? The *Bemba* case highlighted similar issues; thus, we must ask: Are the problems here analogous or distinct?

This chapter explores interlocutory decisions on evidence from the pretrial stage onward, including the Trial and the Appeal decisions. Throughout all stages, a common characteristic emerged: there was always at least one judge who expressed concern about the insufficiency of the prosecutorial evidence to prove guilt beyond a reasonable doubt.

4 Gbagbo Interlocutory Decisions on Evidence

> One can be convinced of a "forest" without evidence of the nature and location of particular "trees".[31]

31 ICC-02/11-01/11-534, October 9, 2013 Amicus Curiae Observations by Professors Robinson, de Guzman, Jalloh and Cryer, at para 42.

4.1 *Assessment of Evidence in Pre-trial Decisions for* Gbagbo

The *Gbagbo* case had faced evidentiary difficulties since 2013, at the confirmation of charges stage. The case's final Trial decision of no case to answer was confirmed by the Appeal Court. The Court issued many interlocutory decisions on evidence matters throughout the entire judicial process from 2013 until the no case to answer application in 2018.

This case is the only one among the other two examined in the book in which pre-trial decisions are discussed. The reason is that from when charges were confirmed at the early stage, the judges had antithetical views regarding the quality of evidence and how to evaluate it. Judge Wyngaert's dissenting decision said that the evidence, even at its highest standard, could not confirm the charges against Gbagbo. When later we read the no-case-to-answer decision of the Trial Court, the Majority said that the evidence taken at its highest standard could not lead a reasonable Court to convict the accused.

In June 2013, the Pre-Trial Chamber's Majority issued a decision adjourning the hearing of the confirmation of charges, asking the Prosecution "to consider providing further evidence or conducting further investigation concerning all the charges".[32] The 2013 Pre-Trial Court noted that the Prosecution's case "relied heavily on NGO reports and press articles" regarding the case's key elements. The Court considered that this evidence did not represent "the fruits of a full and proper investigation".[33] It also noted that incidents were solely proven by anonymous hearsay, which made it difficult for the Court to attribute much probative value and, finally, not to speculate. Also, the Defence could not challenge the evidence. Additionally, the Court said that the adduced information was not enough to make inferences supported by the evidence for the confirmation of the charges.[34] Therefore, the Prosecution should collect further evidence according to Article 61(7) of the Statute.

Both the Prosecution and the Defence requested leave to appeal the above decision. The Prosecution was granted leave to appeal regarding the interpretation of the charges and whether and which of the incidents alleged (by the Prosecutor) should be proved according to the relevant standard for the charges to be confirmed by the Court.[35] According to the Prosecution, this

32 ICC-02/11-01/11-432, 03-06-2013, Decision adjourning the hearing on the confirmation of charges pursuant to Article 61(7)(c)(i) of the Rome Statute, at para 47.

33 *Ibid* at para 35.

34 *Ibid* at para 36.

35 ICC-02/11-01/11-572 16-12-2013, Judgment on the appeal of the Prosecutor against the decision of Pre-Trial Chamber I of June 3, 2013 entitled "Decision adjourning the hearing on the confirmation of charges pursuant to Article 61(7)(c)(i) of the Rome Statute", at para 64.

standard was correctly applied when the Chamber looked at all the evidence "cumulatively" and not at each incident separately.[36] Therefore, the burden of proof should be required only for "material facts", not "subsidiary facts".[37] In December 2013, the Appeal Court confirmed the impugned decision. The Prosecutor should establish to the requisite threshold that a sufficient number of incidents (not each one) relevant to establishing the alleged "attack" took place.

Before the above Appeal Court, amicus curiae observations were submitted after being granted leave. The observations regarding evidence said that "the controversy of the parties and the judges is not whether sufficient evidence is needed" for the confirmation of charges, "but what constitutes sufficient evidence".[38] The Amici Report concluded that because of the absence of feasibility or desirability of direct evidence of thousands of crimes, "UN reports, press articles and NGO reports", along with expert evidence, are necessary and valuable.[39] According to the Report, "Evidence of formal adoption of a policy is not required; a policy need not be formalized and can be inferred from the manner in which the acts occur".[40]

It is true that reasonable inferences of admissible evidence may lead to a conviction. However, conviction is not established if the chain of evidence upon which the inferences are made breaks due to unreliable evidence. When reasonable but antithetical inferences can be made, the circumstantial evidence is insufficient to prove guilt. In 2014, Judge Christine Van den Wyngaert dissented in the Pre-Trial decision regarding the confirmation of charges against Laurent Gbagbo.[41] She said that the evidence, which was primarily anonymous hearsay even taken at its highest standard, could not prove the prosecution's story beyond a reasonable doubt. Judge Wyngaert acknowledged the low evidential standard needed for the charges' confirmation. However, she still decided that the evidence was insufficient not only for proving the charges but even confirming them. In her dissenting decision, she pointed to the insufficiency of the quality of the voluminous prosecutorial

36 *Ibid* at para 27.

37 *Ibid.*

38 ICC-02/11-01/11-534, October 9, 2013 Amicus Curiae Observations of Professors Robinson, deGuzman, Jalloh and Cryer, at para.16.

39 *Ibid* at para 42.

40 *Ibid* at para 4. also ICC-02/11-01/11-572 16-12-2013, *supra* note 35 at para 14 (Judgment on the appeal), the Appeal Court, in its decision did not consider the Amici Curiae observations for reasons related only to the permitted grounds of appeal.

41 ICC-02/11-01/11-656-Anx 12-06-2014, June 12, 2014, Dissenting Opinion of Judge Christine Van den Wyngaert.

evidence, which was primarily anonymous hearsay. She said that the Majority perceived the evidence indicating certain inferences regarding Gbagbo's criminal responsibility; however, alternative and antithetical to criminal responsibility inferences could also be made.

Finally, the Majority decision of the 2014 Pre-Trial Chamber confirmed the charges against Gbagbo. In the evidence, verbs such as "shows", "demonstrates", and "indicates" were used without an analysis of what kind of evidence it was. Nowhere in the majority's decision was any reference to anonymous hearsay, as in Judge Wyngaert's decision.

4.2 *Assessment of Evidence in* Gbagbo and Blé Goudé *Interlocutory Trial Decisions*

> Rather, the changes appear to have been based on the presumed shortcomings of the common law-inspired approach of conducting adversarial criminal trials and the assumption that abandoning this approach would ipso facto make things more efficient.[42]

> J'aimerais également rappeler une chose aux parties. La Chambre est composée de juges professionnels qui sont parfaitement capables de faire la différence entre l'ouï-dire et l'observation directe, la corroboration de la non-corroboration, les sources anonymes des sources qui ne sont pas anonymes, et la Chambre est tout à fait en mesure d'accorder à tout cela la valeur juste. Donc, ce n'est pas la peine de gesticuler tout le temps et de vous lever, parce que la Chambre est composée de juges qui ont quand même une certaine connaissance de la question.[43]

On March 22, 2014, Blé Goudé surrendered to ICC custody. In December 2014, Pre-Trial Chamber I, with Judge Wyngaert partly dissenting, confirmed the charges against Blé Goudé.[44] In March 2015, the cases against Gbagbo and Blé Goudé were joined.[45]

---

42 ICC-02/11-01/15-498-Anx1 04-05-2016, at para 9, Decision adopting amended and supplemented directions on the conduct of the Proceedings, Dissenting opinion of Judge Geoffrey Henderson. Judge Henderson referred to the change made between the decisions of September 3, 2015 and January 19, 2016 as explained in this section.

43 Judge Cuno Jakob Tarfusser, ICC-02/11-01/15-T-46-Red-FRA, June 6, 2016, 13 lines 7–13.

44 ICC-02/11-02/11-186, 11-12-2014, Decision on the confirmation of charges against Charles Blé Goudé; ICC-02/11-02/11-186-Anx, 11-12-2014 Partly Dissenting Opinion of Judge Christine Van den Wyngaert.

45 ICC-02/11-01/15-1, 11-03-2015, Decision on Prosecution requests to join the cases of *The Prosecutor v. Laurent Gbagbo* and *The Prosecutor v. Charles Blé Goudé and related matters*.

5 The Great Admissibility Delay: Who Needs Timely Decisions?

In September 2015, the Trial Court decided that the evidence would be assessed freely, considering relevance, prejudice, and probative value issues. Evidence that would not be regarded as *prima facie* relevant or with probative value would not be admitted. When ruling on admissibility, the Court would consider "any prejudice the evidence may cause to a fair trial or the fair evaluation of the testimony".[46] The approach looked at a combination of continental and adversarial free assessment regarding rulings on admissibility. However, the Court did not clarify the stage when it would decide on admissibility. This left room for the upcoming decision of January 2016.

In January 2016, the same Court decided on the submission and admission of evidence.[47] The parties had unanimously agreed to determine admissibility on a rolling basis at the time of evidence submission.[48] Surprisingly, despite this unanimity, the majority of the Court decided to rule on admissibility only at the final judgment stage. Three core reasons were offered: The Court wanted to "assess" each piece of evidence by considering all the evidence.[49] It is unclear, however, whether the assessment the Court mentioned was relevant to the admissibility or weight of evidence. In its second reason, the Court referred to the danger of "partial knowledge of the case" when ruling on a rolling basis. This suggests a concern about weight. It also said that the rulings' deferral would help the Court by avoiding "multiple and possibly contradictory" decisions for the same piece of evidence. It added that it is not exceptional that relevance "only emerges in light of material submitted at a later stage".[50] The third reason was to "ensure that all the evidence submitted will be subjected to a uniform treatment".[51] However, it is not clear what "uniform treatment" means in legal terms with respect to the relevance, prejudice and probative value of different pieces of evidence.

Finally, the majority of the Trial Court emphasized the importance of admissibility rulings on a rolling basis only for jury trials, not for panels of professional judges as at the ICC.[52] The Court also said that the Majority expects the parties to be prepared "to cover eventualities", conduct investiga-

46 ICC-02/11-01/15, September 3, 2015, Directions on the conduct of the proceedings, at para 51.
47 ICC-02/11-01/15, January 29, 2016, Decision on the submission and admission of evidence.
48 *Ibid* at paras 1–2.
49 *Ibid* at para 13.
50 *Ibid* at para 14.
51 *Ibid* at para 15.
52 *Ibid* at para 16.

tions and prepare their cases "in the light of all submitted evidence".[53] However, even though counsels' professionalism demands adequate and effective preparation, paradoxically, the "eventuality" here seems to also include the admissibility of evidence. This is relatively obscure and not exactly fair, especially when a trial is complex with voluminous untested evidence.

Judge Henderson dissented and mentioned the unanimous approach of all the parties to the admissibility rulings. Most importantly, he said that when evidence admissibility is not addressed on a rolling basis for reasons related to the Chamber's truth-seeking mandate, the Prosecution cannot know, at the end of its case, whether it has met the burden of proof or not.[54] In his analysis, he clearly explained the importance of admissibility decisions for the parties to prepare their cases and adduce substitute evidence. The Defence, especially, must be able to make an informed decision on how to proceed, in silence or by giving evidence. Without knowing admissibility issues, the Defence would be in darkness.[55]

The common law view of Judge Henderson showed that admissibility during the final judgment phase is problematic, especially if pieces of evidence are determined inadmissible after the parties have closed their cases. Correctly, Judge Henderson differentiated between *prima facie* and ultimate admissibility. Ultimate admissibility is related to the weight of evidence, not its relevance, probative value, and prejudice. However, the continental tradition is not trained to understand this distinction. The case law Judge Henderson referred to follows the common law distinction regarding evidence admissibility, not the continental *all-in, and we will check in the end.*

Not surprisingly, Judge Henderson discussed prejudice and how important it is to address it before the trial concludes, but continental thinkers are not familiar with the concept of prejudice.[56] They connote prejudice with the concept of bias, so they perceive it necessary only for common law jury trials. The distinction between prejudice and bias is an unknown concept in the continental tradition. No evidence case law has ever been produced in continental systems for prejudice (not bias), as understood in the common law evidence law. Interestingly, in many foreign languages, linguists confuse prejudice with bias, and prejudice is often seen as synonymous with bias and vice versa. Specifically, linguists frequently treat "prejudice" and "bias" as if they are

---

53 *Ibid* at para 18.

54 ICC-02/11-01/15-405-Anx 01-02-2016, Dissenting Opinion of Judge Henderson, at para 8.

55 *Ibid* at paras 9–10.

56 *Ibid* at para 24.

interchangeable or synonymous. However, in the context of a fair trial, prejudice means more than that.

6 Prejudice in Adversarial Common Law Terms

To understand prejudice when admitting evidence in an adversarial trial we need to explain that prejudice is dichotomized in to moral and reasoning prejudice. Moreover, when assessing the probative value of the offered evidence, prejudice must be outweighed. The admissibility of similar fact evidence in legal proceedings is fraught with challenges due to the inherent risks of propensity reasoning, which involves inferring guilt based on a defendant's past behaviour. This type of reasoning can undermine the fairness of a trial. Historical practices, judicial struggles with excluding relevant evidence, and the balance between probative value and prejudicial impact all contribute to the complexity of this issue. The following breakdown explores these challenges and the principles governing the use of similar fact evidence, highlighting the importance of distinguishing between reasoning prejudice and moral prejudice.

According to Canadian evidence law, particularly as elucidated in the *Handy* case, the prejudice test for similar fact evidence is as follows:[57]

a. Strength of evidence and judicial assessment on probative value vs. prejudice:
   - **Evidence relevance (contribution)**: The evidence should significantly contribute to proving a matter in issue without unfairly prejudicing the defendant. In similar fact evidence, inferences must align with common sense, intuitive probability, and the improbability of coincidence.
   - **Judicial determination**: The judge must determine that the evidence is strong enough on a balance of probabilities and that the probative value (believability and informativeness) of the evidence outweighs potential moral and reasoning prejudice.

b. Countervailing factors in assessing prejudice:
   - **Inflammatory nature and alternatives**: Factors such as the inflammatory nature of similar acts and whether the prosecution can prove its point with less prejudicial evidence are crucial.

57 *R. v. Handy*, [2002] 2 S.C.R. 908, 2002 SCC 56. *See also* David Paciocco, Palma Paciocco, & Lee Stuesser. *The Law of Evidence*, 8th ed. (Toronto, Irwin Law, 2020) 44–46, 52–55, 93–96.

- **Court considerations:** The court must also consider potential distractions from the main charge and undue time consumption.

c. Moral prejudice (prejudgment):
- **Definition:** Occurs when evidence causes a judge or jury to form a negative opinion of the accused based on moral disapproval rather than factual evidence.
- **Example:** Testimony about domestic abuse might cause the jury to view the accused negatively, making them more likely to believe the worst about him.
- **Propensity reasoning:** While propensity reasoning is not outright prohibited and is often inevitable, it is forbidden when based solely on the accused's bad character.

d. Reasoning Prejudice:
- **Definition:** Refers to prejudices that distract the jury from focusing on the specific charge due to inflammatory evidence.
- **Example:** Multiple incidents or victims might distract the jury, leading them to judge the accused based on past behaviour rather than the incident being tried.

Lawrence M. Friedman observed that:

> Everyone who watches American trials on TV or in the movies is familiar with the rituals: One lawyer tries to sneak in some damning piece of evidence, the opposing lawyer leaps up and cries out, in wounded dignity, "Objection", and the judge either overrules or sustains. These evidence rules are strict; they encourage the lawyers, therefore, to find some artful dodges to get around the rules or to shoehorn into the courtroom and into the tender ears of the jury bits of fact and opinion that, strictly speaking, are verboten. The other side will, of course, object.[58]

It is possible that continental legal scholars have this in mind when they refer to technical evidence rules. However, *Handy,* above, reflects a more evolved functional evidence law, rather than strict evidence rules. Although Article 69.4 of the ICC Statute includes provisions for assessing relevance, probative value, and prejudice concerning the admissibility of evidence, this forms a framework for developing evidence law rather than constituting evidence law itself.

---

58 Lawrence Meir Friedman. *American Law in the Twentieth Century* (New Haven, CT: Yale University Press, 2004), 267.

7 The Web of Evidence and the Typicality of Hearsay Admissibility

A rule that documents can only be submitted "through a witness" has no basis in the Statute or the Rules.[59]

In June 2016, the Trial Court discussed the Prosecutor's application to submit prior-recorded testimonies, conditionally, under Rules 68(2)(b) and 68(3). The Court accepted the Prosecution's request, with Judge Henderson partially dissenting. Both accused appealed the decision. The Appeal Court confirmed the Trial Court's Majority decision, with Judge Ozaki partially dissenting.

The antithetical views in these decisions are closely related to hearsay evidence admissibility. The discussion largely turned to whether in-person testimony in trials is the rule, whether the principle of orality is overrated, and the importance of expeditiousness in trial proceedings. As for the admissibility of hearsay, the majority in both Courts ended by saying that Rule 68 provides for typical criteria, not an in-depth analysis.

Rule 68 of the Rules of Procedure and Evidence of the ICC was amended in 2013 to include exceptions to the principle of orality. But, nowhere in the introduction and adoption of these amendments is it said that the admissibility of hearsay evidence is a typicality.

On the contrary, the reason the Rule was amended was to include prior recorded testimonies when these are related to the acts and conduct of the accused; when a person is dead or presumed dead or when a person, even with due diligence, cannot appear in court; and when the person who gave the prior recorded testimony has been subjected to interference. These provisions would allow the ICC to carry on with evidence if certain criteria were met and the witnesses could not or did not appear. This was a way to reduce lengthy proceedings and "streamline" evidence presentation before the Court. The proposed amendments were based on the ICTY's rules.[60]

In the amendment proposal, it was made crystal clear that the principle of orality (Article 69.2) is a general principle, and Rule 68 is the principle's exception. The exception was made mainly because the ICC does not have subpoena power to compel a witness to appear before the Court. Therefore, some flexibility was needed by the Court to hear evidence that could not be

59 ICC-02/11-01/15-573-Red, June 9, 2016, Decision on the Prosecutor's application to introduce prior recorded testimony under Rules 68(2)(b) and 68(3), at para 9.

60 ICC-ASP/12/37/Add., 31.10.2013, Study Group on Governance Working Group on Lessons Learnt: Second report of the Court to the Assembly of States Parties, Annex II.A, Recommendation on a proposal to amend Rule 68 of the Rules of Procedure and Evidence (Prior Recorded Testimony), at paras 3–4.

heard if the witness was not present. It was made clear that fairness and the rights of the accused should be safeguarded.[61] For this reason, specific reference was made to Article 69.4, which inter alia provides that the probative value of the admitted evidence must outweigh prejudice. Another important point in the analysis of the proposed amendment was related to terminology. When the "chapeau" Rule 68 refers to the term "introduction" of evidence, it equates to admissibility.[62]

Let's turn now to the two interlocutory decisions which dealt with the prior recorded testimonies in the Gbagbo case. The Trial Court emphasized that the "essence" of Rule 68(2)(b) "is to allow for streamlining of the evidentiary proceedings by not calling some witnesses in person, even if they are available".[63] The Court did not explain which factors indicated that the probative value of the submitted evidence outweighed its prejudice and which secured sufficient indicia of reliability. However, this is a process strictly required by Rule 68 and is related to admissibility, not to weigh evidence. It seems as if the Court forgot that Rule 68 is an exception, which provides an adversarial principled approach to hearsay admission not a free all-in continental process, and this demanded analysis and reasoning. Finally, the Trial Court considered it important to admit the submitted hearsay by the Prosecution because, as it said, those testimonies, along with the parties' evidence, would "form a web of evidence" and would allow the Court "to appreciate how the events unfolded on the ground".[64]

Here, the so-called web of evidence the Court stated needs some discussion. It is true that when the admitted circumstantial evidence provides a web with no holes, or in other words, a chain without broken links and the conviction is the only logical outcome, the Court should convict. However, the Court did not say this. It said that the ongoing collection of evidence would form an evidence web. However, a large amount of supposedly relevant evidence with reliability frailties and prejudicial stains cannot form a reliable web of circumstantial evidence. Circumstantial evidence, as with all kinds of evi-

---

61 *Ibid* at paras 5–6, 12.

62 *Ibid* 22 at para 13. "Two points of terminology should also be noted. First, the WGLL notes that the term 'introduction' is used in the chapeau of the current rule 68 and in the text of Article 69(2) of the Statute.11 However, the terms 'submit' or 'submitted' are used in Articles 69(3) and 74(2) of the Statute. The WGLL has decided to retain the word 'introduction' in the rule 68 amendment proposal in all cases in which the Chamber itself is admitting evidence. The WGLL understands that the term 'introduction' refers to the general admission of evidence in this context".

63 ICC-02/11-01/15-573-Red, *supra* note 59 at para 11.

64 *Ibid* at para 38.

dence, needs admissibility scrutiny, especially when it is hearsay. Mountains of unreliable and prejudicial evidence can only make a web of garbage.

The admissibility scrutiny and analysis were imperative because the Court would use the submitted hearsay as circumstantial evidence. However, the Trial Court admitted the evidence for trial expeditiousness and, during the hearing, confirmed its ability to distinguish evidence issues without admissibility rulings due to the panel's judicial professionalism.[65] As for the prior recorded testimonies' sufficient indicia of reliability, the Court rather equated reliability with authenticity, which is only part of reliability. Impressively, for an admitted hearsay, where the witness referred to his knowledge from other hearsay, the Court said that, since the testimony was taken by the office of the Prosecution and the witness said how he learnt what he learnt, indicia of reliability had been met.[66] Maybe the continental approach of the Court blurred its view.

Ultimately, it still remains unclear how trial expeditiousness was met here through Rule 68. Only one witness's prior recorded testimony was admitted under Rule 68(2)(b). The other prior recorded testimonies that were admitted under Rule 68(3) were related to witnesses who would finally appear before the Court because their evidence was materially in dispute. However, Rule 68(3) says that if the witness is present and does not object to his prior recorded testimony being submitted and the parties can examine him/her, the Court may admit the previously recorded testimony. Here, the witnesses were not still present. Both the quality and the ratio of the admission are problematic.

Judge Henderson partially dissented. He acknowledged that even if hearsay is not inadmissible, this does not mean that the Court should systematically admit hearsay evidence through Rule 68.[67] The "all-in" evidence admissibility process is wrong. Especially for indicia of reliability, he said that Rule 68(2)(b) has no room for a formalistic approach. He declined to offer a menu of potential indicia of reliability but acknowledged some essentials that must be considered: (a) competence to testify about the fact; (b) a basis for assessing credibility; and (c) coherence of the evidence with other evidence.[68] In other words, he proposed a basic check of whether the proposed hearsay is good enough to be admitted and evaluated later. This is a threshold reliability

65 ICC-02/11-01/15-T-46-Red-FRA, June 6, 2016, 13 lines 7–13. *See* also ICC-02/11-01/15-573-Anx-Red, 13-06-2016 Partially Dissenting Opinion of Judge Henderson, at para 14.

66 ICC-02/11-01/15-573-Red, *supra* note 59 at paras 19, 22.

67 ICC-02/11-01/15-573-Anx-Red, 13-06-2016, *supra* note 24 at para 8.

68 *Ibid* at para 27.

assessment. His dissenting opinion, again, described the difficulty of accessing admissibility questions when evaluating the weight of evidence at the end of the trial. It also shows that the Court should be more vigilant when using the exception of Rule 68 instead of in-person testimonies.

Following an appeal by the defence in November 2016, the Appeal Court's majority analysis regarding admissibility was related to whether the required "sufficient indicia of reliability", according to Rule 68.2(b)(i), needed analysis, as suggested by Judge Henderson. The Appeal Court said that an analysis was not necessary because the Rule provided for formality questions, not in-depth ones. Therefore, it stated:

> An assessment of "indicia of reliability" under rule 68.(2)(b)(i) of the Rules of Procedure and Evidence can be more cursory in nature so that, even if some factors, such as the witness's competence to testify about the facts, the internal consistency of the statement and potential inconsistencies with other evidence in the record, are not taken into account during this assessment, *they may still be considered when assessing the probative value of the evidence.*[69] [emphasis added]

The problem with the quoted paragraph is that the Appeal Court seems to confuse the evidence's sufficient indicia of reliability for admissibility reasons with the evidence's ultimate weight assessment. This shows the rift between Henderson's approach and the Appeal Court's Majority that follows here.

The absence of the Trial Court's admissibility analysis and reasoning for admitting hearsay evidence according to Rule 68 exceptions was a core element in Judge Ozaki's partially dissenting opinion. She also strongly emphasized the importance of not "lightly displacing" the *Bemba* decision, which requested the Trial Court to make clear judgements on admissibility issues.[70] *Bemba* said that the Trial Court, when making admissibility decisions, may take into account factors such as:

> (i) whether the evidence relates to issues that are not materially in dispute; (ii) whether that evidence is not central to core issues in the case,

69 ICC-02/11-01/15 OA 8, November 1, 2016, Appeal Chamber Judgement on the appeals of Mr Laurent Gbagbo and Mr Charles Blé Goude against the decision of Trial Chamber I of June 9, 2016 entitled "Decision on the Prosecutor's application to introduce prior recorded testimony under Rules 68(2)(b) and 68(3)" at paras 3, 96.

70 ICC-02/11-01/15-744-Anx 16-12-2016, Partially Dissenting Opinion of Judge Kuniko Ozaki, at paras 7–8, 11–12, 15.

> but only provides relevant background information; and (iii) whether the evidence is corroborative of other evidence.[71]

Bemba also said that the Court should provide a cautious analysis item by item according to Article 69(2). The Trial Court in *Gbagbo* characterized the submitted evidence "important", but this is not a requirement provided by Rule 68.[72] Prejudice analysis is mandatory because important evidence can be prejudicial. Moreover, the term "important" evidence is not self-explanatory. Relevance and reliability afford a robust admissibility discussion, as Judge Henderson also suggested.

The Appeal Court also said that Rule 68(2)(b) "does not provide any indication as to the factors that a Trial Chamber may or should consider in deciding whether prior recorded testimony has sufficient indicia of reliability".[73] Notwithstanding that the *Bemba* decision had set factors, the Appeal Court not only ignored it but said:

> The factors referred to in the Bemba OA 5 OA 6 Judgment are not requirements but, rather, factors that may be considered in assessing whether the introduction of prior recorded testimony under rule 68(3) of the Rules is prejudicial to or inconsistent with the rights of the accused or with the fairness of the trial generally.

It is not clear why the Appeal Court tried to ignore or diminish the importance of the Interlocutory decision. This *Bemba* decision was issued in 2011. In 2013, Rule 68 was amended. The criteria the Appeal Court set in *Bemba* were included in the amendment and are now clear in Rule 68(2)(i). *Bemba* emphasized the need for admissibility analysis and precluded a wholesale admission of evidence without relevance, reliability, and probative value versus prejudice analysis per evidence item. The adoption of different terms such as factors, requirements, or criteria with reference to *Bemba* does not discard the Court's duty to provide a reasoned decision for admission of evidence when

---

71 ICC-01/05-01/08 OA 5 OA 6, May 3, 2011, Judgment on the appeals of Mr Jean-Pierre Bemba Gombo and the Prosecutor against the decision of Trial Chamber III entitled "Decision on the admission into evidence of materials contained in the prosecution's list of evidence" at para 78.

72 ICC-02/11-01/15-573-Red, *supra* note 59 at para 38. *See also* ICC-02/11-01/15-744-Anx 16-12-2016, *supra* note 70 at para 14.

73 ICC-02/11-01/15 OA 8, *supra* note 69 at para 97.

statutory exceptions. Besides, the *Gbagbo* Court's interpretation of terms as factors, requirements or criteria seems problematic if not legally insubstantial.

The Trial Court in *Gbagbo* had to decide whether some prior recorded statements met the criteria of the exceptions set by Rule 68. When a court decides on statutory exceptions, it is rather necessary for fairness reasons to make clear assessments. Here, it did not happen. It is important to note that the analysis of the Rule 68 amendment, especially for the term "sufficient indicia of reliability", said that the ICC jurisprudence will eventually develop relevant factors.[74]

The discussion of both the Appeal and the Trial Court in the *Gbagbo* interlocutory decision emphasized that the criteria of the Rule 68 exception are limited to formality. The alleged clarification by the Court is not only unclear but also superfluous. It would be more efficient if the Court's decision could help the ICC's jurisprudence to develop more secure steps in the admissibility phase. It should be necessary for the Court to clearly distinguish between threshold and ultimate reliability, moral and legal prejudice, relevance and probative value. It would be helpful towards evolution if the ICC, especially the continental-inspired judges, clearly issued decisions where evidence admissibility and evidence weight were distinct. These are two different processes of evaluation of evidence. The first takes place during the hearing, and the second at the judgment phase. According to its legal framework, the ICC has plenty of discretion. This room is not to avoid precise and concise admissibility decisions.

8 Clear Signs to the Road of No Case to Answer

> Indeed, the Chamber has an obligation to ensure that the case record remains focused and free from evidence that lacks relevance or probative value.[75]

Until now, it has been made clear that the *Gbagbo* Trial Court would only rule on admissibility at the final decision stage. In an interlocutory decision in December 2016, the Court, with Judge Henderson dissenting, admitted more prosecutorial evidence. Some of the evidence had no name, date, or signature. Judge Henderson, again, said that this approach was unfair not only for the Defence but also for the Prosecution. It could end up with the

74 ICC-ASP/12/37/Add., *supra* note 60 at para 22. The Appeal Court also referred to para 22.

75 ICC-02/11-01/15-773-AnxI, 13-12-2016 Dissenting Opinion of Judge Henderson, at para 15.

Prosecution ignoring whether she ever met the burden of proof. As he said, admissibility rulings need to take place sometime. Therefore, the delay in rulings could not help time efficiency. Additionally, the Parties were required to pay attention to which evidence had been admitted or not by the Court.[76] Judge Henderson's language in this dissenting decision was quite strong, but not without a good reason. He could see that the pile of unreliable evidence was growing, and this could not end well.

Despite acknowledging that some pieces of evidence lacked *prima facie* relevance or probative value, the Majority still said that any affirmative ruling on the admission or exclusion of evidence would deprive the Court of freely assessing the entire evidence material at the end. Moreover, any admissibility ruling would have been made with only partial knowledge of the case.[77] By its decision, the Court admitted 135 pieces of evidence of ambivalent or absent relevance and indicia of reliability. The Court called this process good trial management. Following appeals by both the accused, the Appeal Court confirmed, in July 2017, that the Trial Court had not erred in applying its discretion to rule on admissibility later.[78]

In January 2018, the Prosecution's final witness concluded their testimony. In February, the Trial Court invited the Prosecution to submit a trial brief with a detailed narrative about its case and a detailed explanation regarding which of the submitted evidence supported the charges.[79] The Prosecution, in March 2018, submitted a brief called mid-trial brief clarifying that (a) the weight of evidence had not yet been addressed; (b) the requested brief could not be "more onerous than a response to a 'no case to answer' motion"; and (c) the brief was not intended to be a closing brief.[80] The Defence filed observations primarily highlighting the poor quality of the Prosecution's evidence, indicating clearly the "no case to answer" avenue.[81]

---

76 ICC-02/11-01/15, December 9, 2016, Decision concerning the Prosecutor's submission of documentary evidence on June 13, July 14, September 7, and September 19, 2016; ICC-02/11-01/15-773-AnxI, *supra* note 44.

77 ICC-02/11-01/15, *supra* note 46 at para 35.

78 ICC-02/11-01/15 OA11 OA12, July 24, 2017, Judgment on the appeals of Mr Laurent Gbagbo and Mr Charles Blé Goudé against Trial Chamber I's decision on the submission of documentary evidence.

79 ICC-02/11-01/15, February 9, 2018, Order on the further conduct of the proceedings, at para 10.

80 ICC-02/11-01/15, Public with Confidential Annexes 1, A, B, C, D and E. Prosecution's Mid-Trial Brief submitted pursuant to Chamber's Order on the further conduct of the proceedings (ICC-02/11-01/15-1124), at paras 9–10.

81 ICC-02/11-01/15-1158-Conf., 09-02-2018, and ICC-02/11-01/15-1158-Corr-Red, 25-04-2018 Public Redacted Version of "Corrected Version of 'Defence's written observations on

In June 2018, again, with Judge Henderson dissenting, the Trial Court accepted more evidence submitted by the Prosecution without ruling on admissibility.[82] Judge Henderson offered some specific examples from the prosecutorial evidence that lacked relevance in a matter in issue and indicia of reliability. Using strong language again, he underscored the difficulty the Court would face in making an informed decision without admissibility criteria.[83] He also emphasized the cluttering of the case record with insufficient evidence, jeopardizing both fairness and expeditiousness.[84]

In the same month, June 2018, in another decision, the Trial Chamber declared the Prosecution's case closed and asked the Defence to make precise and concise submissions as to whether the prosecutorial evidence was insufficient to reasonably support a conviction.[85] The Court had opened the door for a no-case-to-answer motion. The Prosecution requested the Court to provide guidance upon the applicable standard of proof of a no-case-to-answer motion. She discussed case law and emphasized that a qualitative assessment of evidence at this stage was illogical given the Trial Court's submission and admission regime for the final stage.[86] The decision issued by a single Judge (Judge Tarfusser) on behalf of the Trial Court, rejected the Prosecution's request to define the standard of proof of a no-case-to-answer motion as unnecessary.[87]

Given the entire contradiction in the Judges' views, the question arises: Did the Trial Court's Majority in the *Gbagbo* case deliberately avoid making admissibility rulings, or were they simply unaware of how to make them?

---

the continuation of the trial proceedings pursuant to Chamber's Order on the further conduct of the proceedings (ICC-02/11-01/15-1124)", April 24, 2018, ICC-02/11-01/15-1158-Conf-Corr. (Blé Goudé Defence observations); ICC-02/11-01/15-1157-Red 03-05-2018, Version publique expurgée des « observations de la Défense présentées à la suite de l'ordonnance de la Chambre « on the further conduct of the proceedings » du 9 février 2018 (ICC-02/11-01/15-1124) » (ICC-02/11-01/15-1157-Conf) (Laurent Gbagbo Defence observations).

82 ICC-02/11-01/15, June 1, 2018, Decision concerning the Prosecutor's submission of documentary evidence on April 28, July 31, December 15 and 22, 2017, and March 23, and May 21, 2018.

83 ICC-02/11-01/15-1172-Anx 01-06-2018, Dissenting Opinion of Judge Geoffrey Henderson, at paras 7–10.

84 *Ibid* at paras 4–5, 12.

85 ICC-02/11-01/15, June 4, 2018, Second Order on the further conduct of the proceedings, at para 10.

86 ICC-02/11-01/15, June 8, 2018, Urgent Prosecution's motion seeking clarification on the standard of a "no case to answer" motion, at para 29.

87 ICC-02/11-01/15, June 13, 2018, Trial Chamber I, Decision on "Urgent Prosecution's motion seeking clarification on the standard of a 'no case to answer' motion", at para 13.

It is possible that the Majority's continental judicial thinking process was unfamiliar with the concept of evidence law as it pertains to admissibility rulings. It is crucial to clarify that, in contemporary common law, ruling on admissibility is not a mechanical response to exclusion objections. The ancient common law rule – if hearsay, it is de facto "out" – no longer applies with such simplicity. Modern common law rulings on admissibility aim to safeguard fairness by examining whether the weaknesses in evidence may prejudice the accused.

9 The *Gbagbo and Blé Goudé* "No-Case-to-Answer" Motions

> The law is there to be upheld in all its rigour, not to serve as an excuse to satisfy political or even humanitarian goals.[88]

In June 2018, both accused Gbagbo and Blé Goudé filed motions for a no-case-to-answer case due to the insufficient prosecutorial evidence and requested the acquittals of both accused. The Prosecution requested a holistic evaluation of her evidence.[89] The Trial Court issued an oral decision in January 2019, with Judge Herrera-Carbuccia dissenting. The Majority decided that the Prosecutor had not satisfied the burden of proof, according to Article 66, concerning several core constitutive elements of the crimes as charged and, therefore, the Defence should not submit further evidence.[90] Presiding Judge Tarfusser said that Judge Herrera-Carbuccia had conducted "a superficial *prima facie* review", which led her to the view the trial should continue.[91]

Judge Herrera-Carbuccia, in her dissenting opinion, said inter alia that the Court had mistaken both for not defining the standard of review for a no case-to-answer decision and for applying the prosecutorial burden of proof beyond a reasonable doubt. She explained that, for a no-case-to-answer decision, the Prosecution needed to offer evidence upon which a reasonable Trial Chamber

88 ICC-02/11-01/15-1263-AnxB-Red 16-07-2019, Trial Decision, Reasons of Judge Geoffrey Henderson, Preliminary Remarks, at para 10. [Henderson decision]

89 ICC-02/11-01/15-1207 11-09-2018, Prosecution's Response to Defence No Case to Answer Motions, at para 7.

90 ICC-02/11-01/15-T-232-ENG ET WT, Transcript of January 15, 2019; ICC-02/11-01/15-1234, January 15, 2019, Dissenting Opinion to the Chamber's Oral Decision of January 15, 2019.

91 ICC-02/11-01/15-T-234-ENG, January 16, 2019, at 4–5.

"could" (not "would") convict.[92] She also questioned how the Majority decided on acquittal without individual admissibility rulings.[93]

After six months, in July 2019, the Trial Court issued three separate decisions, two concurring.

10 The Prosecutor Claims a System of Evidence, the Majority Declares "No Case to Answer"

> Being less demanding and rendering judgments based on "systems of evidence" of questionable quality may lead to more convictions and even a vacuous sense that we are doing something to "end impunity". However, the law is there to be upheld in all its rigour, not to serve as an excuse to satisfy political or even humanitarian goals. If we cease abiding by this principle the ICC will become a court in name only and we will no longer be able to do justice for anyone.[94]

The Prosecution called on the Court to conduct a holistic evaluation of the submitted evidence, assessing it as a whole and evaluating it as a "system of evidence".[95]

The phrase "system of evidence" lacks a clear legal definition, and its origins are uncertain. Nonetheless, in 2016, Judge Kuniko Ozaki, in this case, emphasized the importance of the judicial certainty principle and highlighted the unfairness of proceedings when the importance of different pieces of evidence is assessed "within a perceived system of evidence". She noted that such a system "is not only vulnerable to unprincipled application but is also not amenable to meaningful interlocutory review".[96]

Judges Tarfusser and Henderson decided to end this trial and acquit both accused.

In Judge Henderson's almost one-thousand-page decision, which contained the Majority's evidence analysis, it was confirmed that when a no-case-to-answer application is decided, according to the standard in *Ruto and Sang*,

92 ICC-02/11-01/15-1234, *supra* note 90 at paras 43–44, 48.

93 *Ibid* paras 46–47.

94 ICC-02/11-01/15-1263-AnxB-Red, *supra* note 88 at para 10.

95 ICC-02/11-01/15, September 10, 2018, Prosecution's Response to Defence No Case to Answer Motions, ICC-02/11-01/15-1207 11-09-2018 1/10 EC T, at para 7.

96 ICC-02/11-01/15-744-Anx 16-12-2016 1/7 EC T OA8, *supra* note 70 at paras 13–13, regarding prior recorded testimonies according to the Rule 68.

the prosecutorial evidence must be taken at its highest standard, assuming it is credible and reliable. However, the ICC judges cannot be prevented from assessing the quality of evidence when considering whether a reasonable court would convict. This decision, with its far-reaching implications, led to the acquittal of both accused.[97]

Judge Henderson emphasized that the absence of admissibility rulings left the submitted evidence unfiltered. This led to unanswered questions regarding reliability, probative value, and prejudice.[98] Although admissibility rulings would have struck out many pieces of evidence, he clarified that he had considered all the evidence admitted.[99] Still, there was a no-case-to-answer in *Gbagbo and Blé Goudé*.

Henderson's decision analysed the prosecutorial evidence offered for corroboration to prove guilt. There was no direct prosecutorial evidence for the entire case. While this is not uncommon, circumstantial evidence must produce a tight net where guilt is the only logical inference. Otherwise, it is insufficient to prove the accused committed the alleged crime. If the evidence is still inadequate after the prosecution closes her case, the trial should not continue. Continuation would be incompatible with the burden of proof and the presumption of innocence.[100] In this case, the circumstantial prosecutorial evidence could lead to alternative inferences of guilt. Therefore, the trial should be discontinued.

Especially for hearsay evidence, Judge Henderson said that even when hearsay has "considerable" probative value, information about credibility and reliability is mandatory for both admissibility and weight evaluation. Still, the Prosecution did not provide such information.[101] For example, regarding documentary evidence, several signed documents had signatures with questionable authenticity. Documents were moved to multiple places. Evidence regarding origin and authenticity was not offered. Other documents were found ten months later in the Presidential Palace, but no evidence was provided regarding tampering. His authenticity analysis was related not only

97 Henderson decision, *supra* note 88 at para 3. See also, ICC-01/09-01/11-2027 05-04-2016, Trial Chamber V(a), *Prosecutor v. Ruto and Sang*, Decision on the Defence Applications for Judgments of Acquittal, Reasons of Judge Fremr, para. 144; Reasons of Judge Eboe-Osuji, paras 105–125.

98 Henderson decision, *supra* note 88 at paras 4–7.

99 *Ibid* at paras 36–38.

100 *Ibid* at paras 14–15.

101 *Ibid* at paras 42–44.

to an admissibility problem but also to a weight problem. Inevitably, the absence of authenticity negatively affected both stages.[102]

Regarding corroboration, he said that although there is no corroboration requirement, the evidence assessment does not happen in isolation. When a piece of evidence helps to prove the accuracy of another piece, reliability and credibility are core elements proved from other independent evidence. The strength of evidence does not come from its large amount but from its relevance to the fact at issue. Therefore, corroboration happens when two pieces of evidence can independently confirm the fact. The connection of different pieces of evidence for corroboration reasons must be based on their relevance and their probative value regarding a single fact, not different facts that are similar. In legal terms, multiple unreliable pieces of evidence cannot produce corroborative evidence that proves a fact.[103]

For circumstantial evidence, he said that despite its ability to have the same value as direct evidence, its Achilles heel is that wrong inference may be drawn from true but "mischaracterized" circumstantial facts. For conviction reasons, the prosecution must prove beyond a reasonable doubt that the only reasonable inference is guilt.[104] In this case, the plethoric prosecutorial evidence could prove guilt only through a "giant inference".[105] This was impermissible. The required inference cannot be giant because it exceeds reasonableness.

Judge Henderson clarified that the enormous amount of submitted evidence couldn't overshadow the legal question the Court should answer. Could the prosecutorial evidence prove beyond a reasonable doubt the accused created or executed a plan or policy to commit crimes against humanity on the population of Abidjan? The evidence was insufficient, even when taken at its highest standard. The Court should acquit.[106]

10.1 *The Minority's Opinion: There Is a Case to Answer – Proceed with the Trial*

Judge Herrera-Carbuccia's dissenting opinion, which favoured the continuation of the trial, suggested that a reasonable court could convict both the accused. In her three-hundred-page decision, she rather reveals a continental approach. There is no analysis of evidence evaluation, although she confirmed

102 *Ibid* at para 35–38.
103 *Ibid* at paras 46–50.
104 *Ibid* at para 51.
105 *Ibid* at para 1899.
106 *Ibid*, Preliminary remarks, at para 2.

her assessment of both direct and circumstantial evidence despite the absence of direct evidence.[107] Judge Herrera-Carbuccia said that a judge has significant discretion when considering types of evidence.[108]

However, judicial discretion cannot overrule the prosecutorial burden of proof. The consideration of the evidence for admission assessment differs from the consideration for weight assessment. The continental system does not provide this distinction because it does not have admissibility barriers, except for unlawfully gathered evidence. The evaluation of circumstantial evidence for weight reasons (not admissibility) needs strong evidence without frailties, which, when tested, cannot afford any other logical outcome except guilt.

Judge Herrara-Carbuccia said:

> If we allow a president in a democratic society who refuses to step down in the aftermath of a contested election to target citizens of that society and commit crimes against humanity with impunity, we fail to comply with the values and purposes enshrined in the Rome Statute and espoused by the international community.[109]

It seems as if she took for granted that Gbagbo committed the crimes because he did not want to step down. This was the proposed prosecutorial narrative. However, the proposed motive did not equate to proof of intent. When looking carefully at the decision of Judge Herrara-Carbuccia, her conclusions are similar to the inferences the Prosecution called the Court to make. Nothing is wrong with this. However, those inferences would be permissible if they were logical outcomes, not logical jumps. Jumping to conclusions after a series of events is probably common for juries, but it is impermissible for a judge in an adversarial trial. So, for example, when she referred to crimes committed by the Ivorian Defence and Security Forces, she concluded that these acts were committed within the context of a state policy. No evidence evaluation was offered to explain what proved the conclusion.[110]

Was this a reasonably proven conclusion based on tested evidence or an assumption from an untested motive? It seems that the reasoning of the dis-

---

107 ICC-02/11-01/15-1263-AnxC-Red 16-07-2019 6/300 Dissenting Opinion Judge Herrera-Carbuccia, at para 5 and at para 136, where Judge Herrara-Carbuccia confirmed the existence of direct evidence.

108 *Ibid* at para 5.

109 *Ibid* at para 6.

110 *Ibid* at para 10.

senting opinion used the alleged motive as the first building block to create a domino of assumptions based on untested contradictions of the evidence. The difference between motive and criminal intent is clear in common law. Case law has paid particular attention to differentiating between the common and legal usage of the terms *motive* and *intent*. Motive is not part of a crime, and it's always a question of fact and evidence.[111] In continental law, the motive is found mainly in sentencing provisions where it might play an aggravating or mitigating factor, except for the criminal provisions that require a racial motive as a constituent of the crime.

Especially in the Gbagbo case, the motive offered by the prosecution should be proved. It was essential to prove whether Gbagbo believed he lost the elections, which he didn't. If he didn't, the entire tower of the prosecutorial inferences was rather problematic. Judge Henderson paid particular attention to this in his reasoning for the majority.[112]

In another example, Judge Herrara-Carbuccia said that the evidence presented was insufficient to absolve Gbagbo from criminal responsibility.[113] However, it is important to note that, in the context of the ICC, the burden of proof lies with the prosecution, not the accused. While such reasoning might be more acceptable in a continental court system, which often operates without a stringent prosecutorial burden, it fails to meet the legal standards required in an adversarial trial like those conducted at the ICC, where the prosecution must prove guilt beyond a reasonable doubt.

---

111 *See R.v.Steane* [1947] 1 All E.R. 813. The Court clarified that where a particular intent is a necessary constituent of the offence charged that intent must be proved by the Crown just as any other fact necessary to constitute a crime. *See also Lewis v. The Queen*, [1979] 2 S.C.R. 821. The Supreme Court of Canada clarified: "Accepting the term 'motive' in a criminal law sense as meaning 'ulterior intention', it is possible, upon the authorities, to formulate the following propositions: (1) As evidence, motive is always relevant and hence evidence of motive is admissible. (2) Motive is no part of the crime and is legally irrelevant to criminal responsibility. It is not an essential element of the prosecution's case as a matter of law. (3) Proved absence of motive is always an important fact in favour of the accused and ordinarily worthy of note in a charge to the jury. (4) Conversely, proved presence of motive may be an important factual ingredient in the Crown's case, notably on the issues of identity and intention, when the evidence is purely circumstantial. (5) Motive is therefore always a question of fact and evidence and the necessity of referring to motive in the charge to the jury falls within the general duty of the trial judge 'to not only outline the theories of the prosecution and defence but to give the jury matters of evidence essential in arriving at a just conclusion'. (6) Each case will turn on its own unique set of circumstances. The issue of motive is always a matter of degree".

112 Henderson decision, *supra* note 88 at para 301.

113 ICC-02/11-01/15-1263-AnxC-Red 16-07-2019 6/300, *supra* note 107 at para 519.

The major difference between Judge Henderson's and Judge Herrara-Carbuccia's opinions is how they evaluated the evidence. While Judge Henderson analytically provided the evidence and discussed the contradictions among testimonies about the same fact, Judge Herrara-Carbuccia did not. Judge Henderson's decision explained the evidence frailties and why a reasonable Court could not convict if based on the submitted evidence. His work revealed a principled approach to evidence evaluation familiar to common law thinkers.

For instance, Judge Henderson meticulously analysed testimonies of three witnesses concerning the events on Boulevard Principal on February 25, 2011.[114] Judge Henderson found that while each witness's testimony about the events on Boulevard Principal appeared credible on its own, each was significantly contradictory when compared to the other. This raised serious doubts about their overall truthfulness, making it unreasonable to rely on these testimonies for any conclusive judgment.

Judge Henderson's detailed view:

> Therefore, while the accounts of P-0436, P-0442 and P-0109 are plausible when seen in isolation, they are incompatible in relation to a number of significant aspects of the narratives they provide. Since their respective accounts cannot all be entirely true at the same time, this raises serious questions about their truthfulness altogether. Considering that only one of the three testimonies can be truthful in its entirety and there is no possibility to determine which one this is, it would be difficult for a reasonable trial chamber to reach any conclusion based on this evidence.[115]

Judge Herrara-Carbuccia did not rigorously evaluate the evidence or address its frailties and contradictions. Her perspective, viewed through a continental lens, was anticipated. However, according to the Statute and the prosecutorial burden of proof, her approach was flawed. The free evaluation of evidence at the admissibility stage does not absolve the prosecution from proving the quality of evidence required for conviction. While it is true that there was substantial evidence indicating the commission of crimes, the evidence was insufficient to establish guilt beyond a reasonable doubt. Judge Herrara-Carbuccia's decision failed to assess the quality of the evidence, the inherent contradictions, and the multiple inferences that the circumstantial evidence

114 Henderson's decision, *supra* note 88 at paras 1640–1666.

115 *Ibid* at para 1666.

could support. Consequently, her decision was incomplete within the adversarial framework of the ICC trial, where a thorough evaluation of evidence is paramount.

The above discussion reveals a common law approach of Judge Henderson's reasoning, while Judge Herrara-Carbuccia's is continental. They both had antithetical views on the same evidence issues.

10.2 *Agreement in Disagreement: A Continental Perspective in a Common Law Decision*

Let's now examine the views of Judge Tarfusser, who, like Judge Henderson, agreed to end the trial proceedings with a no-case-to-answer decision. Although they reached the same conclusion, their separate opinions reveal distinct conceptual approaches to evidence issues. Since Judge Henderson's perspective has been previously analysed as representing the majority, I will focus on three major points from Judge Tarfusser to illustrate his continental way of thinking.

Regarding the standard of proof, Judge Tarfusser argued that discussions about the standard and evidence admissibility were unnecessary because the Prosecutor's evidence failed to support the charges against the accused. He preferred evaluating all evidence at the end of the trial rather than making rolling admissibility decisions, as this ensures a holistic view. Tarfusser disagreed with Henderson's preference for ongoing admissibility rulings, believing that assessing the authenticity and weight of evidence simultaneously at the trial's conclusion is more effective.[116] Here, it becomes evident that Judge Tarfusser cannot distinguish between admissibility evaluation and weight evaluation, unlike Judge Henderson. He fails to appreciate the procedural efficiency gained by excluding inadmissible evidence. Furthermore, he does not recognize that authenticity is established at the admission stage rather than at the end of the trial. However, his approach remains purely continental.

The most fascinating part is Judge Tarfusser's view on the Prosecutor's duties. He criticized the Prosecutor for selectively applying standards to incriminating versus exculpatory evidence, further highlighting the weakness of the Prosecutor's case. This rigidity, as noted by Judge Tarfusser, is seen as a major shortcoming, as trials naturally involve shifts in focus due to witness

---

116 ICC-02/11-01/15-1263-AnxA 16-07-2019 1/90 EK T Opinion of Judge Tarfusser, at paras 67–74.

testimonies, requiring parties to adapt their strategies. He emphatically said that the Prosecutor has a duty to investigate the truth and request acquittal if the evidence is insufficient for a conviction. This duty is even more crucial for the ICC Prosecutor due to the statutory requirement under Article 54(1)(a) of the Statute to investigate incriminating and exonerating circumstances equally.

However, Article 54(1)(a) deals with the duties and powers of the Prosecutor concerning investigations. These duties do not extend to trial proceedings, as happens in the classic continental systems, where the prosecutor has a duty to investigate the truth during trial.[117] During the ICC trial, the Prosecutor has the burden to prove guilt beyond reasonable doubt (Art. 662 and 663). Judge Tarfusser criticized the Prosecutor for not adjusting her narrative in response to new information revealed during the trial, maintaining the same story from the pre-trial stage to the present. He underscored the Prosecutor's duty to seek the truth and request acquittal if the evidence is insufficient. Judge Tarfusser noted the Prosecutor's failure to address inconsistencies in her case, with only limited and insufficient attempts to adapt her narrative.[118]

The major outcome of Judge Tarfusser's separate decision was the glaring insufficiency of the prosecutorial evidence. His reasoning remains firmly rooted in the continental tradition, even though he ultimately reached the same conclusion as Judge Henderson, who employed a common law approach.[119]

11 Circumstantial Evidence in Focus: The Canadian Common Law Lens

In *Bemba*, we saw that the ICC faced again trouble evaluating circumstantial evidence. We analysed the Canadian approach that was identical to Judge Eboe-Osuji's and Judges Wyngaert and Morrison's. The discussion in *Bemba* was whether the Trial Court had made the required qualitative assessment of the circumstantial evidence, not a quantitative one, for conviction reasons. The Appeal Court said that if the factual basis of the circumstantial evidence

117 Kai Ambos et al., eds., *Core Concepts in Criminal Law and Criminal Justice: Anglo-German Dialogues*, Vol. 1. (Cambridge: Cambridge University Press, 2020) 343–348.

118 ICC-02/11-01/15-1263-AnxA 16-07-2019 1/90 EK T, *supra* note 116 at para 104.

119 *See* Judge Tarfusser's reference to his legal background. *Ibid* at para 3: "The reasons for this opinion are rooted in the profound differences between my legal background and approach of my fellow judges".

is weak, the inferences drawn from it will be even weaker.[120] We also discussed the Canadian evidence law approach via case law and theory.[121]

What is interesting in *Gbagbo* is the suggested inferences made by the Prosecution's narrative after she identified an unproven motive. If we go back to *Villaroman*,[122] we see the Supreme Court of Canada to clarify the difference between rational versus reasonable inferences. It explained:

> The words "rational" and "reasonable" are virtually synonyms: "rational" means "of or based on reasoning or reason"; "reasonable" means "in accordance with reason". [...] There is an advantage of using the word "reasonable". It avoids the risk of confusion that might arise from using the word "reasonable" in relation to "reasonable doubt" but referring to "rational" inferences or explanations when speaking about circumstantial evidence.[123] [...] [emphasis added]
>
> When assessing circumstantial evidence, the trier of fact should consider "other plausible theor[ies]" and "other reasonable possibilities" which are inconsistent with guilt. [...] "Other plausible theories" or "other reasonable possibilities" *must be based on logic and experiences applied to the evidence or the absence of evidence* not on speculation.[124] [emphasis added]

The Canadian Court explained that even though speculation and plausible theory may not have a clear line between them, the basic question is "whether the circumstantial evidence, viewed logically and in light of human experience, is reasonably capable of supporting an inference other than that the accused is guilty".[125] The other inferences must be reasonable, not simply possible.[126]

120 Separate opinion of Judge Christine Van den Wyngaert and Judge Howard Morrison, ICC-01/05-01/08-3636-Anx2, 08-06-2018, at para 12; and Concurring Separate Opinion of Judge Eboe-Osuji, ICC 01/05-01/08-3636-Anx3, June 14, 2018.

121 *See* the analysis in Section 3.6, "Circumstantial Evidence at the ICC and in Common Law".

122 *R. v. Villaroman*, [2016] 1 S.C.R. 1000.

123 *Ibid* at paras 33–34.

124 *Ibid* at para 37.

125 *Ibid* at para 38.

126 *Ibid* at para 42, with reference to *R. v. Dipnarine* 2014 ABCA,584 A.R. 138.

If we go back to Judge Herrara-Carbuccia's dissenting opinion that the evidence was insufficient to release Gbagbo from criminal responsibility,[127] we have to stop and explain the following:

In *R. v. Khela,* the Supreme Court of Canada, clarified that the defence does not need to prove certain facts consistent with the inference of innocence.[128] Otherwise, the prosecutorial burden of proof will not only disappear but also be reversed on the accused. Thus, only the inference of guilt must be based on proven facts, not the inference of innocence. This shows an error of law in the dissenting opinion of Judge Herrara-Carbuccia. But this is probably related to the fact that the continental system has not evolved evidence law via case law to answer similar problems.

Now, the question is whether there is any particular danger when making inferences from circumstantial evidence. The danger is that the jury may unconsciously:

> *"fill in the blanks" or bridge gaps* in the evidence to support the inference that the Crown invites it to draw [...] *The mind may also "take a pleasure in adapting* circumstances to one another, and even straining them a little, if need be, to force them to form parts of one connected whole".[129] [emphasis added]

The ICC trials do not operate as jury trials. However, the continental legal system has historically lacked substantive discussion and evolution of case law regarding the dangers of circumstantial evidence and its relation to the prosecutorial burden of proof. The prosecutorial burden of proof has not been a fundamental aspect of continental legal systems. Consequently, professional judges trained within these systems, without exposure to similar evidence problem discussions and case law analysis, cannot adequately familiarize themselves with the judicial thinking process necessary for evaluating circumstantial evidence. As a result, these judges tend to apply the standards they are familiar with from their own legal traditions rather than the appropriate standards required for ICC trials.

---

127 ICC-02/11-01/15-1263-AnxC-Red 16-07-2019 6/300, *supra* note 107 at para 519.

128 *R. v. Khela,* 2009 SCC 4, at para 58. See also the reference to *R v. Bui,* 2014 ONCA 614, at para 28; *R.v. Defaveri,* 2014 BCCA 370 at para 10.

129 R. *v.* Villaroman, *supra* note 122 at para 26.

12 Appeal Decision: Scrutinizing the Burden and Standard of Proof in No Case to Answer

> Indeed, the Trial Chamber's findings must be appreciated in the context of a violent political history, including a civil war that had remained unresolved at all material times.[130]

The Appeal Court upheld the Trial decision with three concurring opinions. This discussion focuses on two appellate decisions – one from the majority and one from the minority – that present antithetical views, encapsulating the continental versus common law debate in evidence evaluation.

The key difference between a decision that acquits an accused after a full trial and a decision that acquits an accused after the prosecution has closed its case is the role of the defence. In the latter scenario, the defence has no obligation to respond to the prosecution's case. However, in both situations, the prosecution in adversarial trials bears the burden of proving guilt beyond a reasonable doubt. The distinction lies in whether a rebuttal by the defence is necessary. Suppose the presumption of innocence and the prosecutorial burden are well understood. In that case, it is clear that the prosecution must establish proof beyond a reasonable doubt at the close of its case, not after the defence presents its evidence.[131] In *Gbagbo*, there was no rebuttal.

The Trial Court declared the case a no-case-to-answer. The Prosecution appealed. The Appeal Court's majority upheld the Trial decision. It issued one appeal decision with five separate opinions, three of whom made the majority.

The appeal against the Trial decision regarding the standard of proof rested on two main arguments: (1) the standard was unknown; and (2) the evidence should not be evaluated, or if it did, every piece of it should be evaluated in a system of evidence via a holistic approach.

To understand the issues of circumstantial evidence and the standard of proof, let's examine the typical process a court follows to convict or acquit based on circumstantial evidence (See Table 4.1):

---

130 ICC-02/11-01/15-1400-Anx1-Red 03-04-2021 2/135 RH A, Separate Concurring Opinion of Judge Eboe-Osuji, at para 234.

131 *See also* J. A. Coutts, "No Case to Answer: A Postscript" (1963) 27:1 J Crim L 68, at p.69: "The question is whether the standard of proof required of the prosecution *at the end of its case* differs from that required of it *at the end of the case*. It is difficult to see why any distinction should exist or, indeed, how it could do so. Whenever the accused is content to make no defence, the end of the prosecution's case is the end of the case" [emphasis added].

TABLE 4.1 Key principles in criminal trials and no-case-to-answer motions

Adversarial criminal trials & ICC	Principle	Description
Complete trial	Burden of proof	The burden of proof beyond a reasonable doubt is always on the prosecution.
Standard of proof	Beyond a reasonable doubt	The level of certainty and the degree of evidence necessary to establish proof in a criminal case is "beyond a reasonable doubt".
	Conviction based on circumstantial evidence	When the evidence is circumstantial and the only reasonable inference is guilt, the court should convict because the prosecution has proved guilt beyond a reasonable doubt.
	Acquittal based on circumstantial evidence	If the circumstantial evidence allows for reasonable inferences other than guilt, the prosecution has not met the required standard of proof, and the court should acquit.
No-case-to-answer after Prosecution's closing case	Burden of proof	The burden of proof beyond a reasonable doubt remains on the prosecution.
Standard of proof	Reasonable tribunal inquiry	The court must ask whether, based on the evidence presented by the prosecution, a reasonable tribunal could convict the defendant.
	Highest standard of prosecutorial evidence	The court should take the prosecution's evidence at its highest standard, assuming it is credible and reliable, and determine if it is sufficient to support a conviction.
	Multiple reasonable inferences	If the evidence allows for multiple reasonable inferences, including innocence, the court must rule that there is no case to answer, meaning the prosecution has not met its burden of proof.

Circumstantial evidence in criminal trials:

1. **Burden of proof:** The burden of proof beyond a reasonable doubt is always on the prosecution.
2. **Conviction based on circumstantial evidence:** When the evidence is circumstantial and the only reasonable inference is guilt, the court should convict because the prosecution has proved guilt beyond a reasonable doubt.
3. **Acquittal based on circumstantial evidence:** If the circumstantial evidence allows for reasonable inferences other than guilt, the prosecution has not met the required standard of proof, and the court should acquit.

No-case-to-answer with circumstantial evidence:

1. **Burden of proof:** The burden of proof beyond a reasonable doubt remains on the prosecution.
2. **Reasonable tribunal inquiry:** When the prosecution closes its case and a motion for no-case-to-answer is filed, the court should ask whether a reasonable tribunal could convict based on the evidence presented.
3. **Highest standard of prosecutorial evidence:** The court should take the highest standard of prosecutorial circumstantial evidence and determine if the only reasonable inference is guilt.
4. **Multiple reasonable inferences:** If the court finds that the evidence allows for multiple reasonable inferences, it should not continue the trial because the prosecution has not met its burden of proof; thus, a rebuttal is unnecessary.

One of the core appeal discussions was about the standard of proof and whether Judges Tarfusser and Henderson disagreed. The Appeal decision, particularly Judge Eboe-Osuji's separate opinion, highlights these concerns. Conversely, Judge Bossa's dissenting opinion suggests that the confusion may stem from continental legal principles.

In Judge Eboe-Osuji's opinion we find some parts related to the analysis here. One is the holistic approach discussion. We referred in *Bemba* (Chapter 2) to the difference between holistic and atomistic. Given that this decision has attracted criticism for its atomistic approach, later discussed, here we will focus on a comparative analysis of Judge Eboe-Osuji regarding this issue. He stated that the evaluation of evidence as a whole is unquestionable. He clarified that it stems easily from common law jurisprudence. In his opinion he included a great number of common law decisions to explain a better interpretation of the Rome Statute. He said that it is universally agreed that someone cannot be convicted if there is reasonable doubt. However, the holistic approach to evaluating evidence is not a free pass to ignore glaring gaps indicating doubt. Being sure to convict is much easier said than done. It is especially challenging without brushing inconvenient doubts under the rug. He referred to Australian and Canadian cases to emphasize the necessity of evaluating the totality of evidence.[132]

Judge Eboe-Osuji gave an example regarding evidence evaluation with respect to a holistic approach:

> Let's consider a criminal case with five binary items of evidence. Each item allows only a "Yes" or "No" answer to whether it proves guilt. Holistic evidential evaluation deems it unreasonable to ignore the "No" items, even when they are outnumbered by "Yes" items. This is especially true when "No" answers pertain to critical aspects like identifying the accused or their presence at the crime scene. This dilemma persists regardless of how many times the evidence set is replicated.[133]

Regarding the standard of proof beyond reasonable doubt, he acknowledged it as a complex and challenging principle for judicial systems to uphold. He drew guidance from common law precedents to ensure clarity and consistency in its application.[134]

In the UK, the Court of Appeal mandates that juries must be "sure" of guilt before convicting, underscoring the necessity of absolute certainty in the judicial process. Similarly, Canadian model jury instructions emphasize that proof must closely approach absolute certainty rather than mere probable guilt, applying this stringent standard to the totality of evidence rather than individual pieces. In the US case *Victor v Nebraska*,[135] Justice Ginsburg articulated that in criminal cases, the government's burden is to leave jurors "firmly convinced" of guilt. Any real possibility of innocence mandates acquittal, reflecting the high threshold required for conviction. The Canadian Supreme Court in *R v. W(D)* elucidated this standard through a tripartite approach: if the jury believes the accused's evidence, acquittal is mandatory; if the jury disbelieves the accused but harbours reasonable doubt, acquittal is still required; and if no reasonable doubt remains, the jury must determine if the prosecution's evidence meets the rigorous standard of proof beyond reasonable doubt.[136]

---

132 ICC-02/11-01/15-1400-Anx1-Red 03-04-2021 2/135 RH A, *supra* note 130 at para 120-121, with reference to *R v B* (G) [1990] 2 SCR 57, p 77a [Supreme Court of Canada]; *Chamberlain v R* (1984) 58 AJLR 133, p 139 [High Court of Australia].

133 ICC-02/11-01/15-1400-Anx1-Red 03-04-2021 2/135 RH A, *supra* note 100 at para 122–123.

134 *Ibid* at paras 128–133.

135 *Victor v. Nebraska*, 511 U.S. 1 (1994) at para 27.

136 *R v W(D)* [1991] 1 SCR 742, at p. 758 [Supreme Court of Canada].

Blackstone's ratio, asserting, "It is better that ten guilty persons escape than one innocent suffer", epitomizes the rigorous demand for certainty in criminal convictions. This principle affirms that a fair trial inherently entails an uncertain outcome, necessitating acquittal where proof of guilt does not unequivocally meet the high standard.

And he explained that these stringent principles informed the *Bemba* Appeal decision, where the Court asserted that convictions necessitate the Trial Chamber's "sure" or "firmly convinced" belief in the accused's guilt. Absent this standard, a conviction cannot be sustained, highlighting the judiciary's obligation to uphold the integrity of reasonable doubt.

A significant and perceptive insight of Judge Eboe-Osuji was his interpretative approach to the Rome Statute. He drew on common law jurisprudence and specific interpretations from common law Supreme Courts. He focused on the English word "shall" in Article 74.5 of the Statute and its context. Judge Eboe-Osuji emphasized the importance of studying how supreme courts and leading legal experts in English-speaking countries interpret and handle this word. This examination will help the court understand its proper usage and implications within the law, highlighting the importance of common law principles in shaping the understanding of the Statute's provisions.[137]

Judge Eboe-Osuji introduced the functional approach of the Canadian Supreme Court regarding inadequate judicial reasoning, citing seminal Canadian precedents. The Canadian approach, which emphasizes looking beyond technical slips to achieve substantial justice, is crucial for interpreting the Statute. Adopting this functional approach at the ICC Appeals Chamber is wise. It ensures the ICC transcends mere technicalities to achieve substantial justice, enabling the Appeals Chamber to effectively address and resolve comparable issues, thereby ensuring fair and just outcomes.[138]

He also emphasized that there is no practical reason to insist that the Rome Statute or the Rules of Procedure and Evidence provide explicit instructions against adopting the New Zealand model. Therefore, the ICC Appeals Chamber should consider this model and avoid overly rigid interpretations that create unnecessary challenges for the judges of the Trial Chambers. This approach provides a more practical and flexible framework, especially when there is no substantive justice-related reason to enforce such rigidity.[139]

Judge Eboe-Osuji's view not only uses the clarity of the common law thinking process but also incorporates an international approach to inter-

137 ICC-02/11-01/15-1400-Anx1-Red 03-04-2021 2/135 RH A, *supra* note 130 at paras 134–144.
138 *Ibid* at paras 142–180.
139 *Ibid* at para 189.

preting the Statute. This perspective can help the ICC navigate issues successfully.

In her dissenting appellate opinion, Judge Balungi Bossa had an antithetical view of the majority regarding the standard of proof. She noted that the Trial decision lacked clarity, and there were contradictory statements, divergent interpretations, and disagreement among judges on the standard of proof. This confusion impacted legal reasoning, transparency, predictability, and evidence assessment. There was also disagreement on the legal basis for the no-case-to-answer decision, specifically between Article 66(2) and Article 74.

Judge Bossa clarified her views saying that:

> During the decision hearing, Judge Tarfusser, on behalf of the majority, stated that the Prosecutor failed to meet the burden of proof under Article 66 but did not clarify the standard used. The majority did not apply the beyond reasonable doubt standard of Article 66(3) but did not specify an alternative. Judge Tarfusser criticized the Prosecutor's evidence as "exceptionally weak" and referenced Judge Herrera-Carbuccia's dissent, suggesting the majority had applied the beyond reasonable doubt standard, creating immediate confusion.

Judge Henderson applied a modified standard, assessing the reliability and credibility of the evidence, rejecting the beyond reasonable doubt standard at the no-case-to-answer stage. Conversely, Judge Tarfusser later suggested the beyond reasonable doubt standard should apply for terminating trial proceedings, contradicting his earlier statement. Despite agreeing on the acquittals, Judges Tarfusser and Henderson had different views on the applicable standard, causing ongoing uncertainty.

The lack of clarity persisted after the judges' opinions were filed, with continued disagreement on whether the beyond reasonable doubt standard applied. This affected the transparency and predictability of the proceedings and contributed to further legal errors. Judge Henderson saw the legal basis for the no case to answer decision in Article 66(2), while Judge Tarfusser questioned this and pointed to Article 74 as the only basis for ending trial proceedings.

The absence of a defined standard created legal uncertainty, affecting the fairness and transparency of the trial. Judge Henderson's rejection of the beyond reasonable doubt standard contrasts with Judge Tarfusser's later assertion of it, highlighting deep-seated differences in judicial reasoning.

The entire debate in Judge Balungi Bossa's decision is perplexing, centring on allocating the burden of proof and the appropriate standard to be applied.

Judge Tarfusser's reasoning displayed inconsistencies, which finally did not affect the outcome as confirmed by the Appeal Majority decision. However, his reference to Article 74 was relevant only to the no-case-to-answer decision. It did not influence the burden or standard of proof under Article 66. Conversely, Judge Henderson's perspective seems incomprehensible from a continental viewpoint. This is likely due to the lack of tradition in the continental system regarding no-case-to-answer decisions. In continental jurisdictions, once a case progresses to trial, issuing a no-case-to-answer decision is not permitted.

Judge Morrison's statement is illustrative of common law experience:

> When I was sitting as a judge in the UK in jury trials, on many occasions, I had submissions of no case to answer at the halfway stage, i.e., at the close of the prosecution case [...] a prima facie case is simply evidence upon which a reasonable trier of fact could convict. It seems to me that that is a fairly simple way of approaching it.[140]

Furthermore, Judge Balungi Bossa's call for clarity on the standard of proof is even more bewildering when coupled with references to an ICC appellate decision concerning the standard for confirming charges.[141]

Judge Ibáñez Carranza, in her well-reasoned decision that meticulously considered common law precedents, identified legal errors in the impugned decision. She argued that the standard for a no case to answer is lower than beyond a reasonable doubt. Judge Ibáñez Carranza clarified that in this case, a prima facie assessment of the evidence, taken at its highest standard, could lead to a conviction, and therefore the Court should proceed with the trial.[142]

Examining the views of Judges Morrison and Ibáñez Carranza, we notice that Judge Morrison's discussion of a "prima facie case" emphasizes the sufficiency of the prosecution's evidence to support a conviction if uncontradicted. Judge Ibáñez Carranza's reference to a "prima facie assessment" focuses on the preliminary evaluation of whether the evidence, taken at its highest, a reasonable Court could convict.

---

140 ICC-02/11-01/15-1400-Anx4-Red 01-04-2021 1/192 SL A, Dissenting Opinion of Judge Luz del Carmen Ibáñez Carranza to the Judgment on the appeal of the Prosecutor against the oral verdict of Trial Chamber I of January 15, 2019 with written reasons issued on July 16, 2019, at paras 332–333, for the quote in Judge Ibáñez Carranza's decision.

141 *See* ICC-02/05-01/09-73, February 3, 2010, at para 36 and footnote 69 with reference to *The Prosecutor v. Omar Hassan Ahmad Al Bashir*.

142 ICC-02/11-01/15-1400-Anx4-Red 01-04-2021 1/192 SL A, *supra* note 140 at paras 322–359.

While taking the evidence at its highest standard is essential to consider whether the prosecution's case, if uncontradicted, has met the "beyond a reasonable doubt" standard, Judge Ibáñez Carranza's approach, without a concurrent analysis of circumstantial evidence, and the so-called lower standard raises issues. She contended that Judge Henderson's alternative inferences from the evidence, other than guilt, were speculative.[143] However, the Appeals Chamber's majority did not share this view.

It appears there is a lack of consensus among ICC judges on evaluating evidence. In this case, the prosecutorial evidence permitted alternative interpretations beyond the singular inference of guilt required for circumstantial evidence. Ambiguity persists regarding how speculation is perceived by continental judges, who evaluate evidence freely. Unlike common law judges, who systematically address speculation through case law and with respect to the prosecutorial burden, continental judges do not address speculation in their case law.

13 Criticism of "The Other Poisoned Chalice"[144]

> The ultimate principle is that you must put no man on trial under the forms of judicial proceedings if you are not willing to see him freed if not proven guilty. If you are determined to execute a man in any case, there is no occasion for a trial; the world yields no respect to courts that are merely organized to convict.[145]

The no case to answer decision in the *Gbagbo* case received significant criticism. Some supported that the *Gbagbo* acquittal was particularly damaging for the ICC, highlighting either the OTP's inability to successfully prosecute high-profile cases or the judges' failure to fully understand the OTP's case, both of which are concerning for the Court's effectiveness.[146]

---

143 *Ibid* at para 403.

144 Darryl Robinson, "The Other Poisoned Chalice: Unprecedented Evidentiary Standards in the Gbagbo Case? (Part 1)". EJIL: Talk. (2019 Nov 5). https://www.ejiltalk.org/the-other-poisoned-chalice-unprecedented-evidentiary-standards-in-the-gbagbo-case-part-1/.

145 Robert H. Jackson, "The Rule of Law among Nations" (1945) 31:6 ABA J 290, 293. See this reference in Judge Eboe-Osuji's separate opinion ICC-02/11-01/15-1400-Anx1-Red 03-04-2021 2/135 RH A, *supra* note 130 at para 45.

146 Mark Ellis. "The Latest Crisis of the ICC: The Acquittal of Laurent Gbagbo" (2019) 28 *Opinio Juris*. online: https://opiniojuris.org/2019/03/28/the-latest-crisis-of-the-icc-the-acquittal-of-laurent-gbagbo/. *See* a more neutral approach from Justice Info Net, "Why

In 2013, at the confirmation of charges' proceedings, Darryl Robinson, Margaret deGuzman, Charles Jalloh, and Robert Cryer participated as Amici Curiae in the pre-trial proceedings concerning the confirmation of charges against Laurent Gbagbo before the Appeals Chamber. The Appeals Chamber granted permission for them to submit their observations, which addressed crucial legal and evidentiary standards for establishing an "attack" under Article 7(2)(a) of the Rome Statute for crimes against humanity.

The Amici Curiae argued that the Pre-Trial Chamber's decision misunderstood the necessary scale of an attack, the requirement for formal policy adoption, and the evidentiary burden to prove policy elements. They maintained that evidence of policy does not need to be specific to each incident but can be deduced from the overall pattern of conduct. They also noted that the motives of individual perpetrators are not critical for establishing the existence of a policy, as it can be inferred from the systematic occurrence of the acts. The document called on the Appeals Chamber to provide clear guidance to ensure that the International Criminal Court (ICC) can effectively prosecute crimes against humanity. This guidance should align the ICC's interpretation with established legal precedents and practical realities, ensuring that the legal standards are coherent with the broader jurisprudence and practical considerations in prosecuting such crimes.

After the decision was issued, Robinson argued that focusing solely on the accused's interests with ungrounded standards is a poisoned chalice.[147] This is the opposite of what Robert Jackson warned about at Nuremberg. Jackson cautioned that an unfair trial for the accused is a poisoned chalice for the tribunal itself. In his three-part series, Robinson examined the ICC's evidentiary standards in the *Gbagbo* case. He called the standards used as legally unprecedented and epistemologically unsound. He noted that the Majority

---

the ICC Acquitted Laurent Gbagbo and Charles Blé Goudé", September 17, 2019, online: https://www.justiceinfo.net/en/42384-why-icc-acquitted-laurent-gbagbo-charles-ble-goude.html; Another view said that despite the ICC's acquittal of Gbagbo and Blé Goudé, the State's role remained in ensuring justice through investigation, prosecution, and reparations for human rights violations to prevent recurrence and strengthen social cohesion. ICTJ, "With Gbagbo and Blé Goudé Acquitted, What Is Next for Victims in Côte d'Ivoire?", ICTJ.org, (February 4, 2021), online: https://www.ictj.org/news/gbagbo-and-bl%C3%A9-goud%C3%A9-acquitted-what-next-victims-c%C3%B4te-d%E2%80%99ivoire.

147 *See* Darryl Robinson, supra note 114; "The Other Poisoned Chalice: Unprecedented Evidentiary Standards in the Gbagbo Case" (Part 2), November 6, 2019; https://www.ejiltalk.org/the-other-poisoned-chalice-unprecedented-evidentiary-standards-in-the-gbagbo-case-part-2/; and (Part 3) November 6, 2019, https://www.ejiltalk.org/17618-2/.

viewed the evidence through a Cartesian lens, dismissing it when it would be significant under traditional legal standards. Robinson questioned the procedural economy and the mandate for "best" evidence, advocating for practical and holistic standards that rely on experience and warranted inferences.

Robinson suggested that ICC judges, previously criticized for being too pro-conviction, may have overcorrected by adopting overly stringent standards favouring the accused. According to his analysis of the *Gbagbo* trial, incriminating evidence was scrutinized in isolation, often dismissed based on conjectured possibilities rather than reasonable doubts. Judges failed to assess the cumulative improbability of multiple exonerating theories, leading to the Prosecution's case dismissal. Potentially exonerating evidence was accepted uncritically, furthering the imbalance. A narrow and flawed approach to corroboration focused on isolated details rather than broader patterns. Unrealistically high standards for document authentication and minor inconsistencies led to rejecting credible evidence, complicating the prosecution of crimes against humanity. The "Cartesian approach" sought unattainable certainty and logical rigor.

It is interesting to summarize what the Cartesian method is to understand Robinson. René Descartes, a seventeenth-century French philosopher, famous for his phrase *cogito, ergo sum* (I think, therefore I am), developed a method for acquiring genuine knowledge.

> And, just as in pulling down an old house, we usually reserve the ruins to contribute towards the erection, so, in destroying such of my opinions as I judged to be Ill-founded, I made a variety of observations and acquired an amount of experience of which I availed myself in the establishment of more certain. And further, I continued to exercise myself in the method I had prescribed.[148]

Descartes, in his work *Discourse on the Method*, emphasized the relentless pursuit of truth, advocating for a method known as Cartesian doubt. This method systematically questions all ideas, principles and beliefs that can be doubted, even if they are commonly accepted as true. To acquire genuine knowledge, one must use doubt as a tool to deconstruct established beliefs and ideas. By rigorously examining each component, knowledge can be reconstructed based on the remaining indubitable truths. This process of decon-

148 Rene Descartes, *A Discourse on Method (of Rightly Conducting One's Reason and of Seeking Truth in the Sciences)* (Project Gutenberg EBook-No. 59, 2016) 27.

struction and reconstruction ensures that the foundations of knowledge are built on certainty rather than assumption.[149]

Robinson said that despite the extensive evidence presented by the Prosecution, including testimonies, documents, and physical exhibits, the Majority found no case to answer. He favoured Judge Herrera-Carbuccia's more context-aware, holistic approach, which he found to be consistent with national and international practice.

Robinson's comparative lens is challenging. Let's use the circumstantial evidence problem. The challenge in comparing Cartesian doubt with the Canadian approach to circumstantial evidence lies in the fundamental nature of each method. Cartesian doubt is a philosophical approach aimed at deconstructing and reconstructing knowledge by questioning all ideas and beliefs. In contrast, the Canadian approach to circumstantial evidence in criminal law deals with evaluating factual evidence to determine guilt beyond a reasonable doubt.

However, we can find a point of comparison in the underlying principle of seeking truth and certainty. Both methods involve a systematic approach. Cartesian doubt systematically questions beliefs, while the Canadian approach systematically evaluates pieces of evidence. Descartes seeks philosophical certainty, while the Canadian legal system seeks legal certainty (proof beyond a reasonable doubt).

Both processes involve analysis and reconstruction. Cartesian doubt deconstructs and reconstructs knowledge, while circumstantial evidence requires piecing together facts to form a coherent narrative, where the only logical inference is guilt. While Cartesian doubt focuses on ideas and beliefs, its rigorous analytical framework can be metaphorically applied to the Canadian approach to circumstantial evidence. In both cases, components (ideas or facts) are meticulously examined to reach a conclusion grounded in certainty.

Just as Descartes uses doubt to discard uncertain beliefs, the legal system uses scrutiny to discard unreliable evidence. Descartes reconstructs knowledge of certain truths, similar to how the legal system reconstructs facts based on credible evidence to establish guilt. By focusing on the principles of systematic analysis and the pursuit of certainty, we can draw a meaningful comparison between Cartesian doubt and the evaluation of circumstantial evidence in the Canadian legal system. Both methods, despite their different contexts, aim to build conclusions that are as certain and reliable as possible.

149 *Ibid* at 5–66.

I rather find the circumstantial evidence approach quite Cartesian. While Robinson may have a point, rigorously scrutinized circumstantial evidence ensures a fair trial only if guilt is the unequivocal and sole logical inference. This exacting scrutiny surpasses mere doubt; it is an indispensable and principled approach to achieving a fair trial. Furthermore, the level of scrutiny required to establish guilt must be exceedingly more rigorous than that applied to ideas and beliefs, as a person's very freedom and life depend on the outcome.

Finally, Robinson strongly suggested an invigorated comparative dialogue on international criminal evidence law. I cannot be more in agreement. However, the suggested comparative dialogue must first acknowledge the exceptional challenges of gathering evidence after atrocities. Equally important is upholding the mandate of a fair trial as an uncompromised rule. A fair trial transcends both holistic and atomistic interpretations; it is a fundamental principle that must be maintained.

Understanding the historical discussions on the ideal model for an international tribunal is crucial, as highlighted by Cassese.[150] It is clear that the adversarial model can secure fairness through the prosecutorial burden of proof. In the *Gbagbo* case, the evidence was not as well-organized as the meticulously documented evidence from the German archives in the Nuremberg Trials.[151] Nevertheless, acquittals still occurred in Nuremberg, indicating that justice was served despite the immense suffering of the people.

Changing the Rome Statute to adopt a continental trial model is now inapplicable, making the current observation both positive and of significant importance. Whether viewed through adversarial or continental, holistic or atomistic lenses, the backbone of a fair criminal trial is that the prosecution must bear the burden of proof beyond reasonable doubt. Therefore, ensuring effective prosecution critically depends on strengthening the quality of evidence rather than proceeding to trial without robust evidence.

As Robinson emphasized, the most important discussion is on ICC's evidence law. This dialogue must acknowledge the exceptional challenges of gathering evidence after atrocities and uphold the mandate of a fair trial as an uncompromised rule. A fair trial transcends both holistic and atomistic interpretations; it is a fundamental principle that must be maintained.

150 Antonio Cassese, *International Criminal Law: Cases and Commentary* (Oxford: Oxford University Press, 2003) 376–381.

151 See Holocaust Encyclopedia, "Combating Holocaust Denial: Evidence of the Holocaust Presented at Nuremberg", online: https://encyclopedia.ushmm.org/content/en/article/combating-holocaust-denial-evidence-of-the-holocaust-presented-at-nuremberg.

ICC needs no conviction tally to justify its value. It only needs to do justice as it should be done.[152]

14 Conclusion

The *Gbagbo and Blé Goudé* case underscores the divergent judicial perspectives on evidentiary issues within the ICC. However, the presence of opposing views does not inherently lead to contradictory outcomes. Significantly, Judge Tarfusser, who favoured a continental approach, concurred with Judge Henderson in determining that the evidence was overwhelmingly insufficient to secure a conviction. This consensus was notably reached prior to the trial's conclusion, immediately following the Prosecution's presentation of its case.

This scenario brings to the forefront a critical legal issue: the prosecutorial burden of proof beyond reasonable doubt in cases based solely on circumstantial evidence. The rulings of both the Trial and Appeal Courts offered profound insights into the judicial interpretation and evaluation of circumstantial evidence. It became apparent that the continental judicial approach was less effective in rendering clear assessments compared to the common law approach, which is deeply rooted in adversarial criminal trials.

Ultimately, this case underscores the imperative for developing a distinct ICC-specific body of evidence law. More importantly, it highlights the necessity for ICC judges to gain proficiency in handling evidence within an adversarial trial framework, thus ensuring the protection of the fundamental right to a fair trial.

---

152 ICC-02/11-01/15-1400-Anx1-Red 03-04-2021 2/135 RH A, *supra* note 130 at para 46.

CHAPTER 5

The Case of Ongwen

1 The Situation in Northern Uganda (2002–2005)

> In December 2003 I received a referral from the Government of Uganda, the first state referral in the history of the Court. [...]. The criteria for selection of the first case was gravity. We analyzed the gravity of all crimes in Northern Uganda committed by the LRA and Ugandan forces. Crimes committed by the LRA were much more numerous and of much higher gravity than alleged crimes committed by the UPDF.[1]

The Uganda situation reveals a serious chasm between the South and the North of Uganda, with political dimensions. However, the North and the South are not two different states. The origin of this division can be traced back to the British colonization (1894–1962), and it is primarily related to social class. The North provided a great pool of labour hands, soldiers, and police officers. At the same time, the South represented Uganda's elite.[2] However, over the years, it seems that a persistent feature between the North and the South has been inequality.[3]

In this situation, we notice that the vast majority of the victims were from the Acholi tribe who lived in North Uganda.[4] This case related to a rebel group known as the Lord's Resistance Army (LRA), responsible for committing crimes against the Acholi while fighting against the government. The defendant, Dominic Ongwen, an Acholi, was an LRA brigadier.

1 ICC-OTP-20051014-109, Statement by the Chief Prosecutor Luis Moreno Ocampo on the Uganda Arrest Warrants. Press Conference on the Uganda Arrest Warrants, October 14, 2005, http://www.icc-cpi.int/news/press-conference-uganda-arrest-warrants.

2 See Heike Behrend, *Alice Lakwena and the Holy Spirits: War in Northern Uganda, 1985–97* (Athens, OH: Ohio University Press, 2000) 14–19, where she refers to Acholis' ethnogenesis and history and their appearance in North Uganda in 1600 as migrants from Sudan.

3 Chris Dolan, *Social Torture: The Case of Northern Uganda, 1986–2006* (Oxford: Berghahn Books, 2009) at 65. Dolan described the social torture of the Acholi, not the supposed war against the Acholi, and he claimed that this torture over the years went beyond the definition in the Convention against torture.

4 See Alex Moorehead & Jemera Rone, *Uprooted and Forgotten Impunity and Human Rights Abuses in Northern Uganda* (2005) 17:12 (A) (Human Rights Watch, 2005) 2.

 | DOI:10.1163/9789004741010_006

The historical background of this case reveals that the Acholi people endured extreme violence from both the government's army and rebel groups despite both sides allegedly intending to protect them. Under the presidency of Yoweri Museveni, the government forcibly relocated the Acholis to concentration camps to shield them from LRA crimes. Simultaneously, the governmental army committed serious crimes against the Acholi civilians.

The LRA case, known as the Northern Uganda Situation, was referred to the ICC by Museveni in 2003. The ICC Chief Prosecutor Luis Moreno Ocampo never investigated the crimes committed by Museveni's army against the Acholi people. This case was the first state referral since the ICC's inception and the first case where the accused, Ongwen, is both a victim (as an abducted former child soldier) and a perpetrator.

From a historical perspective, the Acholi people have suffered under various political regimes. In this case, however, it seems that the Acholis' long-standing political dissatisfaction with Museveni was exploited by the government. This dissatisfaction was used to legitimize actions against the Acholi, ostensibly in the name of protection from the LRA. Regrettably, this tribe endured decades of hostilities committed by both rebels and the government.

A brief historical account before Museveni's leadership shows that during both the colonial and postcolonial times, except during Idi Amin Dada's dictatorship, a great number of Acholi served in the army and held various governmental positions. However, the stereotype of the Acholi as a "martial tribe" was predominantly cultivated during the colonial period.[5]

After colonization, Milton Obote, a northerner Langi, became the first president of independent Uganda in 1962 (Obote I regime, 1962–1971). In 1971, Idi Amin Dada seized power through a military coup. Immediately after the coup, Amin particularly targeted and murdered hundreds of Acholi, who made up a significant portion of the army, and Langi, because Obote was a Langi.[6] He replaced the Acholi soldiers with troops from West Nile and Sudan, and he attacked and killed thousands of civilian Acholi people. The surviving Acholi, who were middle class and elite, were sent into exile.[7] Many Acholi and Langi

5 Adam Branch, "Exploring the roots of LRA violence: political crisis and ethnic politics in Acholiland", in Tim Allen & Vlassenroot Koen, eds., *Lords Resist Army Myth Real* (London: Zed Books, 2010) 31.

6 Henry Kyemba, *State of Blood: The Inside Story of Idi Amin*, 1st ed. (New York, NY: Putnam Pub Group, 1977) 75, 77.

7 Branch, *supra* note 5 at 29.

who fled the country formed a political movement against Amin and the Uganda National Liberation Army (UNLA). In 1973, Museveni, from South-West Uganda, who later became the President of Uganda, formed the Front for National Salvation (FRONASA) resistance. In 1978, Amin invaded Tanzania. In 1979, rebel groups and the Tanzanian Army invaded Uganda, bringing Idi Amin Dada's brutal dictatorship to an end.[8]

A second presidential period for Milton Obote (Obote II regime) started in 1980 following a rather questionable election, which was not well accepted by the South, the "anti-Amin activists".[9] In both Obote's presidential periods the Acholi people participated in the army and held administrative governmental positions. However, Obote did not manage to reinstitute their former political and administrative power.[10] One year later, in 1981, Museveni formed a rebel movement and an army, the National Resistance Army (NRA). He moved to the bush and started an armed uprising against Obote. Obote's governmental army (UNLA), with Acholi soldiers, faced Museveni's guerrilla warfare.[11] By 1990, many soldiers in Museveni's army were Tutsis from Rwanda.[12]

Tito Okello, Obote's general, an Acholi, overthrew Obote through a military coup and became the president of Uganda for six months (1985–1986). He attempted to form a coalition government, but Museveni did not compromise. Despite the Nairobi peace agreement signed by Museveni and Okello in December 1985, Museveni did not maintain the peace but instead took control of Uganda's capital, Kampala, in January 1986.[13] Reports say that "many northerners were lynched in Kampala".[14] However, in his inauguration speech, Museveni declared: "The people of Uganda should only die from natural causes which are not under our control, but not from fellow human

8 Tim Allen, *Trial Justice: The International Criminal Court and the Lord's Resistance Army* (London, New York: Zed Books, 2006) at 29.

9 *Ibid.*

10 Branch, *supra* note 5 at 29–30.

11 Allen, *supra* note 8 at 29.

12 Dolan, *supra* note 3 at 63. See also the term "Tutsi Empire" in relation to Museveni's government, at 90.

13 Robert Gersony, *The Anguish of Northern Uganda – Section 1 – Uganda* (Washington, D.C., USA: Government of United States of America, 1997) 12. *See also* Allen, *supra* note 8 at 30. The Nairobi peace talks are known as "Nairobi peace jokes", Lucima Okello, ed., *Protracted Conflict, Elusive Peace: Initiatives to End the Violence in Northern Uganda* (London: Conciliation Resources, 2002) 24, online: https://rc-services-assets.s3.eu-west-1.amazonaws.com/s3fs-public/Protracted_conflict_elusive_peace_Initiatives_to_end_the_violence_in_northern_Uganda_Accord_Issue_11.pdf.

14 Okello, *supra* note 13 at 89.

beings".[15] Since that day, Museveni has remained the President of Uganda.[16] However, the North neither supported his election nor his re-elections.

Soon after Museveni's victory, many of Okello's forces fled to North Uganda and Sudan. A resistance movement was created in Juda, Sudan, and Acholi professional soldiers formed the Uganda People's Democratic Army (UPDA).[17] But not all the former Acholi soldiers joined the resistance. Many returned to Acholiland. Given the Acholi belief in spiritual power, guidance and prophecy, divine healing and witchcraft, it was thought that these soldiers needed to get purified from their sins.[18] According to the elders, they were carrying evil spirits, including the spirits of those they killed. Therefore, the Acholi faced two enemies: one internal, the evil spirits attracted by the Acholis former soldiers, and one external, Museveni's army.[19]

A stationed governmental battalion (NRA) in Acholiland started to commit crimes against the Acholi people.[20] The rebel group Uganda's People Democratic Army (UPDA) resisted by attacking the governmental army positions. Museveni's army response against the Acholi civilians was brutal. Torture, murders, and rapes were reported to have been committed by his army. Gradually, by the end of 1986, the UPDA resistance forces dramatically lost power and weapons.

During the same year, in August , an Acholi woman, Alice Auma "Lakwena", who was neither a politician nor a military person, formed the Holy Spirit Mobile Forces, known as Holy Spirit Movement (HSM). She was guided by the spirit of Lakwena to fight against Museveni's army and impure former

15 Richard J Reid, *A History of Modern Uganda* (Cambridge, UK: Cambridge University Press, 2017) 79.

16 *Ibid* at 82–84 for the discussion on Museveni's re-election over the years.

17 Okello, *supra* note 13 at 21. Tim Allen, "Understanding Alice: Uganda's Holy Spirit Movement in Context" (1991) 61:3 Afr J Int Afr Inst 370–399 at 371.

18 Regarding the impurity of the soldiers see Behrend, *supra* note 2 at 28–29. Behrend says that until 1988 the primary Acholi explanation for deaths was related to witchcraft, at 28. Regarding the Acholi religious beliefs and Christianity *see also* Allen, *supra* note 8 at 31–33; Allen, "Understanding Alice", *supra* note 17 at 386–388.

19 Behrend, *supra* note 2., talks about the "internal threat" and the "external threat" or "internal" and "external enemy" at p. 26–27. Similarly, Branch, *supra* note 5 at 32–33, talks about the "internal" and the "external enemy".

20 Behrend, *supra* note 2. p. 24–25. Allen, *supra* note 8 at 34 says that Alice Lakwena claimed that NRA soldiers had kidnapped and imprisoned youngsters. *See also*, Okello, *supra* note 13 at 89, where it is said that, in August 1986, NRA/FEDEMU/UFM (all of which constituted the NRA Army) "executed scores of civilians at Namokora, Akilok, Oryang and Padibe".

governmental Acholi soldiers.[21] Alice was a *nebi*, a Christian diviner, possessed by the spirit of Lakwena, and had established a remarkable healing cult with large following.[22] That year, she developed an army of thousands of soldiers and gained a number of victories against Museveni's army. The Acholi people believed in her powers and supported her. During the same period another Acholi, Joseph Kony, who was also possessed and guided by the spirits, formed the United Holy Salvation Army (later renamed LRA). It is said that he wanted to merge with Alice Lakwena, but she did not accept merging her army with Kony's.[23] However, in November 1987, Alice's army moved into the South and was defeated by Museveni's army. Alice fled to Kenya on a bicycle.[24]

Kony, like Alice, was neither a politician nor a military person. He had been trained as a spirit medium, an *ajwaka*.[25] After Alice's defeat, he became the new leader of the resistance. Kony, during the entire period of the civil conflict, continued calling for:

> (a) an all-party "National Conference" followed by general elections; (b) the creation of a Religious Affairs Ministry to "see an end to the use of witchcraft and sorcery by promotion of the Ten Commandments"; (c) rehabilitation of the economy and rehabilitation of the country's infrastructure; (d) national unity (through inter-tribal marriages and language instruction); (e) education for all; (f) policies encouraging foreign investment; (g) the independence of the judiciary; (h) the formation of an ethnically balanced national army; (i) improved diplomatic relations with neighbouring states; and (j) relocation of Uganda's administrative capital to Kigumba in Masindi district.[26]

In 1987, Dominic Ongwen was abducted at the age of nine by Kony's army. In 1988, the Acholi people supported peace negotiations among all the factions and the government. Museveni's government signed a peace agreement only with the rebel group Uganda's People Democratic Army (UPDA). Kony also wanted to participate in the peace talks, but the governmental army

21 Behrend, *supra* note 2 at 25, 43.

22 Allen, *supra* note 8 at 33. *See also* his discussion on whether Alice had related her Movement with Christianity and whether Lakwena had anything to do with the Holy Ghost even though Alice adopted this Christian approach, at 35. Allen says that what was happening was strange: "spirit mediums emerged as military commanders" at 31.

23 *Ibid* at 38.

24 *Ibid* at 36.

25 *Ibid* at 38.

26 *Ibid* at 43.

attacked him before the talks.[27] UPDA soldiers who did not take the opportunity of amnesty laws merged with Kony's army. The notorious UPDA commander Odong Latek joined Kony.[28] The governmental army was attacking, Kony's army was responding, and the cycle of violence escalated. This reached a peak in 1991 when Museveni launched a huge operation called "Operation North".

Kony not only opposed the government but also attacked the Acholi in their villages and later in the camps set up by the government. Kony considered the people living in the camps to be government supporters, and he executed those Acholi who did not follow his army's orders.[29] Although in early 1990, the government had established camps ostensibly to protect the Acholi people from Kony, this displacement did not actually happen voluntarily but rather forcibly by Museveni's troops. Moreover, those who refused going to the camps or the so-called protected villages were perceived as rebel allies.[30] It seems that for the Acholi civilians, blind submission to both sides was the only way to avoid being murdered.

Human Rights Watch reported in 2005: "Since 1996, the government has used the army to undertake a massive, forced displacement of the population in the north and imposed severe restrictions of freedom of movement".[31] The report notes that during these years, the crimes committed by the governmental army against the civilians in the camps included wilful killings, torture, rape, arbitrary arrest, and detention. This report states: "The situation has become so serious that some civilians seem to view such outright abuse at the hands of the soldiers as normal".[32] The same source said that the LRA committed wilful killings of civilians, torture, rape, and abductions. However, during LRA attacks in the camps or during movement through rural areas, Kony forbade his army to commit rapes against women and girls.[33] Museveni's continuous tolerance regarding his army's crimes, especially those committed by the 11th Battalion in the Gulu district, in conjunction with the lack of police

27 Okello, *supra* note 13 at 31.

28 Allen, *supra* note 8 at 38.

29 *See* Moorehead & Rone, *supra* note 4 at 9 and at 16.

30 *See* Dolan, *supra* note 3 at 76.

31 Moorehead & Rone, *supra* note 4 at 4.

32 *See* Dolan, *supra* note 3 at 144–147, where he explains the "access to protection" for the people who lived in the camps. He makes it clear that there was neither protection nor security.

33 Moorehead & Rone, *supra* note 4 at 21.

forces in the camps, seems more than problematic and rather suspicious.[34] It seems that the camps were the perfect spot for the prey to be completely exposed so that all sides could easily target it.

Chris Dolan argues that the violations committed by the "supposed protectors" against civilians in the camps were "double" and "triple violations". The so-called protector, the government, committed crimes against the protected and failed its duty to protect (double violation). Furthermore, the protectors were locals (triple violation). Therefore, these violations had "more disastrous social and psychological impact" than those committed by a "clearly defined enemy". Moreover, Museveni, the President of Uganda, was the Commander-in-Chief of the institution from which the perpetrators came.[35] Dolan's view in 2009 is both interesting and disturbing, especially when one thinks of the ICC Chief Prosecutor's statement in 2015: "Crimes committed by the LRA were much more numerous and of much higher gravity than alleged crimes committed by the UPDF".[36]

The Museveni government's response to the above Human Rights Watch report was the following: "There is a well-established function[ing] accountability structure in the IDPC (Internally Displaced People Camp) for any abuses by the government officials more especially the UPDF". Regarding the crimes committed by the governmental army the Government said: "We note that most complaints are fronted by opposition Members of Parliament to malign the UPDF".[37]

---

34 *Ibid* at 24–36 for crimes the government army (UPDA) committed against the Acholi; *ibid* at 14–23 for the crimes committed by the LRA. *See also*, Human Rights Watch, *World Report 2005 | Human Rights Watch* (New York, NY: Human Rights Watch, 2005) 173. Regarding the crimes against the Acholi by the governmental army and the genocide discussion against the Acholi *see* Olara A Otunnu, "The Secret Genocide", (October 2009), *Foreign Policy*. https://foreignpolicy.com/2009/10/19/the-secret-genocide/, especially in respect to the conditions and death rates in the camps. *See also* Branch's discussion on the governmental responsibility for violence and "the narrative of government innocence", Adam Branch, "Dominic Ongwen on trial: The ICC's African dilemmas" (2017) 11:1 *Int J Transitional Justice* 30–49 at 43–45.

35 Dolan, *supra* note 3 at 152. *See also* at 159-188, his discussion on the devastating consequences of those violations to civilians, such as physical, psychological, and cultural debilitations.

36 ICC-OTP-20051014-109, *supra* note 1. Susana SáCouto & Katherine Cleary, "The gravity threshold of the International Criminal Court" (2007) 23: Am. U. Int'l L. Rev. 807, 851.

37 Moorehead & Rone, *supra* note 4 at 41. (To avoid misunderstanding, the UPDF army is the governmental army. The UPDA army is the rebel group).

It is shocking however, that nowhere were the Acholi people ever protected. Tragically, their enemy constantly was changing brutal faces and was everywhere in both material and spiritual worlds.

Between 1994 and 1999, Kony who had moved his headquarters and his army (LRA) to South Sudan openly received the support of the Sudanese government. Omar al-Bashir, the president of Sudan, argued that his support of the LRA was a direct response to the support Museveni gave to the Sudan People's Liberation Movement and Army, who were opposed to al-Bashir.[38] With Sudanese support, Kony committed a number of ferocious attacks.[39]

In 1999 the Museveni government passed an Amnesty Bill, enforced in 2000, for those of the rebel groups' members who would return and conform to the government. In December of 1999, the governments of Sudan and Uganda, under pressure from the Carter Center, agreed, on papers only, to "stop supporting cross-border rebel groups".[40]

Interestingly though, the most successful and long-lasting President of Uganda, the educated president with powerful political connections who implemented plans of aggressive economic development in the South, did not manage to protect the Acholis. He tolerated his army's crimes against the Acholis and dramatically failed in his government's peace negotiations. Looking at the North, the Acholi, and the LRA as a unified problem, it seems that this particular manifestation of Museveni's incompetence was related to the political importance of the peril's long duration and its northern origin. The Southerners, the elite, and the entire non-Acholi population needed Museveni's protection. The enemy was the North, which stereotypically was different in a rather primitive, superstitious, and violent way.[41]

After 2001, the LRA was included in the USA Terrorist Exclusion List. In 2002 Museveni and al-Bashir declared their alliance to fight the LRA terrorists. The Ugandan Iron Fist I and II military operations against the LRA material-

---

38 ReliefWeb, "Sudan-Uganda: Bashir says support for lra rebels has ceased", *ReliefWeb*, (August 2001), online: https://reliefweb.int/report/sudan/sudan-uganda-bashir-says-support-lra-rebels-has-ceased.

39 Allen, *supra* note 8 at 49.

40 *Ibid* at 51, 73.

41 *Ibid at 48-49 for* Tim Allen's discussion on the "political uses" of the LRA, *See also* Dolan, *supra* note 3 at 72–103, where he discusses the dynamic between LRA and Museveni's government; *ibid* at 91: since 1986 the LRA had survived longer than any other Ugandan rebel group; *ibid* at 72: from a quantitative point of view the governmental army was more powerful and effective against other rebel groups; *ibid* at 109: the government's response to the LRA was military rather than negotiate a true peace, which also favoured the existence of the "shocking" displacement camps.

ized with the help of Sudan. Regrettably, during these operations, civilians abducted by the LRA were killed by Museveni's army.[42]

The same year as these deadly operations (2002), the government of Uganda signed the Rome Statute and the ICC's jurisdiction in Uganda started. On December 2003, Museveni referred the LRA to the ICC. On January 29, 2004, a rather highly criticized joint conference was held in London with the ICC's Chief Prosecutor Luis Moreno Ocampo and Museveni announcing Uganda's referral. Museveni declared that he would amend his amnesty law to exclude the LRA leadership ensuring that they could be brought before the ICC. It was clear that many LRA members were themselves victims, but the amnesty law would help them reintegrate into the society. No concern, however, was given for Ongwen who was an Acholi victim of the LRA, an abducted former child soldier, the youngest of the five accused in the "LRA leadership".[43]

In July 2004, Luis Moreno Ocampo started investigations in Uganda. Even though many thousands of civilians had suffered all these years, including the period under investigation (2003–2005), at the hands of both the governmental forces and the LRA, the investigations covered only the LRA,[44] because it was determined that it committed graver crimes.[45] However, William Schabas has characterized, using the gravity of crimes as a determinant, a "legalistic formula" which permitted a political decision to look judicial.[46]

On July 8, 2005, five arrest warrants were issued against five LRA persons. The investigation's focus was six hugely ferocious attacks against civilians that the LRA carried out between 2002 (the year the Rome Statute was ratified) and

---

42 Allen, *supra* note 8 at 51. For the inclusion of the LRA among the terrorist groups, *ibid* at 72.

43 ICC-20040129-44, ICC – President of Uganda refers situation concerning the Lord's Resistance Army (LRA) to the ICC (January 24, 2004), http://www.icc-cpi.int/news/icc-president-uganda-refers-situation-concerning-lords-resistance-army-lra-icc.

44 ICC-OTP-20051014-109, *supra* note 1. *See also* the criticism against the ICC for not investigating the Ugandan government crimes and the political role of Museveni: Human Rights Watch, "ICC: Investigate All Sides in Uganda" (February 4, 2004) *Hum Rights Watch*. https://www.hrw.org/news/2004/02/04/icc-investigate-all-sides-uganda. Mark Kersten, "Why the ICC won't prosecute Museveni" (March 17, 2015) *Justice Hub.org*. https://justicehub.org/article/why-the-icc-wont-prosecute-museveni/. Kevin Jon Heller, "Poor ICC Outreach – Uganda Edition" (September 22, 2015), *Opinio Juris*. http://opiniojuris.org/2015/09/22/poor-icc-outreach-uganda-edition/.

45 *See* Moorehead & Rone, *supra* note 4 at 41–51 for the UPDF's impunity.

46 William Schabas, *Unimaginable Atrocities: Justice, Politics, and Rights at the War Crimes Tribunals* (Oxford: Oxford University Press, 2012) 89. For criticism, *see also* Mark Kersten, "Yeah, Right… ICC Officials Say There's No Evidence Against Ugandan Military" (May 5, 2016) *Justice Conflict*, online: https://justiceinconflict.org/2016/05/05/yeah-right-icc-officials-say-theres-no-evidence-against-ugandan-military/.

2005. The leader of the LRA, Joseph Kony was described by Moreno as "the absolute leader of the LRA and controls life and death within the organisation" and "that he orders the movements of his forces and dictates the types of military and civilian targets of the LRA attacks".[47]

In 2011, the U.S., with one hundred special forces, supported African troops in hunting the LRA leader, Joseph Kony.[48] In 2013, the U.S. offered a reward for information leading to Kony, Odhiambo, and Ongwen.[49] Among the five people against whom arrest warrants had been issued by the ICC Prosecutor, two are still at large: Joseph Kony, the Commander in Chief of the LRA; and Vincent Otti, the Vice-Chairman and second in command. Okot Odhiambo, the Deputy Army Commander, and Raska Lukwiya, the Army Commander, died. Only one, the fifth in line, the brigadier and abducted former child soldier Dominic Ongwen voluntarily surrendered to the ICC on January 16, 2015 in Bangui of the Central African Republic.[50] One year later, in 2016, Museveni said that the "ICC is a useless body"[51] and "a bunch of useless people".[52]

Since 2017 the hunt for Kony has been relaxed, as he is no longer considered a big threat.[53] However, the LRA is still alive, but every year it commits fewer killings and kidnappings.[54]

---

47 ICC-OTP-20051014-109, *supra* note 1. at 4–5.

48 BBC News, "LRA rebel Dominic Ongwen surrenders to US forces in CAR", BBC News (January 7, 2015), online: https://www.bbc.com/news/world-africa-30705649.

49 BBC News, "US offers up to $5m for leads on Uganda warlord Kony", *BBC News* (April 3, 2013), BBC News, online: https://www.bbc.com/news/world-africa-22017853.

50 ICC-02/04-01/05, Report of the Registry Source on the voluntary surrender of Dominic Ongwen and his transfer to the Court in the case of *The Prosecutor v. Joseph Kony, Vincent Otti, Okot Odhiambo, Dominic Ongwen*, January 22, 2015.

51 *See* Luksaka Times, "Zambia : Museveni praises South Africa's decision to leave ICC as he arrives in Zambia for Uhuru celebrations", Lusakatimes.com (October 23, 2016), online: https://www.lusakatimes.com/2016/10/23/museveni-praises-south-africas-decision-leave-icc-arrives-zambia-uhuru-celebrations/.

52 *See* New Vision, "ICC a bunch of useless people – Museveni", *New Vis* (May 12, 2016), online: https://www.newvision.co.ug/articledetails/1424384.

53 *See* Juliette Hattem, "Joseph Kony is still at large. Here's why the U.S. and Uganda were willing to give up the hunt", *The Washington Post* (April 22, 2017), online: https://www.washingtonpost.com/news/worldviews/wp/2017/04/22/joseph-kony-is-still-at-large-heres-why-the-u-s-and-uganda-were-willing-to-give-up-the-hunt/.

54 *See* Crisis Tracker (online: https://crisistracker.org/), which tracks atrocities that the LRA commits. The report shows the LRA was still active in March 2022. Crisis Tracker, "A Central African girl escaped from the LRA Achaye faction and fled to Zemio after being held captive by the armed group for 2 years. A combatant from the armed group went searching for the girl in nearby communities", Crisis Tracker (March 20, 2022), online: https://crisistracker.org/incidents/377378.

Many leaders in North Uganda opposed the ICC investigation stating that it will lead to instability while negotiations for peace were on the way. Many supported the position that all the LRA people should benefit from the Amnesty Act[55] and get back to their society and that the ICC should investigate the government's army crimes. When Ongwen surrendered, it was thought that he would be tried by the Ugandan International Criminal Division. However, Museveni claimed that, since Ongwen was not arrested in Uganda, he had no authority to order his trial in Uganda.[56]

Ongwen was charged by the ICC with an indictment containing 70 allegations of war crimes and crimes against humanity.[57] His trial opened on December 6, 2016. During the trial, his defence argued duress and mental incapacitation according to Article 31 (1.a &d). The Court rejected both defences and convicted him of 61 counts.[58] He was sentenced to 25 years imprisonment.[59] The ICC Trial Court accepted that the displacements of the Acholi people, in some cases, happened forcibly. However, even if only for historical accuracy, there was no mention of the crimes Museveni's army committed against the civilians.[60] The Court stated that "the LRA hostility towards people living in internally displaced persons (IDP) camps is at the core of the present case".[61]

The Appeal Court, in 2022, upheld the Trial decision by majority.[62] Judge Luz del Carmen Ibáñez Carranza dissented and considered Ongwen's dual status of victim and perpetrator. The sentencing analysis follows later in the chapter.[63]

The above brief historical analysis sheds light on the background of this case. However, since Museveni's leadership (1986), the Northerners were the enemy of the Southerners. Ongwen was born in the Acholi community, and he

55 Moorehead & Rone, *supra* note 4 at 55–56.

56 Kersten, *supra* note 45. *See also*, Barrie Sander, "Why is Museveni Allowing Dominic Ongwen to be Sent to the ICC?" *Justice Conflict* (January 15, 2015), online: https://justiceinconflict.org/2015/01/15/why-is-museveni-allowing-dominic-ongwen-to-be-sent-to-the-icc/.

57 ICC-CPI-20160323-PR1202, Press Release, March 23, 2016, ICC Pre-Trial Chamber II confirms the charges against Dominic Ongwen and commits him to trial.

58 ICC-02/04-01/15, February 4, 2021, *The Prosecutor v. Dominic Ongwen* (Trial Judgement).

59 ICC-02/04-01/15, May 6, 2021, *The Prosecutor v. Dominic Ongwen* (Sentence).

60 *The Prosecutor v Dominic Ongwen*, 2021 Trial Chamber IX at 9–13. ICC-02/04-01/15, Trial Chamber IX, February 04, 2021, 11.

61 *Ibid* at 12.

62 ICC-02/04-01/15-2023, December 15, 2022, Judgment on the appeal of Mr Dominic Ongwen against the decision of Trial Chamber IX of May 6, 2021 entitled "Sentence".

63 ICC-02/04-01/15-2023-Anx1, Partly dissenting opinion of Judge Luz del Carmen Ibáñez Carranza, 15-12-2022.

was abducted by the LRA in 1987 when he was almost nine years old. He is not a political leader but a brigadier of a brutal rebel group with Christian fundamentalistic characteristics mixed with spiritual guidance, prophecy, and superstition. His tribe, his abduction, his child soldiering, the war, and the horrific LRA environment is Ongwen's background. In the entire social and political background of the North Uganda Situation since 1986, when Museveni took over Kampala with his rebel group and became the President of Uganda, Ongwen, was rather an insignificant personality. Despite the attempt to label his trial as the trial of the notorious Lord's Resistance Army, Ongwen was both a perpetrator and a victim, and probably a political scapegoat.

2 Part One: Conviction

2.1 *Defining the Central Legal Question of This Case*

This is the only case among the three discussed in this book that is divided into two parts: one related to the trial and conviction, and the other to the sentencing trial. The reason for the division is that, unlike the *Bemba* and the *Gbagbo* and *Blé Goudé* cases, Ongwen was convicted.

The trial on Ongwen's criminal responsibility included considerations of issues like duress and mental disorder. However, the focus here is not on Ongwen's criminal responsibility per se nor on the severity of the sentence. Rather, it is on how and whether the Court evaluated evidence related to the affirmed defences for conviction and sentencing purposes. This includes the burden and standard of proof. Additionally, it examines whether the Court addressed Ongwen's moral blameworthiness given the totality of his background.

2.2 *The Evidence Regime, the Burden, and the Standard of Proof in* Ongwen

> The ICC system is substantially different from the classic common law system. Firstly, the bench is made up of professional judges who will decide on the guilt of the accused. Because of their professional background and experience, it is not necessary to shield them from unreliable or irrelevant evidence, because they disregard such evidence automatically.[64] [emphasis added]

64 Judge Bertram Schmitt, "Legal Diversity at the International Criminal Court Reflections of a Judge" (2021) JICJ 485–510, at 495. Interestingly the Rome Statute does not mention the phrase "professional judges" but uses the following as alternative qualifications:

The following analysis does not pertain to the determination of whether Ongwen was mentally incapacitated or acting under duress in relation to the crimes for which he was convicted. Rather, the focus here is to examine whether Ongwen's trial elucidates issues concerning the burden of proof and its implications for the right to a fair trial.

In Ongwen's trial, we will scrutinize the ongoing interplay between admission and submission of evidence. This trial foregrounds the persistent myth surrounding continental (professional) judges and their purported automatic proficiency in adjudicating within an adversarial framework. This myth is encapsulated in the assertion that "common law evidence rules are technical and designed for juries". Our examination will reveal the frequent reappearance of this myth and highlight the critical implications of this stereotypical misconception.

2.3 *Was the Submission Regime Truly "Firmly Established"? An Inquiry*

An ongoing controversy regarding the admissibility of evidence arose among ICC judges as the *Ongwen* case advanced through pre-trial preparations and interlocutory motions. The two distinct approaches, labelled submission and admission, stem from the statutory framework governing the court's proceedings. Under the submission regime, all determinations of evidence admissibility would be deferred until the deliberation phase of the trial, regardless of any objections raised by the parties concerning specific pieces of evidence. The presiding court would then address the admissibility of evidence in its final judgment, considering its relevance to the decisions at hand.

Under the admission regime, the court is required to rule on issues of admissibility during the trial hearing. Opinions varied on the precise timing for these rulings, but concerns about ensuring trial fairness generally dictated that such determinations be made before final submissions and deliberation. This approach aligns with the adversarial common law system, where parties control the evidence introduced to support their cases.

In contrast, the submission approach aligns with the traditional continental trial model, where the judge assumes a more dominant, hierarchical role. However, in the classic continental tradition, concepts of relevance and pro-

---

Article 36.3(b). Every candidate for election to the Court shall: (i) have established competence in criminal law and procedure, and the necessary relevant experience, whether as judge, prosecutor, advocate or in other similar capacity, in criminal proceedings; or (ii) have established competence in relevant areas of international law such as international humanitarian law and the law of human rights, and extensive experience in a professional legal capacity which is of relevance to the judicial work of the Court.

bative value, balanced against the potential for prejudice, do not typically determine admissibility. Instead, evidence is only excluded if it is proven to have been obtained illegally.

The *Ongwen* decision refers to two significant *Bemba* cases, one of which is discussed in Chapter Three of this book. To fully grasp the nature of the controversy, it is essential to consider both cases. This examination will also illuminate the role of precedent in the ICC and how the continental tradition typically selects which precedents to follow, or how it chooses to demonstrate preference for one over another.

The first case, *The Prosecutor v. Bemba*,[65] involves prosecution for war crimes and crimes against humanity. The second derivative case, *The Prosecutor v. Bemba et al.*, pertains to the administration of justice crimes allegedly committed during the prosecution of Mr. Bemba.

In *Prosecutor v. Bemba et al.* (2015), the Trial Chamber articulated that it would defer issues of evidence admissibility until the deliberation stage of the trial. The Chamber justified this approach as consistent with its "right and duty" to the free assessment of evidence pursuant to Rule 63(2) of the ICC Rules of Procedure and Evidence.[66] In March 2018, the Appeal Chamber, in the same case, *Bemba et al.*, agreed and held that the Court has the option to follow either the *submission* or the *admission regime* of evidence. It preferred the *submission regime* because it permitted the Court to evaluate admissibility at the evaluation stage, where it would decide guilt or innocence. However, this did not require the Court to make separate admissibility rulings in its judgment.[67]

In dissent, Judge Henderson argued against the *submission* regime, highlighting the diverse legal cultures that must coexist under the Statute's compromise. He stated:

> I do not agree with my colleagues that the approach followed by the Trial Chamber is a fair reflection of the compromise at Rome which created a hybrid system. On the contrary, in my respectful view, the approach approved by my colleagues has effectively *undermined the*

65 ICC-01/05-01/08, *The Prosecutor v. Jean-Pierre Bemba Gombo.*

66 ICC-01/05-01/13, September 24, 2015, *The Prosecutor v. Jean-Pierre Bemba Gombo et al.*, Decision on Prosecution Requests for Admission of Documentary Evidence (ICC 01/05-01/13-1013-Red, ICC-01/05-01/13-1113-Red, ICC-01/05-01/13-1170-Conf), paras 10, 11–13.

67 ICC-01/05-01/13 A A2 A3 A4 A5, March 8, 2018, *The Prosecutor v. Jean-Pierre Bemba Gombo* et al., paras. 585, 597–598. *See also* the analysis at paras. 586–601.

> *compromise reached by the States Parties between the Common Law and the Romano-Germanic legal traditions.*[68] [emphasis added]

Specifically, with respect to ruling on admissibility, he added:

> The Statute's admissibility regime is thus considerably *less formal* than what exists in most Common Law jurisdictions and *offers more flexibility and discretion* to the judges. However, and this is crucial, otherwise, the compromise would not work, it does not dispense with the need to consider the question of admissibility of evidence altogether.[69] [emphasis added]

In his explanation for his conclusion, he began by describing his opponents' views as representing a "caricature" of the common law system, portraying it as "atomistic" in contrast to the purportedly superior "holistic" approach of the continental system.[70] In common law practice, subject to a judge's residual discretion to raise an evidentiary issue, rulings are typically made only after an objection and submission from a party. Demonstrating a more subtle understanding of the common law evidence approach, he offered two purposes for admissibility rulings:

> Firstly, to *provide notice to the parties as to the purpose* for which the evidence has been entered into the case record; i.e. what the tendering party aims to prove by it (possibly in conjunction with other evidence) and, second, to *ensure that the Chamber receives all necessary information* to make a fully informed evaluation of the exhibit's evidentiary weight.[71] [emphasis added]

More importantly, his critique was premised on the nature of an adversarial procedure and the fair trial interests of the parties who need to know whether they must adjust their strategy in response to an admissibility ruling.[72] By the time the deliberation stage is reached, it is too late for such adjustments. Judge Henderson rejected the majority's view that "it is not possible to make fully

68 ICC-01/05-01/13-2275-Anx, March 8, 2018 Separate Opinion of Judge Geoffrey Henderson, paras. 38–55.
69 *Ibid* at para 38.
70 *Ibid* at para 41.
71 *ibid* at para 42.
72 *Ibid* at para 45.

informed admissibility rulings before all the evidence is in" emphasizing that this suggests the common law decisions are ill-informed:

> To suggest *this amounts to saying that thousands of judges on Common Law benches throughout the world have for centuries been making ill-informed decisions*. Such a suggestion is plainly wrong. Indeed, as any experienced Common Law judge knows, decisions on relevance, probative value and prejudice are made on the strength of the parties' submissions. If the tendering party is of the view that the Chamber must assess these factors in light of other evidence that is still to be submitted, they have the responsibility *to point this out to the Chamber who may then admit such evidence de bene esse*.[73]

Judge Henderson clearly held the view that the *submission regime* misunderstood the compromise in the Statute of Rome and attempted, on evidence matters, to move from an adversarial, party-driven process that respected fair trial rights to a regime of judicial primacy.[74]

In the *Bemba* case, three months later the Appeal Court, in June 2018, by a majority, reversed the Trial decision and entered an acquittal.[75] This was a circumstantial evidence case where the appellate majority concluded that considering solely admissible evidence, the Prosecutor had not proved that guilt was the only reasonable inference. With respect to the Trial Court's approach to evidence admissibility, the separate decisions that comprised the appellate majority specifically addressed this point. Judge Eboe Osuji referred to Judge Henderson's dissent *in Bemba et al.* and said:[76]

> Having carefully considered the reasoning of the Majority and that of Judge Henderson in that appeal, I am in the fullest accord with Judge Henderson and I fully adopt his opinion and fully recommend it.

The joint opinion of Judges Van Den Wyngaert and Morrison referred to the *submission* approach used in *Bemba et al.*, and concluded that, while the sub-

73 *Ibid* at para 46.

74 *Ibid* at para 38.

75 ICC-01/05-01/08-3636-Red, Judgment on the appeal of Mr Jean-Pierre Bemba Gombo against Trial Chamber III's "Judgment pursuant to Article 74 of the Statute", June 8, 2018, Appeals Chamber, Decision.

76 ICC-01/05-01/08-3636-Anx3, June 14, 2018 *Bemba* Appeals Chamber, Concurring Separate Opinion of Judge Eboe-Osuji, para 297.

mission approach may be acceptable for certain offenses, it is not suitable for the more serious cases. For crimes under Article 5 the Trial Court must rigorously apply admissibility criteria to avoid cluttering the case record with inferior evidence:

> Whereas this may have been unproblematic in the context of a case relating to offences against the administration of justice. We are of the opinion that it is not appropriate in cases relating to article 5 of the Statute. In this respect we agree with our colleagues Eboe-Osuji and Henderson. Not only is it necessary to rule on the admissibility of all evidence submitted by the parties, the Trial Chamber must also apply the admissibility criteria of article 69 (4) of the Statute sufficiently rigorously to avoid crowding the case record with evidence of inferior quality. We are confident that, if this had been done in the present case, many of the problems that we have identified in this section would not have arisen.[77]

Thus, three of the five judges on the *Bemba* appeals panel accepted Judge Henderson's complete rejection of the submission regime in *Bemba et al.* and concurred with his reasoning for that conclusion.

Now, we can begin to examine *Ongwen* with a newfound appreciation for the lively debate over evidence admission among ICC judges. However, in *Ongwen*, the die had already been cast by an interlocutory decision, and in July 2016, the *Ongwen* Court issued directions for the conduct of proceedings.[78] The Chamber confirmed that it would follow the rulings developed in the cases of *Laurent Gbagbo and Charles Blé Goudé*,[79] *Bemba et al.*,[80] and *Bosco*

77 ICC-01/05-01/08-3636-Anx2, June 8, 2018 (*Bemba* Appeals Chamber), Separate Opinion of Judge Van den Wyngaert and Judge Morrison, para 18.

78 ICC-02/04-01/15, July 13, 2016, Trial Chamber IX, Initial Directions on the Conduct of the Proceedings.

79 ICC-02/11-01/15-405, January 29, 2016, *The Prosecutor v. Laurent Gbagbo and Charles Blé Goudé*, Decision on the submission and admission of evidence. *See* ICC-02/11-01/15-405-Anx, Dissenting Opinion of Judge Henderson.

80 ICC-01/05-01/13-1285, September 24, 2015, The Prosecutor v. Jean-Pierre Bemba Gombo, Aimé Kilolo Musamba, Jean-Jacques Mangenda Kabongo, Fidèle Babala Wandu, and Narcisse Arido, Decision on Prosecution Requests for Admission of Documentary Evidence (ICC-01/05-01/13-1013-Red, ICC-01/05-01/13-1113-Red, ICC-01/05-01/13-1170-Conf).

Ntaganda.[81] On the question of evidence, the Court stated that it "will recognise their formal submission" and:

> [w]ill consider the relevance, probative value and potential prejudice of each item of evidence submitted *when deliberating the judgment*, though it may not necessarily discuss these aspects for every item submitted in the judgment itself.[82] [emphasis added]

Additionally, the Court stated that "consistent with its approach of deferring admissibility considerations, it will not set limitations on how it will consider any submitted evidence".[83] Clearly, this was the *submission* approach.

The Trial decision, issued on February 4, 2021,[84] followed suit on the evidentiary issue but with surprising confidence and notwithstanding the acceptance of Henderson's dissent by three judges in *Bemba*. After reiterating the view that a Trial Court has the option of choosing *submission* or *admission*[85] the Court held that the *submission* regime:[86]

> [*i*]s *now firmly established in the practice of the Court*. It has been adopted in numerous cases and, as recalled, *its foundation in the Statute* was recently confirmed by the Appeals Chamber, which, on the basis of an in-depth analysis, concluded that it was consistent with the legal framework of the Court – including the plain language of Articles 69(4) and 74(2) of the Statute and Rule 64 of the Rules – *as well as with the corresponding exact intentions of the drafters of the relevant legal instruments*, as made clear by their drafting history. A series *of other documents*, authored by judges or other experts in international criminal law, have also *confirmed the legitimacy* of such procedure. [emphasis added]

But what about Judge Henderson's rejection that was adopted by the three judges in the *Bemba* appeal? How can one say that the *submission regime*

81 ICC-01/04-02/06-619, June 2, 2015, *The Prosecutor v. Bosco Ntaganda*, Decision on the conduct of proceedings; ICC-01/04-02/06-1340, May 27, 2016, *The Prosecutor v. Bosco Ntaganda*, Decision on Defence request for admission of documents used during the testimony of Witness P-0933, para 5.

82 ICC-02/04-01/15, July 13, 2016, *supra* note 78 at para 24.

83 *Ibid* at para 29.

84 ICC-02/04-01/15-1762-Red 04-02-2021, Trial Judgement at para 237.

85 *Ibid* at para 239.

86 *Ibid* at para 241.

was "firmly established"? Searching through the text and the numerous voluminous footnotes, the primary source for this conclusion was the Appeal decision in *Bemba et al.* No mention is made of the *Bemba* decision or the earlier dissent of Judge Henderson in *Bemba et al.* No effort was made to reconcile the contradiction between these two cases.

In its Closing Brief, the Defence rejected the submission regime in the *Bemba* Appeal decision (2018). This included specific references to the opinions of Judges Wyngaert and Morrison, as well as Judge Henderson's critique, which they relied upon. The *Ongwen* Defence argued that the submission regime had been explicitly rejected in the *Bemba* Appeal decision.[87]

The Defence, in its Closing Brief, had just spent three paragraphs referring to the rejection of the submission regime in the Appeal decision in *Bemba* (2018), including specific references to the opinion of Judges Wyngaert and Morrison, as well as Judge Henderson's critique upon which they relied. The Ongwen Defence was arguing that the *submission regime* had been rejected in the *Bemba* Appeal decision. The *Ongwen* Court characterized the defence's submission as "untenable":[88]

> This proposition by the Defence is based exclusively on a remark expressed *in a minority opinion appended* to a judgment rendered by the Appeals Chamber on another appeal. The Chamber considers the Defence submission in this respect *untenable*. [emphasis added]

In a convoluted and lengthy footnote, the Court attempted to argue that the appellate judges in the *Bemba* case could not be relied upon due to their misinterpretation of distinguishing *Bemba et al.*, which concerned offences related to the administration of justice rather than war crimes. Furthermore, by characterizing the Defence argument as based on "a remark in a minority opinion", the Court overlooked the fact that three judges of the Appeal Court in *Bemba* endorsed the so-called minority opinion, thus forming a more recent majority.[89]

The *Ongwen* Court went to great lengths to explain why the submission regime was either superior or, at least, did not cause the problems its oppon-

87 ICC-02/04-1/15, March 13, 2021 Public, with Confidential Annexes A-B and Public Annexes C-H ICC-02/04-01/15-1722-Corr-Red 13-03-2020 1/198 RH T, Public Redacted Version of "Corrected Version of 'Defence Closing Brief'", filed on February 24, 2020 at paras 99–101.

88 ICC-02/04-01/15-1762-Red 04-02-2021, *supra* note 84 at para 234 fn. 252.

89 Ibid.

ents raised. Much of this discussion repeats or expands points made in *Bemba et al.*[90]

When the Ongwen Court asserted that the *submission* evidence regime had been "firmly established in the practice of the Court" and "adopted in numerous cases", it relied on the *Independent Expert Review of the International Criminal Court and the Rome Statute System* and the *Paris Declaration on the Effectiveness of International Criminal Justice* to legitimize this claim.[91] Ironically, both documents merely affirm the ICC's discretion to select its method and emphasize the Court's obligation to assess admissibility. Neither document suggests or implies that the submission regime is preferable.

The *Paris Declaration* in 2017, under the title "Expediency", recommended an ongoing consideration and evaluation of the practice of delaying, either completely or partially, the determination of the admissibility of evidence until the deliberation stage of a trial:

> Continue reflecting upon the practice of totally or partially postponing to the deliberation stage the assessment of the admissibility of the evidence presented.[92]

The Independent Review in 2020 stated clearly that there was not necessity to settle the disagreement by officially deciding in favour of one approach over the other through a specific regulation:

> The suggestion made is that the difference should be resolved in favour of one or the other through a Regulation on the matter. That is not considered necessary.[93]

It's rather perplexing that the Trial Court in Ongwen cited these documents to argue that the submission approach is firmly established. Why would the Court rely on sources that merely affirm the ICC's discretion without explicitly endorsing one method over the other?

---

90 *Ibid* at paras. 238–245. Judge B. Schmitt presided over both the *Bemba et al.* and *Ongwen* trials, where he affirmed the view that the Rome Statute provides trial judges with the discretion to choose between the submission or admission regimes. In both cases, he chose the submission regime.

91 *Independent Expert Review of the International Criminal Court and the Rome Statute System*, Final Report, September 30, 2020, paras 546–550. *Paris Declaration on the Effectiveness of International Criminal Justice*, October 16, 2017, para 21.

92 *Paris Declaration, supra* note 91 .

93 *Independent Expert Review, supra* note 91 at paras 546–547.

Let us closely examine the various justifications provided in *Ongwen* for adopting the submission regime. In its 2016 directions, the Court supported its choice of the submission approach with the following reasons:[94]

(i) The Chamber can assess *more accurately the relevance and probative value* of a given item of evidence *after having received all* of the evidence being presented at trial.
(ii) A significant amount of *time is saved* by not having to assess an item's relevance and probative value at the point of submission and again at the end of the proceedings.
(iii) There is no reason for the Chamber to make admissibility assessments to screen itself from considering materials inappropriately.
(iv) There is *no reason to assume that professional judges would consider irrelevant or unduly prejudicial material*, noting in particular that the requirement of a reasoned judgment enables the participants to verify precisely how the Chamber evaluated the evidence. [emphasis added]

These reasons require some comment. With respect to (i), to the extent that it may be true, it does not preclude ruling on admission after all evidence is heard but before the parties' final submissions. This would respect trial fairness by giving the parties an opportunity to deal with the Court's evidentiary rulings. As well, the parties would prepare their submissions only on admissible evidence. On the same line, the Court would be advantaged by deliberating only based on all admissible evidence, not encumbered by the entire bulk of all the evidence submitted at trial. Expeditiousness, addressed in (ii), should not be a platform that subordinates the fair trial rights of the accused, especially when objections to evidence have been raised. With respect to (iii) and (iv), these assert the supremacy of the Court, thereby again subordinating the fair trial rights of the accused and undermining the adversarial nature of the proceedings. This is a "trust me regime", a familiar approach to the classic continental systems. By addressing admissibility only at the deliberation phase, the parties face a blind spot about whether more evidence may be needed and how to construct their final submissions.

In 2021, the Trial Court in *Ongwen* reiterated and amplified the same reasons for its choice of the *submission regime* in its judgement.

94 ICC-02/04-01/15, July 13, 2016, *supra* note 78 at para 25.

2.4 *Admissibility Test vs. Evidence Weight: Understanding the Distinction*

The Court in *Ongwen* issued a Trial decision of 1077 pages. The formally submitted evidence recognized by the Court was in total 5149 items.[95] The Office of the Prosecutor presented 109 witnesses and experts, the Defence presented sixty-three witnesses and experts, and the Legal Representatives of the Victims presented seven witnesses and experts.[96]

The Court decided that its truth-seeking mission would have been endangered if it had excluded evidence items for relevance, probative value and prejudice issues before the end of the trial. The Court said that "the relevance and probative value of a given piece of evidence may not be evident in the course of the proceedings but may become so when all the evidence is received and considered".[97] Therefore, "until the end of the trial", the "knowledge" of the Court was "by definition partial".[98]

Regarding relevance, probative value, and prejudice in individual rulings, the Court stated that scrutinizing evidence, when submitted, is necessary only for jury trials and not for professional judges. It emphasized that professional judges are "capable of disregarding" irrelevant material, prejudicial, or with no probative value.[99] The Court's only statutory duty, according to Article 74(5) was to provide a reasoned decision for its determination.[100]

The Trial Court especially for the *submission* and *admission* evidence regime stated:[101]

> Each procedure employs different terminology to reflect the scope of the trial chamber's determination with respect to items of documentary evidence upon their submission by a party: generally, they are *either "recognised as submitted"* within the meaning of Article 74(2) of the Statute, in the first procedure, or are individually "admitted", in the second one. Notwithstanding the difference in concerns, the scope of this determination by a chamber, the consequence of either determination is the same: both indicate, with equal clarity, that the item of evidence is

95 ICC-02/04-01/15, February 4, 2021, *supra* note 58 at para 25.

96 ICC-PIDS-CIS-UGA-02-021/21, Case Information Sheet, online: https://www.icc-cpi.int/sites/default/files/CaseInformationSheets/OngwenEng.pdf.

97 ICC-02/04-01/15, February 4, 2021, *supra* note 58 at para 239.

98 *Ibid* at para 239.

99 *Ibid* at para 246.

100 *Ibid* at para 247.

101 *Ibid* at para 236.

> part of the collection of evidence that the chamber would consider for its eventual decision on the guilt or innocence of the accused. So long as such determination is clear with respect to each item of evidence, parties know with equal precision, irrespective of the procedure employed in each individual case, which items will be considered as part of the deliberation of the final judgment. [emphasis added]

The above statement seems to represent a strange, if not misapprehended, perception of the evidence admissibility assessment process conducted by the ICC. The "recognised as submitted" items of evidence and the "individually admitted" items are not exactly of the same "consequence". These are two different processes with different results. The "individually admitted" process means that when the evidence is submitted, immediately follows an assessment of whether it is admissible or not. Therefore, no admissibility issues will be discussed later in the process for inadmissibility reasons, except in the cases of the *de bene esse* process.[102] According to the "recognised submitted" evidence process, the submission of evidence is not followed by individual assessment and admissibility rulings, but assessment is pending, not vanished.

As we saw above, the Ongwen Court stated that the parties would precisely know "which items will be considered as part of the deliberation of the final judgment".[103] The Court said that the assessment of the evidence was conducted "as part of the deliberation of the judgment" and "emerges from its reasoning",[104] and that "trial chambers have a degree of discretion as to what to address explicitly in their reasoning".[105]

Later the Court said that "each statement made by a witness" was discussed individually in the decision.[106] Finally, the Trial decision provided a kind of admissibility discussion for selected pieces of evidence the Court chose without justifying why others were ignored. For these items, some discussion regarded relevance, reliability, probative value and prejudice, but not necessarily for all four of each selected evidence item.

However, when the ICC in *Ongwen* evaluated the weight of evidence, it seemed to imply that all the submitted evidence items were considered admitted on the face of their submission. Furthermore, when the Court stated that

---

102 A party submits evidence under the condition the admissibility process be addressed in light of further evidence.

103 ICC-02/04-01/15, February 4, 2021, *supra* note 58 at para 236.

104 *Ibid* at para 246.

105 *Ibid* at para 247.

106 *Ibid* at para 260.

any non-excluded evidence was eligible for guilt or innocence determination, it seems like the Court perceived the absence of rulings on admissibility as equal to rulings on admissible evidence.[107] Profoundly, only the non-excluded evidence should a Court consider for determining guilt or innocence. But since the Court neither explicitly stated which evidence was considered as admitted nor whether it admitted all the submitted evidence, this seems rather problematic. The legal issue here is that the reader of an ICC decision needs to know the exact process the Court followed for evidence admissibility, not to hypothesize based on assumptions like: "If the Court refers to specific pieces of evidence, it is acceptable. If it does not, that is also acceptable. The Court is presumed to possess the requisite knowledge, providing no grounds to question its trustworthy judgment". However, for fair trial purposes, the ICC's reasoning needs to be transparent.

The Court stated that relevance and probative value arguments raised by the parties were assessed as part of the deliberation phase with respect to the determination of guilt or innocence:

> Such arguments made by the parties and participants in the course of the trial have been duly considered as part of the Chamber's determination of Dominic Ongwen's guilt or innocence and are addressed and disposed of in the present judgment as appropriate.[108]

However, the phrases the parties' and participants' arguments "have been duly considered" and addressed "as appropriate" by the Chamber are rather vague and unclear. Given that the Court seems to have conflated the admissibility test with the evaluation of evidence weight, the vagueness becomes hugely problematic.

As per the assessment of the relevance, probative value, and prejudice, the Court stated that since they are professional judges, "they are thus able to assess all items of evidence before them properly" and therefore, instead of individual rulings:

> [s]uch assessment – conducted as part of the deliberation of the judgment – emerges from its reasoning, in the context of which "a trial chamber must indeed explain with sufficient clarity the basis for its determination".[109]

107 *Ibid* at para 236.
108 *Ibid* at para 247.
109 *Ibid* at para 246.

It is clear that the *Ongwen* Court, in the Trial decision, wrongfully seemed to synonymize the question of admissibility with the evaluation of evidence weight.[110]

Nevertheless, the ICC's judgement on how the submitted evidence led to a conviction or acquittal is related to the evaluation of evidence weight. Thus, it cannot supersede or preclude the admissibility process. Moreover, nowhere does the legal framework of the ICC provide that judges can choose between an "all-in" evidence process without admissibility assessment or a "pick and choose" process with semi-assessments. It is evident that only the admissible evidence should be evaluated by the ICC. Thus, the admissibility assessment is an inevitable process. If the drafters of the ICC legal framework wanted to disregard admissibility assessments, the provisions related to admissibility, considering relevance, probative value, and prejudice, would be absent from the Statute, as in the classic continental systems. The ICC hybrid model does not imply that some judges may choose the common law tradition while others adhere to the classic continental. Additionally, the ICC trial model does not allow for some panels to decide on admissibility while others do not.

More importantly, it must be emphasized that there is no provision, however outrageous it might seem, that states or even implies that the test for evidence admissibility is equivalent to evaluating the weight of the evidence. This distinction is crucial: admissibility concerns whether evidence can be considered at all based on criteria such as relevance, probative value, and prejudice. Evaluating the weight of the whole evidence involves determining its significance within the context of the entire case. The ICC framework clearly separates these two processes to ensure a fair and rigorous evaluation of evidence. Holistic evaluation does not conflate the two. In contrast, the continental free evaluation of evidence confuses these processes as one.

2.5 *The Fallacy: Reliability Equals Credibility*

In common law, the assessment of the admissibility of evidence, which includes the factor of "relevance", takes a *prominent place in criminal trials*. This is justified by the fact that in a trial by jury, the laypersons decide on the merits of the case, i.e. the innocence or guilt of the accused. *The laypersons, who have no experience* in considering and assessing evidence, *have to be shielded from noncredible and unreliable evidence that would otherwise "contaminate" their minds*. Therefore, it

110 *Ibid* at para 237.

> makes sense to render a decision on the (in)admissibility of each item of nonoral evidence at the moment it is submitted at trial so as to protect the lay jurors from undue influence and limit the evidentiary basis of the case.[111] [emphasis added]

Reliability and credibility are not synonymous legal terms. However, the *Ongwen* Trial Court seemed confident in thinking they were.

The Trial Court in *Ongwen* said that it considered evidence reliability. In the decision, it is stated that several factors were considered for reliability reasons: coherence of the narrative, relation to other evidence, and "richness of details".[112] However, the Statute, according to Article 69(4), has left reliability out. Especially for the reliability issue, the preparatory works show that the drafters of the Statute deliberately "left the Rules silent on this issue" because of the different methods a Court might chose to proceed with admissibility of evidence.[113]

Notwithstanding the reference to reliability in the Trial decision, narrative coherence and richness of details are factors related to credibility, not reliability. When the Court was discussing credibility, it assumed that this was a reliability issue. This could be well understood if we consider that the classic continental systems have not developed a discourse through doctrine or case law on reliability and credibility legal issues and their distinction. Without legal analysis and clarification on these issues, a credible witness is usually considered reliable. Often, a witness who provides a coherent narrative and details is considered, in general terms, a trustworthy person and, therefore, reliable and credible. Honesty is often synonymous with the supposed absence of bias. As well, many witnesses are considered presumptively trustworthy and credible, especially in certain social contexts (i.e., high-ranked state officers, police officers). Moreover, factors such as age, memory problems, inaccurate observations, failure to communicate clearly, and the reasons behind this failure (i.e., PTSD) have not been substantial legal issues for assessing reliability. Even in a case of fatally unreliable testimony, according to common sense, the continental court, following the principle of free evaluation of evidence, may never address this unreliability in its decision. In the classic

---

111 Judge Bertram Schmitt, "Legal Diversity at the International Criminal Court: Reflections of a Judge" (2021) 19:3 JICJ 492. https://doi.org/10.1093/jicj/mqab038.

112 ICC-02/04-01/15, February 4, 2021, Trial Judgment, paras 255–256.

113 Donald Piragoff, "Evidence", in R. S. K. Lee and Håkan Friman, eds., *The International Criminal Court: Elements of Crimes and Rules of Procedure and Evidence* (Ardsley, NY: Transnational Publishers, 2001) 354.

continental systems, the notions of credibility and reliability in Court have a rather social or everyday meaning, not a legal one. Additionally, the courts do not analyse each piece of evidence relied upon to determine guilt. Explicit discussions on reliability, probative value, prejudice, and credibility are absent from the continental Courts' decisions and legal doctrine.[114]

In *Ongwen,* the Court stated: "The same witness may be reliable in one part of their testimony, but not in another", relying upon the earlier decision in the *Ngudjolo* case.[115] However, the *Ngudjolo* Appeal Court did not equate credibility and reliability like the *Ongwen* Court. It held that the two notions are not synonymous.[116] It stated:

> *The evidence of a witness in relation to whose credibility* the Trial Chamber has some reservations may be relied upon to the extent that it *is corroborated by other reliable evidence.* However, the Appeals Chamber also finds that there may be witnesses whose *credibility* is impugned to such an extent that he or she cannot be relied upon, even if other evidence appears to corroborate parts of his or her testimony.[117] [emphasis added]

Credibility and reliability are distinct but related legal notions. Credibility is about the witness's honesty. The trier of fact, based on the circumstances, should assess whether a witness is honest or not. Reliability describes the accuracy of the evidence. Reliability can be affected by the accuracy of a scientific process, or, if it is related to a witness, can be affected by "(a) inaccurate observations, (b) memory problems, (c) a failure by the witness to communicate observations accurately".[118]

The *Ongwen* Court further said that when there were "competing versions of events" in witness testimonies it had to determine the "more probative" version.[119] It's not clear what this "probative version" was for. It should be

114 See Demetra Fr. Sorvatzioti & Allan Manson, "Burden of Proof and L'intime conviction: Is the Continental Criminal Trial Moving to the Common Law?" (2018) 23:1, *Can.Crim.L. Rev.* 113–115.

115 ICC-02/04-01/15, February 4, 2021, *supra* note 58 at para 261.

116 ICC-01/04-02/12-271-Corr, *The Prosecutor v. Mathieu Ngudjolo Chui,* Public Version of Judgment on the Prosecutor's appeal against the decision of Trial Chamber II entitled "Judgment pursuant to article 74 of the Statute", April 7, 2015 at paras 168–169.

117 *Ibid* at para 168.

118 David Paciocco, Palma Paciocco, & Lee Stuesser, *The Law of Evidence*, 8th ed. (Toronto: Irwin Law, 2020) 44–45.

119 ICC-02/04-01/15, February 4, 2021, *supra* note 58 at para 257.

clear that the weight of evidence needed to be evaluated against the prosecutorial burden of proof, not against supposed logical factors that remained unknown. Even though the ultimate gatekeeper for determining guilt or innocence is the trier of fact, the prosecutorial burden of proof never disappears nor shifts before the ICC. Nonetheless, probative value is a term used in Article 69. This is related to evidence relevance and admissibility assessment. Probative value means how informative the evidence is to prove a matter in issue.[120] The probative value of a relevant piece of evidence should outweigh prejudice. Moreover, "competing versions of events" of a witness's testimony may probably indicate an unreliable witness. When the *Ongwen* Court tried to locate the supposed "probative version" of the contradictions of the witness, it purely exercised its free assessment of evidence approach – the continental way of assessment.

In the Trial decision, the Court, for some pieces of evidence, held a rather problematic approach with respect to credibility, the burden of proof, and reasonable doubt. Let's look at the following examples:

The Court's evaluation of witness P-0142:[121]

> The Chamber notes that at times, the witness appeared to be attempting to minimise the implications of the LRA actions as well as his role in the attacks. However, this did not undermine the Chamber's view of his *general credibility*. Indeed, the witness was at times candid about his account of events which incriminated Dominic Ongwen, thus *bolstering the Chamber's view of his credibility given his very positive relationship with Dominic Ongwen.* [emphasis added]

The Court's evaluation of witness P-0231:[122]

> The Chamber notes that the witness testified to having a close relationship with Dominic Ongwen while he was in the bush, and believed that Dominic Ongwen saved his life while they were both in the LRA. *Perhaps, for this reason*, there are aspects of the witness's testimony where he appears to be minimising Dominic Ongwen's actions. For example, the witness claims that he never saw anyone young in Dominic Ongwen's house. Such a statement *is not credible in light of the testimony of other reliable witnesses.* However, the Chamber also notes that much of

120 Paciocco *et al.*, *supra* note 118 at 45–46.
121 *Ibid* at para 269.
122 *Ibid* at para 276.

> the witness's testimony *is consistent with other reliable evidence heard in this case.* [emphasis added]

The Court's evaluation of witness Joseph Okilan (D-0019):[123]

> If you don't follow Kony's commands, that means death is assured for you. In light of all the other evidence, this statement is not credible. In addition, the Chamber considers that a natural explanation for this statement is the fact that the witness occupied a relatively high position in the LRA hierarchy, and was motivated to minimise his responsibility. With this clarification, the Chamber considers Joseph Okilan generally reliable. [emphasis added]

The Court's way of credibility assessment, as viewed through the reasoning "the witness testified that if you don't follow Kony's commands death was the next step because he was motivated to minimise his high position of responsibility", or "since Ongwen saved the life of the witness perhaps for this reason the witness minimised Ongwen's actions", or "the positive relationship of the witness with Ongwen bolsters his credibility", does not explicitly explain how the aforementioned reasons for excluding certain parts of a witness's testimony were justified, nor how the sustainability of any reasonable doubt was overcome by facts or other reliable and credible evidence.

The Court, for witness P-0145, stated:[124]

> However, the Chamber finds other aspects of the witness's testimony credible, particularly with the planning of the Lukodi attack as well as the LRA's policy on the treatment of civilians and Dominic Ongwen's behaviour as an LRA commander. The Chamber also notes that much of the witness's testimony is supported by other reliable evidence heard in these proceedings.

The above paragraph again did not provide any explanation regarding what constituted the "other reliable evidence". One might think of going through the Court's records to find out what happened, but if this is the case, then the so-called reasoned decision of this Trial is decidedly not reasoned. What is important here is not whether Ongwen was planning or could plan the "Lucodi attack" but rather what a reasoned decision means when the burden

123 *Ibid* at para 281.
124 *Ibid* at para 306.

of proof is on the prosecution. When the burden of proof rests with the prosecution, the determination of guilt or innocence does not influence the mandated reasoning process. Even when the prosecution presents a compelling case on the elements of the offences, as seen in the *Ongwen* trial, the Court must still maintain a rigorous approach to evidence issues.

In *Sheppard*,[125] the Canadian Supreme Court Judge Binnie J. said that judges "owe" a duty to give reasons (a) to the public;[126] (b) to the losing party;[127] and (c) to counsel and the appeal courts for appellate review.[128] In *Sheppard*, with reference to *Burns*,[129] it was stated:

> The more problematic situation is where the trial judge renders a decision and gives either no reasons or, as in this case, *"generic" reasons* that could apply with equal facility to almost any criminal case. *The complaint is not that the reasoning is defective but that it is unknown or unclear*.[130] [emphasis added]

In *Ongwen*, the problem is that the reader, in the above reasoning examples, has no clear picture of the Court's credibility assessment. Moreover, the statements of the supposed non-credible witnesses were in favour of the accused. The reasoning for their exclusion was generic and, therefore, unclear. How does this generic reasoning meet fair trial standards? Such vague justifications undermine the transparency and fairness required in judicial processes, leaving significant doubt about the integrity of the Court's decision-making.

Overall in the *Ongwen* Trial decision, the Court appeared to favour the evidence submission regime with an implicit "trust us, we are professional judges" approach. However, this trial, which adhered to the submission regime, lacked the adversarial nature intrinsic to ICC proceedings and failed to adequately address the prosecutorial burden of proof beyond a reasonable doubt. The Trial decision's discussion on this critical prosecutorial burden is notably insufficient. This inadequacy suggests an attempt to prioritize the free evaluation of evidence over the stringent prosecutorial burden of proof, reflecting a traditional continental system approach. This raises significant

125 *Sheppard v. R.*, [2002] 1 S.C.R. 869, 210 D.L.R. (4th) 608.
126 *Ibid* at para 20.
127 *Ibid* at para 24.
128 *Ibid* at para 25.
129 *R. v. Burns*, [1994] 1 S.C.R. 656.
130 *Sheppard*, *supra* note 125 at para 32.

concerns about adherence to fair trial standards and the integrity of the judicial process under the Rome Statute.

2.6 *The Burden and the Standard of Proof for Affirmative Defences in* Ongwen

> The German system of criminal procedure *knows no "parties" with active roles at the trial,* and it knows nothing about a burden of proof being placed on either party; in the German tradition, the criminal process is conceived of as the *court's unilateral endeavour to find the truth, with the prosecution and the defence standing at the side-lines.*[131] [emphasis added]

> The burden and standard of proof are laid out in Article 66 of the Statute. *Naturally,* this judgment *applies this burden and standard of proof to the evidence presented.* [Trial Judgement, at para 85] [emphasis added]

The following discussion is not related to whether Ongwen was or was not mentally incapacitated or under duress for the crimes he was convicted of. The issue here is to examine whether Ongwen's trial reveals the burden of proof questions regarding the fair trial right.

According to the Rome Statute, Article 66(2) states clearly that the burden of proof is on the prosecution, and Article 67(i) states that a reverse of this onus to the accused is not permitted in the ICC's adversarial trial. However, in *Ongwen* the parties held antithetical views regarding the burden of proof question for Ongwen's affirmative defences. Even though it is interesting to examine the parties', the participants', and the Court's responses to this issue, what is rather fascinating is that the Appeal Court in *Ongwen* called for amici curiae submissions on the burden and standard of proof.[132]

Ongwen's Defence raised the affirmative defences of mental incapacity and duress in 2016. In September 2018 his Defence delivered an opening statement and raised the burden of proof issue. In January 2019, the Defence filed a

---

131 Thomas Weigend. "Assuming that the Defendant Is Not Guilty: The Presumption of Innocence in the German System of Criminal Justice" (2014) 8 *Criminal Law and Philosophy* 290.

132 ICC-02/04-01/15 Appeal Chamber, October 25, 2021, Order inviting expressions of interest as amici curiae in judicial proceedings (pursuant to Rule 103 of the Rules of Procedure and Evidence), at paras 5, 8, 10.

motion requesting the Court to issue an immediate decision confirming the burden of proof regarding the defences of exclusion of criminal responsibility as provided by Articles 31(1)(a) and (d) of the Rome Statute.[133] More specifically, the Defence claimed that after the submission of evidence regarding the existence of Ongwen's mental incapacity and duress, the Prosecution had the burden to disprove beyond a reasonable doubt each element of these defences according to Articles 66 and 67(1)(i).[134] The Prosecution replied that "the parties bear no burden to prove or disprove elements of the defences" and only the Court had the "obligation to determine" whether the Defence succeeded or not.[135] The participants, the Victim's Representative, argued that the burden of proof was on the Defence.[136] Remarkably, in this international criminal trial, none of the parties or the participants shared the same view on the burden and the standard of proof.

The Court issued its interlocutory decision with respect to the burden and the standard of proof issue, with reference to the provision of Article 66 (which defines that the burden of proof for guilt is on the Prosecution) and stated that the Court's "interpretations of the applicable law will be set out in its judgment".[137] This position of the Court, when analysed through the lens of common sense, implies that in order for the Prosecution to establish guilt beyond a reasonable doubt, the Prosecutor must effectively disprove the raised affirmative defences. But if Article 66 was self-explanatory as per the defences, according to the Court, why did the parties and the Victims' Representative submit diametrically opposed responses?[138]

Surprisingly, in 2021 the *Ongwen* Court, in its Trial judgement, referred to the Defence's request regarding the immediate ruling for the burden of proof

133 ICC-02/04-01/15, January 28, 2019, Defence Request for the Chamber to Issue an Immediate Ruling Confirming the Burden and Standard of Proof Applicable to Articles 31(1)(a) and (d) of the Rome Statute.

134 *Ibid* at paras 2, 4.

135 ICC-02/04-01/15, April 5, 2019, Decision on Defence Request for the Chamber to Issue an Immediate Ruling Confirming the Burden and Standard of Proof Applicable to Articles 31 (1)(a) and (d) of the Rome Statute, at para 7.

136 *Ibid* at para 8.

137 *Ibid* at para 16.

138 *See* ICC-02/04-01/15-1439, February 7, 2019, Prosecution Response to "Defence Request for the Chamber to Issue an Immediate Ruling Confirming the Burden and Standard of Proof Applicable to Articles 31(1)(a) and (d) of the Rome Statute"; ICC-02/04-01/15-144, CLRV's Response to "Defence Request for the Chamber to Issue and Immediate Ruling Confirming the Burden and Standard of Proof Applicable to Articles 31(1)(a) and (d) of the Rome Statute".

and stated that the Defence had "no right to receive a full legal interpretation by the Chambers on the law at a specific point in the proceedings",[139] but did not explain why. It is awkward that according to the Court's view the Defence had no right to learn where the burden and the standard of proof laid when the accused raised affirmative defences before the ICC. Given that Ongwen's case was the first trial in which the mental incapacity and duress defences were raised before the ICC and the parties and participants held antithetical views on the burden, why did Ongwen's Defence have no right to know how to effectively prepare his defence for fair trial purposes? Furthermore, as per the Defence's argument that they were in darkness and they did not know explicitly where the burden and the standard of proof were lying, the Court stated:[140]

> The Defence argues that it was prejudiced because, had it known the burden of proof during the proceedings, it "may [have chosen] other evidence". This argument is *speculative*. The Defence called numerous witnesses on the matter and submitted numerous items of evidence. *The Defence does not even seek to explain how its evidence would have been different.* In fact, the Chamber considers that in this case where grounds excluding criminal responsibility were alleged by the Defence since the confirmation proceedings and where they form one of the crucial issues in the trial, the possibility of the Defence choosing a path different than the one it chose is purely theoretical. [emphasis added]

It is rather astonishing that the Court seems not to understand or appreciate what is the legal meaning of an effective defence and its core importance to the fair trial right. Moreover, it is staggering that the Court was expecting the Defence to explain before it how Ongwen would shape an effective defence strategy. I avoid commenting on the Court's characterization of the Defence's position as speculative and theoretical.

The question raised by the Defence was not whether they could call more witnesses, as the Court understood, but which witnesses to choose to call or not, to prove what was determined in respect to the burden by the Court. This approach was not "speculative" or "theoretical" but an informed approach for an effective defence strategy. Here, the *Ongwen* Trial Court seemed to have misapprehended the Defence's role in an ICC trial. This approach aligns with

139 ICC-02/04-01/15, February 4, 2021, *supra* note 58 at para 88.

140 *Ibid* at para 89.

the classic continental tradition, emphasizing the dominant role of the continental judge.

When the Trial Court addressed the burden of proof, it also analysed the Defence's ability to submit evidence and examine witnesses. The Court claimed that the exercise of these rights indicated no "prejudice". However, it remains unclear how this analysis addresses the Defence's concerns about the burden and standard of proof, particularly regarding duress and mental state defences.[141] Conflating the Court's potential bias with the accused's right to an effective defence is problematic and does not adequately resolve the Defence's questions.

Finally, as per the burden and standard of proof, the Court stated:[142]

> *When a finding of the guilt of the accused also depends on a negative finding* with respect to the existence of grounds excluding criminal responsibility under Article 31 of the Statute, *the general provisions of* Article 66(2) and (3) on the burden and standard of proof equally apply, operating (as is always the case for the determination on the guilt or innocence of the accused) solely with respect to the facts indispensable for entering a conviction, namely, in this case, *the absence of any ground excluding criminal responsibility and, thus, the guilt of the accused.* [emphasis added]

The Court also said that the absence of a relevant provision in the Statute regarding the burden of proof, with respect to Article 31, is not "a lacuna" because, according to Articles 66(2) and (3), "the burden of proof (incumbent on the Prosecution) and the standard of proof (beyond reasonable doubt) relate to the 'guilt of the accused'".[143]

The Court later stated:[144]

> The onus is on the Prosecutor to prove the guilt of the accused, and, under Article 66(3), in order to convict the accused, the Court must be convinced of the guilt of the accused beyond reasonable doubt.

141 ICC-02/04-01/15, February 4, 2021, *supra* note 58 at paras 89–93.

142 *Ibid* at para 231.

143 *Ibid.*

144 ICC-02/04-01/15, February 4, 2021, *supra* note 58 at para 2588.

The Trial Court finally rejected the Ongwen defences of mental incapacitation and duress.[145] But, nowhere in the Trial decision did the Court say clearly that the Prosecution needed to disprove beyond a reasonable doubt the defences of duress and mental incapacity or that she did so. The Court decided that since it was convinced of guilt beyond a reasonable doubt, consequently, this indicated a negative finding on the raised affirmative defences. Even though this should have been the only logical outcome if the prosecution had disproved the raised affirmative defences, there was an absence of any relevant discussion on the burden and the standard of proof in the Court's Trial decision.

The *Ongwen* Court actually confirmed the Prosecution's argument that the parties had no burden of proof for the raised defences and the Court had the "obligation to determine" the success of the defences. Furthermore, there was no reference in the trial decision explaining why Ongwen's Defence did not raise any reasonable doubt. It appears that the unanimous decision of the Court safely concluded that Ongwen was guilty beyond reasonable doubt of the crimes which he was accused of committing. Therefore, as a side effect, his defences failed.

However, the ICC trials are conducted along adversarial lines, which requires the Court to weigh the admitted evidence against the burden of proof, which lies with the Prosecution. Therefore, the Prosecution has a duty to prove guilt beyond a reasonable doubt. When the Defence raises affirmative defences, it doesn't imply that (a) the accused must, in agony, try to convince the Court; (b) the Prosecution can respond without adhering to the burden and standard of proof; and (c) the Court should decide without considering prosecutorial burden and standard. This approach aligns with the inquisitorial model, not the adversarial, and certainly not the ICC framework.

The Court's approach in *Ongwen,* and especially the way the decision drew the lines of the Court's dominant role, seems similar to the classic continental system's approach. The Trial judgement reiterated that a reasoned decision is the Court's duty. This is correct. However, an ICC decision is only truly well-reasoned if it includes a thorough discussion and analysis of (a) why the Defence did not manage to raise a reasonable doubt for their defences and (b) how the Prosecution disproved beyond a reasonable doubt the elements of

145 *See also* Pascale Chifflet & Ian Freckelton, "The Mental Incapacity Defence in International Criminal Law: Ramifications from the Ongwen Trial Judgment" (2022) 22:4 Int. C. L. R. 751–779, a critique about the Court's difficulty in distinguishing between incapacitation and diminished responsibility in its trial judgement.

each raised defence. Without these critical analyses, the decision lacks the depth and rigour expected in the adversarial ICC model.

Perhaps the classic continental tradition's inexperience with burden and standard of proof explains why the Court, in its decision, did not attempt to interpret and clarify whether the defences of duress and mental capacity should be assessed using an "air of reality" test or a balance of probabilities test. In classic continental systems, there is no discussion regarding the evidential and persuasive burden of different defences and excuses. For instance, defences, such as self-defence, necessity, duress and mental incapacity, are not differentiated with respect to standards of proof, unlike in common law systems.

The question of which party bears the burden of proving a fact or issue is known as the evidential burden. In criminal cases, the evidential burden rests on the prosecution, and the persuasive burden requires proving the case beyond a reasonable doubt, except in instances where a statutory or common law reverse onus applies. The persuasive burden establishes the standard of proof required for a conviction.

If the accused introduces a defence that goes beyond denying an element of the offence, he must meet an evidential and a persuasive burden. This is exactly what the Ongwen Defence wanted to know: the evidential and persuasive burden for the affirmative defences in order to prepare his effective defence.

In common law criminal trials (unlike continental law, which lacks a prosecutorial burden of proof), the two burdens are distinct. The accused satisfies the evidential burden by pointing to or adducing evidence that raises a reasonable doubt on a matter in issue. The persuasive burden means that the accused must persuade the Court regarding the fact he indicated or adduced evidence for. The standard of the persuasive burden depends on the raised defence. For instance, in a defence of incapacity due to the presumption of sanity, the accused's persuasive burden is to the balance of probabilities, but the prosecution must still prove beyond a reasonable doubt that the accused was sane. In cases of self-defence, the air of reality test applies to the accused, and the prosecution must then prove beyond a reasonable doubt that the accused was not acting in self-defence.[146]

If the Court in *Ongwen* had understood the Defence's question and recognized the distinction between the accused's evidential and persuasive bur-

146 Sydney N. Lederman, Alan W. Bryant, & Michelle K. Fuerst, *The Law of Evidence in Canada,* 4th ed. (Toronto: LexisNexis Canada, 2014) 228–229. Similarly, for jury and judge alone trials, at 204.

dens, it would have grasped the significant impact of this issue on the right to a fair trial.

Nevertheless, even if the *Ongwen* Trial Court refrained from interpreting the burden and standard of proof and simply reiterated the precise language of Article 66, it unequivocally established that when affirmative defences of duress and mental incapacity are invoked under Article 31, the prosecution remains responsible for proving guilt, and the standard of proof is beyond a reasonable doubt. This determination is critically important for safeguarding the rights of the accused in future proceedings. However, the principal concern is that the Trial Court's 1,077-page decision did not adequately address or analyse the burden of proof within its reasoning. This gap is perhaps understandable given the Court's adherence to the traditionally vague continental approach regarding the burden and standard of proof in the context of affirmative defences. It is imperative that future judicial panels, equipped with greater expertise in these legal principles, deliver more comprehensive and reasoned judgments when addressing similar defences.

2.7 *Conclusion*

What we observed in the burden of proof discussion in *Ongwen's* affirmative defences confirms the patterns seen in the *Bemba* and *Gbagbo* cases. Although the *Ongwen* Trial Court appeared confident in referencing the prosecutorial burden of proof, its decision did not demonstrate a thorough understanding of its application. This highlights a critical distinction: understanding a legal concept is not the same as merely knowing its legal terminology. Learning definitions is crucial, but relying solely on them, especially initially, can hinder genuine understanding.[147] Common law is not necessarily superior, but it benefits from centuries of experience we lack. While we adopted the terminology of the prosecutorial burden of proof in 2018, we have yet to fully grasp its implications. Thus, it is advantageous to learn from the extensive experience of common law systems.

One may question whether the rules:

> on the amount and persuasiveness of proof necessary for conviction are indeed part of the presumption of innocence, or whether they concern a different issue. Be that as it may, what is problematic is the transfer of the "until proved guilty beyond a reasonable doubt" standard from the

147 The Feynman Technique: Master the Art of Learning, online: https://fs.blog/feynman-technique/.

common-law world, where it originated, to a totally different procedural system like that in Germany.[148]

3 Part Two: Sentencing[149]

> Words and figures cannot adequately portray the physical and psychological harm inflicted on vulnerable children who were brutalized and who lived in constant fear. The loss and grief to their inconsolable families is immeasurable. Their childhood stolen, deprived of education and all human rights, the suffering of the young victims and their families left permanent scars.[150]
>
> BENJAMIN B. FERENCZ

3.1 *Brief Overview*

The Trial Court convicted and sentenced Ongwen to 25 years imprisonment.[151] Ongwen appealed both the conviction and sentence decisions,but the Appeal Court upheld the Trial judgement for conviction. The Majority also upheld the sentencing decision.[152] Judge Luz del Carmen Ibáñez Carranza provided an articulate dissenting opinion, which is in line with the arguments here.[153]

The Trial Court considered the mitigating and aggravating factors listed in the Statute and Rules but in a rather perfunctory manner. Aggravating factors marched in a parade (cruelty, multiplicity of victims, victims particularly defenceless, discrimination on political grounds and discrimination against

148 Weigend, *supra* note 131 at 290.

149 Sorvatzioti, "Proportionality and Moral Blameworthiness in Ongwen's ICC Sentencing Decision" (2023) 23:5-6 at 755–781, Crim L Rev. International Criminal Law Review, 23(5–6), 755–781. https://doi.org/10.1163/15718123-bja10159.

150 Benjamin B. Ferencz, "Ferencz closes Lubanga Case for ICC Prosecution" (August 2011), online: benferencz.org/articles/2010-present/ferencz-closes-lubanga-case-for-icc-prosecution. *See also* the Schauer report, regarding the multiple phycological disorders child soldiers and ex-combatants suffer in countries with war and violence, *The Prosecutor v Lubanga Dyilo*; ICC-01/04-01/06, July 10, 2012, Decision on Sentence pursuant to Article 76 of the Statute, paras 39–49.

151 ICC-02/04-01/15, May 6, 2021, *supra* note 59.

152 ICC-02/04-01/15-2023, December 15, 2022, *supra* note 62 at section entitled "Sentence".

153 ICC-02/04-01/15-2023-Anx1, *supra* note 63, Partly dissenting opinion of Judge Luz del Carmen Ibáñez Carranza, 15-12-2022.

women) with zero analysis of the prosecutorial burden of proof.[154] However, in the "applicable law" section, the Court said that aggravating factors should be proved beyond a reasonable doubt.[155] This became the beginning and the end of the entire analysis.

When the Court considered the defences of duress and mental capacity for sentencing purposes, it rejected them with reference to the conviction reasoning. Sentencing, especially when long periods of imprisonment are in play, requires more. The drafters and signatories of the Rome Statute accepted that, notwithstanding the gravity of the Rome Statute offences, a range of imprisonment penalties would be available to a sentencing court. This should be interpreted as a reflection of proportionality. While gravity is the central feature of any sentencing regime based on proportionality, a significant element should be moral blameworthiness. Here, the Trial Chamber and the majority of the Appeal Court failed to evaluate how Ongwen's life and experiences affected his moral blameworthiness. The Court's narrow-minded view, which reflects a continental approach, ignored the moral blameworthiness evidence without confronting why it is relevant. Relevance is an important issue in evidence law and in the sentencing process.

There is an important controversy between the majority and the minority of the Appeal Court. While four judges did not understand the concept of moral blameworthiness in relation to the social context of *Ongwen*, Judge Ibáñez Carranza accurately explained moral blameworthiness via the concept of moral culpability. Regrettably, the majority decision showed a vague understanding of sentencing analysis and ignored the prosecutorial burden of proof. In antithesis, the minority decision, in a modest and articulate way, *spoke the truth.*

The crux of the discussion that follows is the role of Ongwen's moral blameworthiness and how the ICC misapplied the principle of proportionality.[156] Behind Ongwen's individual circumstances was the Ugandan North Acholi social and political context, which was germane to Ongwen's moral responsibility. Ongwen's situation was a socio-political and international criminal law phenomenon. A mere summary by the Court regarding Ongwen's captivity was inadequate to explain the Court's method for balancing proportionality and determining sentencing.

---

154 A similar lack of analysis is observed in the Trial judgment. Adam Branch, *supra* note 5 at para 131.

155 *Ibid* at para 53.

156 Moral blameworthiness is also known as culpability or moral culpability or moral responsibility and is related to sentencing factors.

3.2 *Gravity in* Ongwen's *Sentence*

The ICC's jurisdiction deals with zenith gravity crimes,[157] where atrocities are sentenced with no mandatory minimums or mandatory life sentences,[158] and mitigating and aggravating factors are determined by the Court.[159]

Although gravity plays a significant role in sentencing determination, the vagueness of the ad hoc criminal tribunals and the ICC case law on sentencing reveals ambiguity, while gravity seems to overlap with aggravating factors.[160] In *Ongwen,* the sentencing Court raised gravity to the "extreme" level without analysis.

It is unclear whether gravity was a jurisdictional issue,[161] or an additional feature for sentencing reasons. For example, the Chamber said, "the gravity of the crime of torture is in the abstract very high".[162] For enslavement, "this incrimination protects the individual's personal liberty, making the crime of enslavement *in abstracto* a crime of considerable gravity".[163] For rape, it referred to the "inherent gravity" of rape and marked its gravity as very high.[164] When the Court looked at the violation of the right to life, liberty, sexual integrity, personal property, the right not to be subjected to cruel or degrading treatment and the right to consensually form a family, it noted that "the extreme gravity of their violations cannot go unnoticed and unaccounted for".[165] However, gravity has one jurisdictional aspect and a sentencing impact. The grave importance of a right's violation is not synonymous with the gravity or the extreme gravity of a crime. The latter is examined only via aggravating factors.[166]

The Court stated that it was aware of Ongwen's crimes' extreme gravity, "especially when considered jointly".[167] Rule 145(3) and Article 77(1)(b) provide possible life imprisonment when justified by the extreme gravity of the crime *and* the individual circumstances of the convicted person. Here the

---

157 M.M. DeGuzman, Shocking the Conscience of Humanity (New York, NY: Oxford University Press, 2020) 35.

158 Article 77(1).

159 Rule 145(2)(a)(b).

160 DeGuzman, *supra note* 157, pp. 170, 174–179, 183. *See also* SáCouto & Cleary, *supra* note 36 at 842, regarding "the amorphous nature of the factors denoting gravity" in sentencing case law of the ad hoc criminal tribunals.

161 Article 17.

162 ICC-02/04-01/15, May 6, 2021, *supra* note 59 at para 157.

163 *Ibid* at para 162.

164 *Ibid* at para 344.

165 *Ibid* at para 393.

166 Rule 145(3).

167 *Ibid* at para 387.

Court added the gravity of each crime and said that this is a life sentence case, but the individual circumstances permit mitigation. This mathematic syllogism is legally erroneous. Only adding extreme gravity to the offender's circumstances can produce a life sentence, not the crimes' gravity alone. *Ongwen* is not a life sentence case. Kony's might be. Ongwen's unique status should count to reduce his imprisonment to not go beyond thirty years.

One aspect of the case that the Court paradoxically viewed only against Ongwen, was the way the LRA treated the kidnapped children. The decision provides an identical description of the suffering Ongwen gave before the Court regarding his life after his abduction.[168] When the Court referred to the "extreme harsh treatment of children", it looked at *Ntaganda*. Ntaganda was not a former child soldier. The Court did not differentiate from *Ongwen* and did not view the child soldiers' treatment as a moral culpability issue in favour of Ongwen, only against him.[169] The Court, for *Ongwen*, stated that "it is clear that he intended such treatment of children abducted and integrated into Sinia".[170] No explanation was offered either for the word *clear* or for Ongwen's purpose of torturing children deliberately despite his well-evidenced indoctrination since he was nine. As for Ongwen's intent, the Court considered his "degree of participation and degree of intent very high in respect of all of the crimes discussed".[171] However, it is unclear what the phrase "very high" intent means in legal terms, even for sentencing.

3.3 *Proportionality in* Ongwen

Today, proportionality plays a role, often a central one, in most domestic sentencing systems. Going back to the 1960s, two major theoretical strands explained the importance of proportionality. One is known generally as *just deserts*, the primary advocate of which has been Andrew Von Hirsch. Here, proportionality is the engine that ought to drive sentencing. The other is referred to as *limiting retributivism,* where proportionality is the brake, not the engine, on sentencing. That means that other considerations determine the sentencing outcomes, but the scheme cannot extend to produce a disproportionate sentence. This theoretical approach is attributed to the seminal work of Norval Morris. Over time, while both these theories have maintained

168 *Ibid* at para 360.

169 *Ibid* at para 361, fn.655.

170 *Ibid* at 363.

171 *Ibid* at para 329. *See also* the phrase "very high", paras 181, 219, 254, 291, 297, 302, 307, 318, 322.

their original focus on the role of proportionality, they have been modified to include factors that produce similar outcomes.[172]

Given the importance put on proportionality by the "just desert" theorists, it is not surprising that they have given the most consideration to understanding the scope of proportionality. Perhaps the clearest and best-developed example is the book *Proportionate Sentencing: exploring the Principles*, by Von Hirsch and Ashworth.[173] The necessary calculus for determining proportionality is an equation between the seriousness of the offence and the seriousness of the punishment.[174] Of course, a major aspect of seriousness is the assessment of comparative intrinsic gravity between one offence and the others (*cardinal proportionality*), which resulted in what would be essentially a ladder of offences.[175] To determine the distance between the rungs of the ladder and what precise sentence, or range of sentence, they represent, Von Hirsch used what he called *ordinal proportionality*. It involved a process of spacing and anchoring that determined more clearly where each offence fit on the ladder by reference to the past sentencing experience of the particular sentencing system with due regard to restraint in setting the top and bottom limits.

On the other side of the equation, looking at the seriousness of the punishment, an essential element of punishment and sentencing is censure. In other words, for the offender, the victim and the public, the sentence serves to blame the offender for the offence. This means that a proportionate sentence needs to be commensurate with the offender's blameworthiness of the offender.[176] This is why just deserts theory distinguished the situation of young offenders or juveniles because they are considered to be, by virtue of their age and lack of maturity, less blameworthy than an adult who commits the same crime. Over time, just deserts theorists have incorporated other considerations into the calculus that distinguish between levels of seriousness based on factors like the degree of criminal responsibility attached to the specific offence, not its general category. This would include the role of the offender in the crime and whether the necessary mental element was one of intention or criminal negligence. Other considerations, referred to by Von

172 Malcolm Thorburn & Allan Manson, "The Sentencing Theory Debate: Convergence in Outcomes, Divergence in Reasoning" (2007) 10: 2 New Criminal Law Review 278–310.

173 Andrew Von Hirsch & Andrew Ashworth, *Proportionate Sentencing: Exploring the Principles* (Oxford: Oxford University Press, 2005).

174 *Ibid* at 63.

175 For a fuller discussion of ordinal proportionality, *ibid* at 137–143.

176 *Ibid* at 134–137.

Hirsch and Ashworth as "equity factors", have also been included in the calculation.[177] These include factors like mental illness short of insanity. Regardless of the label, what we see is the inclusion within the rubric of blameworthiness of factors that encompass aspects of the offender's circumstances which may lessen the deserved sentence. Essentially, what we have seen is a door opening to consider other aspects which may bear on an offender's blameworthiness (culpability).

Inevitably the above proportionality theory has influenced the discussions on international criminal sentencing goals. However, plurality and ambiguity are found regarding the goals of global institutions.[178] Schabas argues that a human rights approach in sentencing does not permit retribution to guide sentencing judges of international criminal tribunals.[179] Ohlin can see only retribution including the death penalty because the offender is a "community enemy". Focusing on the gravity of the crimes and the resulting harm, the sentence must be harsh, vindicating the rule of law.[180] However, D'Ascoli argues that the harm produced by the committed crimes can never be proportionate to the imposed sentence.[181] In *Ongwen*, the Court seems to have used a retributive approach by linking proportionality and Ongwen's culpability only to the harm caused.[182] Despite the Court's approach, a proportionality analysis according to Article 81(2)(a) and Rule 145(1) is mandatory.[183]

177 *Ibid* at 165–179.

178 DeGuzman *supra* note 157 at 27–31.

179 W.A. Schabas, "Sentencing by International Tribunals: A Human Rights Approach" (1996) 7 *Duke J. Comp. & Int'l L.* 461–517. *See also* Frederik Harhoff, "Sense and Sensibility in Sentencing-Taking Stock of International Criminal Punishment in Law at War", in Ola Engdahl & Pål Wrange, eds., *The Law as It Was and the Law as It Should Be*, Vol.22 (Leiden-Boston: Martinus Nijhoff Publishers, 2008) 139–140, where Harhoff proposed "more attention to the reconciliation process", because of the no real impact of general and specific deterrence for war crimes and crimes against humanity. As per the contribution of the ICC to deterrence "on average, it has stronger positive effects on governments than on rebels", Hyeran Jo & Beth A. Simmons, "Can the International Criminal Court Deter Atrocity?" (2016) 70:3, *International Organization* 444.

180 Jens David Ohlin, "Proportional Sentences at the ICTY", in Bert Swart, Alexander Zahar, & Göran Sluiter, eds. *The Legacy of the International Criminal Tribunal for the Former Yugoslavia* (Oxford: Oxford University Press, 2011), 329.

181 Silvia D'Ascoli, Sentencing in International Criminal Law: The UN ad hoc Tribunals and Future Perspectives for the ICC (Oxford: Hart Publishing, 2011), 292–293.

182 Margaret M. deGuzman, "Proportionate sentencing at the ICC", in Carsten Stahn (ed.) *The Law and the Practice of the International Criminal Court* (New York, NY: Oxford University Press, 2015), 936. *Ibid* 935-943 for the proportionality theories' analysis.

183 *See also* DeGuzman *supra* note 157 at 182, and Barbora Hola, "Sentencing of International Crimes at the ICTY and ICTR", (2012) 4:4 *Amsterdam LF* 9.

When looking carefully at Ongwen's case, it is rather difficult to appreciate the utility of the deterrent message of his sentence for the population of former child soldiers. Mark Drumbl argues that no evidence shows the positive results of deterrence, especially when violence is the only "viable survival strategy" for people. Moreover, the "normalization of violence" produces a "deception" hiding the political, historical, social, economic, and colonial factors that led to violence and atrocities.[184] Drumbl promotes the expressive didactic role of punishment, which unlocks the ratio behind punishment, not deterrence. Trial and punishment should mandate "moral unacceptability" for atrocities to build moral norms.[185] Sentencing should respect certain features of transitional justice applicable in national institutions, as in the case of *Mato Oput* in Uganda.[186] Judge deGuzman agrees with Drumbl that norm expression should be the guide and aim of punishment and favours the imposition of less harsh sentences (minimum retributivism), which, in their reasoning, will explicitly reflect deterrence and norm expression for global crime prevention.[187]

The ICC commenced its sentencing case law with *Lubanga*,[188] and said that Rules 145(l)(a) and (b) require the sentence to reflect the culpability of the offender. Therefore, the Court must ensure that the sentence is in proportion to the crime according to Article 81(2)(a).[189] It needs to balance mitigating and aggravating factors along with the offender's circumstances, while additional factors and circumstances to be considered are provided by Rules 145(1)(c) and (2). However, when the Court determines the Article 76(1) *appropriate* sentence, none of the provisions limits the factors to be considered by the Court.[190] The Prosecution must prove aggravating factors beyond a reasonable

184 M. Drumbl, *Atrocity, Punishment and International Law* (Cambridge: Cambridge University Press, 2007) 172.

185 *Ibid* at 174.

186 *Ibid* at 173–176. For an analysis on expressivist punishment theory *see* Joshua Glasgow, "The Expressivist Theory of Punishment Defended" (2015) 34:6 *Law and Philosophy* 601–631. For transitional justice, which represents a "conception of justice associated with periods of political change, characterized by legal responses to confront the wrongdoings of repressive predecessor regimes", *see* N. Roht-Arriaza, "The New Landscape of Transitional Justice", in Naomi Roht-Arriaza & Javier Mariezcurrena, eds., *Transitional Justice in the Twenty-First Century: Beyond Truth versus Justice* (Cambridge: Cambridge University Press, 2006), 1. Regarding transitional and restorative justice, *see* Beatriz E. Mayans-Hermida & Barbora Holá, "Punishing Atrocity Crimes in Transitional Contexts: Advancing Discussions on Adequacy of Alternative Criminal Sanctions Using the Case of Colombia" (2023) 43:1 *Oxford Journal of Legal Studies* 1–31.

187 DeGuzman, *supra* note 182.

188 ICC-01/04-01/06, July 10, 2012, *supra* note 150; *The Prosecutor v Lubanga Dyilo*; ICC-01/04-01/06, July 10, 2012, Decision on Sentence pursuant to Article 76 of the Statute at para 36.

189 *Ibid* at paras 25–26.

190 *Ibid* at para 29.

doubt while mitigating factors must be proved on the balance of probabilities by the Defence.[191]

A proportionality analysis should thoroughly consider the facts of the committed crimes, the offender's personal facts, and the social facts of the case. Being a child soldier is a social and international criminal law phenomenon, not a personal issue or an "unfortunate personal situation".[192] The *Ongwen* Court should also have looked at the cycle of violence during the LRA's wartime and the relevant social facts. The Court referred to proportionality as a sentencing principle,[193] but when it determined the sentence, it rather conflated "Ongwen's personal background with his culpable conduct and the suffering of the victims".[194] As *Lubanga* clarified, the proportionality principle is misapplied if the Court does not provide an analysis of the distinction between: (a) factors relevant to the gravity of the crime, and (b) factors relevant to the offender's degree of responsibility.[195]

3.4 *Raised Defences as Mitigating Factors*

> The holy spirit reported to the chairman [Kony] who selected the soldiers who could be "on stand". All the spirits are with Kony but if you are going to the battle, you feel that something is with you. In the battlefield, they will be doing their duty and take care of you: everyone will feel very strong.[196]

In Ongwen's conviction trial, the Court rejected the raised affirmative defences of duress and mental incapacity. The Defence had argued that his childhood in the bush as an LRA soldier, the LRA martial structure, and Kony's personality, along with his rather metaphysical control over the LRA soldiers, had a tremendous negative impact on both Ongwen's mental health and his ability to make independent decisions. The conviction decision illustrates a rather superior Western approach that perceives arguments related to spiritualistic control and fears in the jungle as scientifically untested by Western

191 *Ibid* at paras 32–34.

192 ICC-02/04-01/15-1819-Anx, May 6, 2021, Partly Dissenting Opinion of Judge Raul C. Pangalangan, para 15.

193 ICC-2/04-01/15, May 6, 2021, *supra* note 59 at para 52.

194 *Ibid* at para 389.

195 See also *Morris, infra* note 229.

196 Former commander's interview, Kristof Titeca, "The spiritual order of the LRA", in Tim Allen & Koen Vlassenroot, eds. *The Lord's Resistance Army: Myth and Reality* (New York, NY: Zed Books, 2010) 64.

methods. However, the question here is not why expert evidence "A" was more understandable by the Court's culture than expert evidence "B" but which aspects of Ongwen's situation were relevant for sentencing purposes.[197]

According to Rule 145(2)(a)(1), the evidence used unsuccessfully to support affirmative defences at trial may be relevant for sentencing purposes but must be evaluated differently. Here, the sentencing decision lacks depth in analysis, especially concerning the rejection of certain mitigating factors, such as those related to Ongwen's mental state. It feels like Ongwen's trauma, culture, and mental state had ornamental effects, not an actual impact on his terrible life. The Court desperately attempted to show a monstrous savage whose life experience as an abducted indigenous child soldier vanished when he freely, wilfully, and happily decided on a career through the LRA hierarchy. In doing so, the Court disregarded expert witnesses who analysed Ongwen's traumatic experiences and their inevitable impact on his captured life.

The circumstances not considered by the Court on sentencing were related to the Uganda-Acholi war and Ongwen's life within a wild rebel group controlled by spirits, mysticism, extreme violence, and fear. He spent 27 years in the bush in continuous war. The Court failed to logically explain how, in its view, Ongwen managed to transform himself into a well-informed rebel military leader and adult man,[198] stained only with a *touch* of childhood unhappiness.

The Prosecution characterized Ongwen's child and adolescent life as "extremely difficult", and requested a one-third reduction of the sentence to be imposed on Ongwen, suggesting 20 years minimum imprisonment for a total joint sentence. Surprisingly, the Court decided that the Prosecution's proposal simply identified a sentence lower than 30 years imprisonment and did not "propose a specific joint sentence".[199] The Court vaguely stated that the mitigating circumstances of Ongwen's childhood, personal background, family circumstances, and "alleged good character" were "duly taken into account".[200]

The Defence requested a short sentence for retributive factors with permission for Ongwen to "undergo all the appropriate rituals in northern Uganda,

197 *See also* Adina-Loredana Nistor, Andrew Merrylees, & Barbora Holá, "Spellbound at the International Criminal Court: The Intersection of Spiritualism & International Criminal Law", in Julie Fraser & Brianne McGonigle Leyh, eds., *Intersections of Law and Culture at the International Criminal Court* (Cheltenham, UK: Edward Elgar Publishing, 2020) 148–149, 162–164.

198 ICC-02/04-01/15, May 6, 2021, *supra* note 59 at para 393.

199 *Ibid* at para 9.

200 *Ibid* at para 63.

including *Mato Oput*".[201] The Court decided that the principle of legality precluded the Court from introducing a traditional justice process.[202]

The Court discussed the determination of each crime's sentence, referring to Article 81(2)(a) and Rule 145(1), which provide the principle of proportionality.[203] With respect to Ongwen's abduction, it said that between 1987 and 2002 Ongwen's life was "extremely difficult" but he adapted into the LRA and its "violent methods". The Court did not emphasize the violence Ongwen suffered and experienced but, instead, focussed on the supposed and unproven wilful adoption of violence by Ongwen. To prove his adoption of violence, the decision stated that in 1996, when Ongwen was 16 years old, he abducted a victim, raped her, and made her his wife.[204] Impressively, the Court decided to use this fact to prove Ongwen's wilful adoption of violence even though Ongwen was not criminally responsible at the time. Ample evidence proved that Kony assigned girls and women to his soldiers. Still, the Court decided that the 16-year-old boy had formed a violent interest in rape and forced marriage, ignored Kony's orders and had adopted the LRA violence thoughtfully and voluntarily.

As per Ongwen's alleged childhood trauma, the Court noted that, soon after his abduction, the nine-year-old Ongwen "was forced to slaughter some people, hang their intestines on a tree and eat beans mixed with their blood", that he said "he collapsed and became unconscious as a result, and that to this day, he cannot forget this image".[205] However, Ongwen, at the sentencing hearing, described this incident as follows:

> They told us *if you want to live kill* these people [...] I was beaten with a wire lock. They *ordered us to slaughter* these people with a knife, remove their intestines and hang their intestines on the tree. Part of their intestines we were ordered to *hang on our necks*, and we were told to say this was electric wire. We did all that. [...] *they put our plate of beans under the people who were dripping*, the bodies that were dripping with blood and the blood was dripping on these plates. They asked us to eat, but I refused. But they told us, *that is what we want you to do*. So *we were*

201 *Ibid* at para 18.

202 *Ibid* at para 26.

203 ICC-02/04-01/15, May 6, 2021, *supra* note 59, para 51, with reference to ICC-01/04-01/06-3122, December 1, 2014 (*The Prosecutor v. Thomas Lubanga Dyilo*, Judgment on the appeals of the Prosecutor and Mr Thomas Lubanga Dyilo against the "Decision on Sentence pursuant to Article 76 of the Statute").

204 *Ibid* at para 84.

205 *Ibid* at para 73.

> *forced* to eat beans mixed with human blood. […] The Acholi culture does not eat humans. When I finished eating, *I collapsed*, and I became *unconscious*. I vomited. That is what happened in my first attempt to escape. […][206] [emphasis added]

It is not clear why the Court summarized Ongwen's horrific experience with a blind eye to analyse Ongwen's childhood trauma and his fear.

The Court focused on Ongwen's supposed resilience and adopted Dr Catherine Abbo's evidence that he had a similar street gang socialization, and his alleged "favourable early childhood experiences" "contributed to his resilience" despite the impact of the daily traumatic experiences on his brain.[207] Impressively, the Court did not positively refer to expert witnesses' reports and evidence in favour of Ongwen but stated that Ongwen's trauma had no lasting consequences related to mental disorder or disease (which was not a sentencing question).[208] Ongwen belonged to a "small minority" who made choices for a "steep and purposeful rise in the LRA hierarchy".[209] The sentencing decision repeated the conviction decision that Ongwen was not forced to commit crimes, and despite the opportunities, he did not escape like others did.[210]

As per the mental incapacity defence in relation to sentencing, the Court repeated the argument of the conviction decision: "The possibility of mental disease or defect was discussed at trial and ultimately excluded in the Trial judgement on the basis of a detailed analysis of evidence, including expert evidence".[211] However, this does not constitute an analysis of its potential impact on sentencing. Mere reference to Ongwen's mental state at the material time of the committed crimes, a conviction prerequisite, does not resemble a sentencing analysis. Strengthening its view on Ongwen's state of mental health, the Court marked its high impression when he "spoke lucidly for one hour and 45 minutes, without a break, sustaining a structured and coherent declaration, while speaking largely freely".[212] However, Ongwen's speech could never negate the Court's failure to analytically reconsider the mental defence for sentencing reasons.

206 ICC-02/04-01/15-T-261,15-04-2021, 6 (lines 14–25), 7 (lines 1–2,4–5, 9).
207 ICC-02/04-01/15, May 6, 2021, *supra* note 59 at para 81.
208 *Ibid* at para 83.
209 *Ibid* at para 85.
210 *Ibid* at para 86.
211 *Ibid* at para 93.
212 *Ibid* at para 104.

With respect to Kony's spiritual powers and control and the horrific punishments or death he imposed on his subordinates, the Court repeated its conviction decision rejecting the defence of duress, saying there was no room for using that evidence for mitigation.[213] The Court disregarded the report and methodology of Professor Titeca about the LRA's "cosmological space" and stated:[214] "The report does not contain any critical assessment of the statements received in particular from Dominic Ongwen, which appear to have been taken at face value".[215] However, Titeca had clarified that he was not examining whether the LRA soldiers had actual help from spirits during fights but whether they believed they did and how this belief affected them.[216] It was crystal clear that Titeca evaluated the effect of the spiritual order on the LRA combatants. From a methodological view, there was no room for critical assessments of the collected qualitative data. It was peculiar that the Court negated Titeca's research. Before the Court, Titeca said that "absolute obedience to the many, and frequently changing spiritual rules" was "the only way to survive life in the bush".[217] He confirmed that the more time someone was in the LRA's spiritual environment, the more influence the spirits had on him.[218] Surprisingly, the Prosecutor commented that "in fact, none of those things are correct in terms of the laws of science".[219]

Looking at the Court's treatment of Professor Titeca's expert evidence as it related to moral blameworthiness, it is hard to understand why the Court was so dismissive. Perhaps this was an example of an inherent Western inability to appreciate the *other*, non-Western "cosmological space" of the LRA, which was related to Ongwen's moral responsibility. The Court either had no intention or was unable to evaluate the importance of Titeca's expert analysis of LRA's spiritual order, the soldier's blind belief in Kony's power to read their minds,

---

213 *Ibid* at paras 110–111.

214 ICC-02/04-01/15-T-197, 9-11-2018, UGA-D26-P-0060, The Prosecution asked Titeca whether his report described factual experiences or cultural truth and he replied: "I am not interested in truth per se" (65, line 6). "I am interested in understanding belief systems as they function" (65 line 9). "What is secondary is whether this is factually true or not" (65, lines 10–11). "What is important is the effect it creates" (66, line 12). "What ethnography as a field tries to do is, again, an emic understanding" (75, line 22).

215 ICC-02/04-01/15, May 6, 2021, *supra* note 59 at para 114.

216 ICC-02/04-01/15-T-197, 9-11-2018, *supra* note 214 at 17 (lines 15–25), 18 (lines 1–6).

217 Allen & Vassenroot, *supra* note 196 at 62.

218 ICC-02/04-01/15-T-197, 9-11-2018, *supra* note 216, Titeca explained that for those who came out of the bush either "the spirit has left them" or "they no longer believe in the spirit and the spirit has left Kony" (102 lines 11–15). However, spiritual beliefs "remained present among individual fighters" (103 lines 9–12).

219 *Ibid* at 78 (line 14).

in conjunction with the entire Acholi culture and spiritualism. The Court also rejected evidence submitted by other witnesses who analysed the LRA environment (Eric Awich Ochen, Awich Pollar), and referred again to its rejection in the conviction decision of the duress defence.[220]

According to Article 69(4) and Rule 63(2), the ICC legal framework incorporated the truth-seeking continental principle, which is not limited to the identification of the crimes. The ICC judge's mandate is to examine and evaluate everything related to the case, the crime and the offender, even when in his favour. Because of the unique LRA regime, the Court needed to hear expert evidence, such as Titeca's, to understand the LRA's operation. Simply hearing this evidence and impressively ignoring whatever favoured Ongwen does not resemble a thorough truth-seeking process by the ICC. Hence, the Trial Court's rejection, especially of Titeca's expert evidence, is hugely problematic.

> Within the Lord's Resistance Army, Joseph Kony, he's the messenger, he's the law, and he is the one who's in contact with these spirits, he is the one who is talking to them and he is the one who is the messenger on them, so when for example, when combatants, or former combatants, say then the spirit said X, Y, Z, in reality this is the leader Joseph Kony who said these things.
>
> While, again, some of these combatants, they had very strong – how would I say – supra-natural experiences, meaning that they themselves had dreams which had predictive powers, they could see the future, they have spoken with animals, they could see strange creatures, and so on. Even after having left the Lord's Resistance Army, they continue believing in these spirits.[221]

3.5 *Proportionality and Moral Blameworthiness in Canada*

> Victims, after all, may be imperfect. Perpetrators may be tragic.[222]

---

220 ICC-02/04-01/15, May 6, 2021, *supra* note 59 at paras 115–116.

221 ICC-02/04-01/15-T-197, 9-11-2018, *supra* note 214 at 19 (lines 5–16).

222 Mark A. Drumbl, "Victims who victimise" (2018) 4:2 *Lond. Rev. Int. Law* 218. Drumbl suggests sentencing mitigation when the *antipodes* of *pure* victim and *ugly* perpetrator meet in a person creating an imperfect victim (with reference to Ongwen). *See also* E.K. Baines, "Complex political perpetrators: reflections on Dominic Ongwen" (2009) 47:2 *The Journal of Modern African Studies* 177–181, regarding child soldiers as victims,

Because the ICC is a sui generis court with a mandate that includes only the world's gravest offences, it is usually a mistake to compare its sentencing framework to domestic systems in which the sentencing scheme must provide a coherent rationale for all offences from the lowest order to the gravest, usually murder and treason. However, sometimes specific circumstances can provide an analogy that permits looking to a domestic system for guidance. This is the case with how Canadian law has refined its conception of blameworthiness when sentencing aboriginal offenders.

Like the Statute of Rome, the statutory framework for sentencing in the Canadian Criminal Code makes it clear that proportionality is the fundamental principle of sentencing. Section 718(1) states that a "sentence must be proportionate to the gravity of the offence and the degree of responsibility of the offender". The Supreme Court of Canada has gone further and refined the term "responsibility of the offender" with the nuanced dimension of "moral blameworthiness", which might relate to the offender's social history and life experience.

Starting in the late nineteenth century, the Canadian government began a campaign of oppression and suppression of its native peoples that has been described by Chief Justice McLachlin as an attempt of cultural genocide.[223] Along with other acts, it included the placement of native children in residential schools and their forced removal for adoption by *white* parents.[224] The discrimination extended into the Canadian criminal justice system resulting in a high degree of over-representation of indigenous people in Canadian prisons.[225] Now, in the twenty-first century, Canada is struggling with how to redress more than a century of ugly and ill-treatment of its indigenous populations. The courts are also struggling with how to sentence Aboriginal offenders who themselves or their ancestors were victims of this state-sponsored campaign of suppression. Eventually, to provide a new lens for

---

agents and perpetrators focusing on Ongwen, and the importance of justice to understand the violence suffered and its reproduction.

223 Beverly McLachlin, "Canada's Chief Justice Calls Treatment of First Nations an Attempt at 'Cultural Genocide'" speech excerpt, CBC Radio (June 1, 2015), online: https://www.cbc.ca/radio/asithappens/as-it-happens-friday-edition-1.3093097/canada-s-chief-justice-calls-treatment-of-first-nations-an-attempt-at-cultural-genocide-1.3095692#:~:text=And%20she%20used%20a%20phrase,Aga%20Khan%20Museum%20in%20Toronto.

224 For a full account of these horrors, *see* The Truth and Reconciliation Commission of Canada, "Summary of the Final Report of the Truth and Reconciliation Commission of Canada", *Honouring the Truth, Reconciling for the Future* (Truth and Reconciliation Commission of Canada, 2015).

225 *See* Supreme Court of Canada, *R. v Gladue*, [1999] 1 SCR 688, paras. 61–65; Supreme Court of Canada, *R. v. Ipeelee*, [2012] SCC 13, paras 56–63.

the sentencing system, the courts have refined the concept of moral blameworthiness to address the situation of Aboriginal offenders in order to recognize their true social and historical context.

With respect to the sentencing of indigenous offenders, the Supreme Court of Canada has said:

> First, *systemic and background factors* may bear on the culpability of the offender, to the extent that they shed light on his or her level of *moral blameworthiness*. [...] Canadian criminal law is based on the premise that criminal liability only follows from voluntary conduct. Many Aboriginal offenders find themselves in situations of social and economic deprivation with a lack of opportunities and limited options for positive development. While this rarely – if ever – attains a level where one could properly say that their actions were not voluntary and therefore not deserving of criminal sanction, the reality is that their constrained circumstances may diminish their moral culpability.[226] [emphasis added]

More recently, the Ontario Court of Appeal, in *R. v. Morris*,[227] was required to consider whether a similar concept of moral blameworthiness applied to anti-Black racism and the sentencing of a young black offender. At the sentencing hearing, substantial evidence was adduced of discrimination and anti-Black racism in the City of Toronto. This included social context evidence by experts as well as evidence of the offender's previous experiences with the police, the educational system and social service institutions. The trial judge imposed a lenient sentence of one-day imprisonment plus 18 months' probation. The prosecution appealed, arguing that the judge erred essentially because he was overwhelmed by the racism evidence and proposed three years imprisonment as the fit sentence.

The Appeal Court rightly confirmed that the trial judge had erred in using the background evidence to diminish the gravity of the offence. However, it confirmed the mitigating relevance of the evidence regarding the offender's life and experiences, including his interactions with police and other institu-

226 *R. v. Ipeelee, supra* note at para 73. *See also,* Supreme Court of Canada *R. v. Anderson*, [2014] 2 S.C.R. 167, the sentencing syllogism regarding proportionality and moral blameworthiness, para 21.

227 Ontario Court of Appeal *R. v. Morris*, [2021] ONCA 680. The accused had been convicted of offences arising from possessing a loaded handgun.

tions, as it related to the dimension of his moral blameworthiness. Unanimously, the five-member court concluded:

> Social context evidence relating to the offender's life experiences may be used where relevant to mitigate the offender's degree of responsibility for the offence and/or to assist in the blending of the principles and objectives of sentencing to achieve a sentence which best serves the purposes of sentencing as described in s. 718.[228]

Specifically, with respect to the offender's background, the Court concluded:

> There can be no doubt that evidence on sentencing, describing the existence and effect of anti-Black racism in the offender's community and the impact of that racism on the offender's circumstances and life choices is part of the offender's background and circumstances. The evidence is not only admissible, it is, in many cases, essential to the obtaining of an accurate picture of the offender as a person and a part of society.[229]

The Court said that a "sentencing process which frankly acknowledges and addresses the realities of the offender's life takes one important step toward the goal of equal justice for all".[230]

Looking now at the ICC, in *Lubanga*,[231] the accused was convicted of conscripting child soldiers under the age of 15. The Court said:

> Mr Lubanga is clearly an intelligent and well-educated individual, who would have understood the seriousness of the crimes of which he has been found guilty. This marked level of awareness on his part is a relevant factor in determining the appropriate sentence.[232]

In the Court's view, Lubanga's degree in psychology increased his culpability since he would have been aware of the consequences of his actions.

228 *Ibid* at para 13.

229 *Ibid* at para 91.

230 *Ibid* at para 106.

231 ICC-01/04-01/06, July 10, 2012, *supra* note 150 at paras 54–56. *The Prosecutor v Lubanga Dyilo*; note 151.

232 *Ibid* at para 56.

Although the Court did not mention *moral blameworthiness*, this is the concept it used.

Looking at *Morris,* the Court emphasized that whether a disadvantaged environment influences the offender or limits his choices is related to his moral blameworthiness for his acts, not to the seriousness of his offences.[233]

Looking at *Ongwen*, the Court gave a nod to his difficult early years, but ignored, both explicitly and implicitly, his life of 27 years in the bush dominated by an ethos of war, cruelty, forced compulsion, indoctrination, spirituality, and lack of education. Surely, this should go to the mitigating dimension of moral blameworthiness. Although the evidence of duress and mental state should have been re-addressed through the sentencing lens,[234] the Court here, simply re-rejected the evidence of the raised defences, not re-addressed it.

Especially for Kony's control, the Court invented an objective standard, without focusing on Ongwen, and said: "LRA members with some experience in the organization did not generally believe that Joseph Kony possessed spiritual powers".[235] Moral blameworthiness is attached only to the specific perpetrator at trial. There is no room for a reasonable person's standard portrayed by other people's perceptions and attitudes. Moreover, there is no explicit explanation of how the Court reached the conclusion that Ongwen, on the balance of probabilities (mitigation's burden of proof), was not influenced by Kony. As well, there is no discussion of the fear factor despite the expert evidence adduced.[236] The *Morris* Court appreciated that constant fear was a reality in Morris' life.[237] The *Ongwen* Court speculated that Ongwen did not suffer fear because some testified he did not. Evidence proved this was not true in real time.[238]

The *Morris* Court stated:

> It was open to the trial judge to find that the evidence of anti-Black racism was connected to, or played a role in, Mr. Morris's strong fear

---

233 *Ibid* at paras 49, 94, 104, 154.

234 Allan Manson, introducing the moral blameworthiness concept, argues that whenever duress may not meet a full defence standard, it may mitigate the sentence, A. Manson, *The Law of Sentencing*, (Toronto, Irwin Law, 2001), p. 140.

235 ICC-02/04-01/15, May 6, 2021, *supra* note 59 at para 112.

236 Tim Allen testified before the Trial Court about the LRA s fear factor, Kony's knowledge of others' thoughts and the LRA people's fear of Kony, UGA-OTP-P-0422 T-28, ICC-02/04-01/15, 16-01-2017, p. 31 (lines 11-25), p. 32 (lines 1–6). *See also*, Titeca *supra* note 73.

237 *Morris, supra* note 82, para 49 with reference to Morris' social history report. Note 229

238 Allen & Vlassenroot, *supra* note 91.

> for his personal safety in the community. That state of mind offered a mitigating explanation for Mr. Morris's possession of the loaded, concealed handgun. Looked at in this way, evidence of anti-Black racism, which played a role in generating the fear that helps explain why Mr. Morris had a loaded gun, is akin, for the purposes of sentencing, to evidence that Mr. Morris had been terrorized by somebody in the community and had armed himself because he genuinely feared that person.[239]

In *Morris*, one can see how life experience and social context evidence may be used by the Court to: (a) mitigate the degree of offender's responsibility; and (b) assist the blending process of sentencing principles and objectives for achieving the sentence which serves the sentencing purposes.[240]

In *Ongwen,* life experiences, fear, and trauma were viewed only when related to LRA's victims, never to Ongwen, who had suffered the same from the LRA. The Court ignored the LRA's social context, which ought to play a mitigating role.

Comparing *Lubanga* or *Ntaganda* to *Ongwen*, the context, the social facts, and the individual circumstance are antipodes. Ongwen's exposure to cruel physical and emotional abuse, the absence of a stable and peaceful environment, education, and normal social connections in the community were circumstances that indicated the possibility of a lower sentence.[241] This was the exact view of Professors Baines, Clarke, and Drumbl when they suggested a sentence lower than 25 years because of Ongwen's "moral development".[242]

President Museveni's backstage role regarding who from the LRA should be accused is well known to all of those who have examined and studied the Uganda Situation. Ongwen was one of the five wanted men. He was the youngest, illiterate, the only former child soldier, and, seriously speaking, not a significant figure for the LRA and the entire Ugandan political arena. But the ICC

239 *Morris, supra* note 82 at para 100.

240 *Ibid* at para 13.

241 *See also,* Ontario Court of Appeal, *R. v. Borde* [2003] 168 O.A.C. 317 at para 32: "systemic and background factors may have played a role in the commission of the offence and the values of the community from which the offender comes", and Ontario Court of Appeal, *R. v. Hamilton* [2004], 189 O.A.C. 90 at para 137 on "the underlying causes" of crimes when they are "very real and are to a large extent the product of circumstances that are either beyond" the accused's "control, or for which (he) cannot be faulted", para 137.

242 ICC-02/04-01/15-1906, December 23, 2021, Submission of Amicus Curiae observations on the merits of the legal questions presented in the "Order inviting expressions of interest as amici curiae in judicial proceedings (pursuant to Rule 103 of the Rules of Procedure and Evidence) of October 25, 2021 (ICC02/04-01/15A)".

had only Ongwen for the entire Uganda Situation.[243] Either it was arduous for the Court to appreciate the many sufferings of Ongwen or the continental inexperience in sentencing analysis confused the Court. The Majority decision does not explain why Ongwen's decision-making was not related to fear, bad surroundings, war, mysticism, and lack of education. Nor does it explain how the Court reached a reasoned conclusion that the former child soldier became a rebel army career man through free will and informed choice. The absence of explanation shows the Court's failure to properly address aspects relevant to Ongwen's moral blameworthiness for mitigation reasons. The Court also enmeshed factors relevant to the crime's gravity with factors relevant to the offender's degree of responsibility. The entire process indicates a proportionality misapplication.

Remarkably, Judge Ibáñez Carranza's dissenting opinion of the sentencing Appeal decision shows the real implications of Ongwen's child soldier life on his personality. Judge Ibáñez Carranza conducted a thorough legal analysis along with a factual analysis based on expert evidence.[244] She evaluated the submitted evidence and emphasized that a fair sentence is a fair trial issue. Her approach showed a broader understanding of moral culpability based on scientific evidence and the law. It was a pragmatic approach which understood Ongwen's moral blameworthiness.

> In particular, in this case, it is of crucial importance to consider *the impact* that Mr Ongwen's abduction, conscription, violent indoctrination, being forced to carry out and participate in criminal acts when he *was still a defenceless child of about nine* years of age, and *his upbringing* in the coercive environment of the LRA had on his personality, the *development of his brai*n and moral values, and future opportunities.
>
> A determination of the appropriate sentence requires thus both a holistic and intersectional analysis that takes into consideration both the blameworthiness of the convicted person and his or her individual circumstances. *Mr Ongwen's condition as a victim did not cease when he turned 18 years old.*[245] [emphasis added]

243 *See also* L.G. Minkova, "Expressing what? The stigmatization of the defendant and the ICC's institutional interests in the Ongwen case" (2021) 34:1 LJIL 235–241.

244 ICC-02/04-01/15-2023-Anx1, *supra* note 63 at paras 136–147.

245 *Ibid* at 3–4.

3.6 *Sentencing Ongwen's "Remorse" and "Good Character"*

Ongwen's Defence requested the Court to recognize the mitigating factors of remorse,[246] and good character.[247] These factors are clearly related to Ongwen's moral responsibility and, therefore, the Court's perception was crucial for determining a proportional sentence.

The remorse discussion in the sentencing decision reveals the Court's lack of understanding of the Acholi culture and Ongwen's testimony before the Court. The Rome Statute identifies remorse as a mitigating factor without setting any standard, let alone a Westernized, dogmatic Christian ideal. It is the ICC's global role and duty to appreciate remorse according to the culture of the accused, not the accused's responsibility to show remorseful behaviour according to a Western court's perception. The truth is that Ongwen surrendered himself to the ICC and stated he felt bad for what happened to the victims, mentioning that he was also a victim.

Ongwen, before the Court, said:

> If you are mindful about the sufferings that I have gone through, then you should not take this judgement, this sentencing with a lot of anger. I request you, I appeal to you that you should also be mindful of the sufferings I went through.
>
> I know that you have heard a lot of evidence before this Court, but of what happened I am also remorseful. I feel bad for the things that have happened. The things that happened on me, on my family were also grievous things. But there is no difference. I was – I'm a person, my parents were also humans. Those other victims that those things happened to them are also humans. So we all went through the same grievous harm. So if indeed you mind about my suffering that I went through, then please look at it because I also want to become free and lead a free life.[248]

The Court decided:

> Dominic Ongwen has not expressed any such remorse. The absence of remorse became very clear during his personal statement at the senten-

246 ICC-02/04-1/15, May 6, 2021, *supra* note 59 at para 42.
247 *Ibid* at para 121.
248 ICC-02/04-01/15-T-261, 15-04-2021, 26 (lines 4–13).

> cing hearing, where, in a display of self-pity, he acknowledged the suffering of (presumably) the victims of his crimes only to claim that his own suffering was equal.[249] [...]
>
> The Chamber cannot overlook the absence, in Dominic Ongwen's submissions during the hearing on sentence, of any expression of empathy for the numerous victims of his crimes – and even less of any genuine remorse – supplanted by a lucid, constant focus on himself and his own suffering eclipsing that of anyone else.[250]

From a sentencing point of view, reaching the Trial Court's conclusion is quite onerous. However, the references of Chief Judge Schmitt to the German system might show an indication of the continental yardstick the Court used to measure remorse in African-Acholi culture.[251] Nevertheless, the ICC serves fairness and justice via a specific legal framework. The judges' national trial experience is helpful but cannot be predominant in ICC decisions. Otherwise, a national legal tradition will hinder the ICC's international and intercultural legal and social mandate. Regrettably, in *Ongwen*, the ICC proved not to have the experience or the willingness to appreciate intercultural remorse, given that Acholi people do not ask for forgiveness the way the Westerners do.

As per the mitigating factor related to Ongwen's good character and especially that he saved the lives of many in the LRA, the Court said:

> When Dominic Ongwen saved lives of other members of the LRA, including by standing up to Joseph Kony, indicate to the Chamber, once more, that Dominic Ongwen was fully able to appreciate the value of human life [...]. Further, they suggest that the circumstances of his upbringing, and stay, within the LRA constituted no obstacle to him forming his own views, and acting accordingly, in spite of the positions of other members of the group, including individuals higher than him in the LRA hierarchy and Joseph Kony himself. These episodes [...] in which Dominic Ongwen helped people in the bush because he "cared about people" cannot but demonstrate further that at no time he lost his

249 *Ibid* at para 42.

250 *Ibid* at para 394.

251 *See* for example ICC-02/04-01/15-T-162-Red-ENG WT 19-03-2018, 37 (line 25), 54 (line 20); ICC-02/04-01/15-T-163-Red-ENG WT 20-03-2018, 4 (line 1), 21 (line 4), 89 (line 25); ICC-02/04-01/15-T-166-ENG CT WT 26-03-2018, 9 (line 24).

> ability to distinguish between right and wrong and to act independently.[252]

The Court here conflated the mitigating factors at sentencing with the mental state defence at trial. It seems as if the ICC twisted the Defence arguments to prove something other than what they were submitted for. This is a rather speculative outcome not proven by the evidence, familiar to continentals who are mainly investigating the truth, not evaluating the evidence.[253] But twisting the sayings, not finding the truth, divulges vengeful shadows among the letters of the alphabet.

3.7 *The ICC's Continental Style of Sentencing in* Ongwen

The Rome Statute provides a separate hearing process for sentencing.[254] This process is foreign to classic continental systems. Continental legal tradition provides separate reasoning for sentencing, but not a separate sentencing trial after conviction. Even if the common law court decides to proceed with a decision on sentencing immediately after conviction, the procedure still requires two separate decisions following two separate processes.[255]

Sentencing in common law represents a separate branch of law and is not synonymous with penology. Penology studies punishment theories, the scope and the types of sentences, and it evaluates their application.[256] Sentencing is not synonymous with punishment. Punishment is the response to a crime by an imposition of a sentence by a court. Sentencing is the judicial process that precedes punishment. It determines and decides a just punishment (sentence) for a particular offender who committed a particular crime. Allan Manson argues that to not confuse sentencing with punishment and to comprehend its role, three prominent aspects need to be distinguished: the importance of sentencing in the criminal justice system, its historical perspectives, and its philosophical and political sources.[257]

---

252 ICC-02/04-1/15, May 6, 2021, *supra* note 59 at para 129.

253 D. Sorvatzioti and A. Manson, *supra* note 114 at p. 114.

254 Rome Statute Article 76(2).

255 The judges of the *ad hoc* tribunals abolished the previously adopted separate sentencing trial because they perceived it as a common law jury trial feature. William A. Schabas, *The International Criminal Court: A commentary on the Rome Statute* (Oxford: Oxford University Press, 2016) 1147–1148.

256 David Scott, *Penology* (London: SAGE Publications, 2008) 7.

257 Manson, *supra* note 234 at 1–4.

For the continentals, a single court hearing is provided by the criminal procedure for both conviction and sentencing. It includes evidence regarding both conviction and sentencing before the parties' closing arguments, even though the accused may have pleaded not guilty.

Both common law and continental judiciaries and practitioners might consider the process of each other's system peculiar. The continental process seems prejudicial and unfair from a common law perspective, given that character and predisposition evidence is adduced before the conviction decision.[258] For the continentals, no matter if the accused pleads guilty or not, the trial will take place because a guilty plea does not have the effect of confirming conviction as in common law. However, in the absence of evidence rules in the continental system, any evidence submission, prejudicial or not, is compatible with the principle of free evaluation of evidence and the Court's truth-seeking mandate without typically affecting the fairness of the trial.[259]

Now, modern common law systems, as the Canadian, that have developed sentencing law have been able to focus and refine discussions related to a more individualized punishment and the role and objectives a sentence should serve. This is the reason behind the nuanced approach of the moral blameworthiness concept seen in Canadian sentencing case law.

Judges who are not experienced in their respective national systems with a separate sentencing hearing perceive sentencing as punishment imposition, a mere side effect of conviction. They are not aware of the functionality of the common law sentencing trial. The reason is that the continental criminal procedure code does not permit a separate sentencing trial. Continental judges do not have tools such as pre-sentence reports, victim impact statements, or separate evidence submissions, including expert evidence. Sentencing determination follows a rather fast-track process where both conviction and sentencing evidence have been presented almost simultaneously.[260] They are accustomed to neither addressing and refining legal issues for sentencing determination nor analysing the burden of proof. Given that the continentals, at least in the European Union, were mandated to include the prosecutorial burden of proof beyond a reasonable doubt in their respective systems in 2018, their inexperience with the burden analysis is rather justifiable.[261]

258 D. Sorvatzioti, "Why Sentencing Needs a Separate Trial in the Continental System", in C. Papacharalambous, ed., *The Aims of Punishment* (Baden-Baden, Nomos, 2020) 160–161.

259 Sorvatzioti and Manson, *supra* note 114 at 114.

260 Sorvatzioti, *supra* note 258.

261 Directive (EU) 2016/343, Article 6, *supra* note 15 at 124–128.

Looking at the *Ongwen* sentencing decision, there is a reference to what is required by the ICC legal framework but no analysis to transparently reveal the judicial thinking process of the Court. A common law approach is found in *Ntaganda.* The Sentencing Court addressed the arguments submitted by the parties on specific legal issues through an explicit discussion of the burden and the standard of proof.[262]

In *Ongwen*, the Court rejected the mitigating factors Ongwen's Defences represented with mere reference to its conviction decision and did not analyse, let alone discuss, the burden and the standard of proof for aggravating or mitigating factors. This has been the continental judicial practice for centuries. Only the minority Appeal decision gave a thorough analysis. Whether the approach is continental or common law, or a marriage of the two, depends on the reasoning, how the Court discusses evidence issues, the burden of proof, and whether there is room in sentencing determination for expert evidence to help define a proportional sentence. Defending the effective survival of the ICC, there is no "inescapable dyad" regarding the applicable legal tradition (too common law/too continental). I suggest there is a "right size" approach.[263] The Statute of Rome gives room to introduce a tailor-made, evolving sentencing case law for the ICC. Paradigms from evolved modern legal orders, such as Canada's, may provide a helpful vehicle for those of the judiciary and lawyers from jurisdictions with less applied experience in refining nuanced concepts of harm, moral blameworthiness, and proportionality.

3.8 *Conclusion*

Ongwen's case illustrates the *rotten social background* of abducted indigenous children who become perpetrators.[264] However, there is an asymmetry between justice and desert when sentencing perpetrators of dual status. We can locate the "unjust" in Ongwen's sentence, but we cannot precisely define the "deserved".[265]

There is no indication that the Rome Statute drafters had in mind perpetrators of international crimes being victims of identical crimes. This does not vindicate the ICC to essentially brush off the dual status of Ongwen. However,

262 ICC-01/04-02/06, November 7, 2019 at paras 212, 214–215, 224.

263 D.Robinson, "Inescapable Dyads: Why the International Criminal Court Cannot Win" (2015) *28:2 LJIL* 324–327.

264 *See also* R.L. Aguiling Pangalangan, "Dominic Ongwen and the Rotten Social Background Defense: The Criminal Culpability of Child Soldiers Turned War Criminals" (2018) 33 *AmU.Int'l L.Rev* 626–632.

265 Thorburn & Manson, *supra* note 172, citing Anthony Bottoms when discussing justice and desert, 285.

the *proper* explanation might be their inexperience in complex sentencing considerations. But the obliteration of *Lubanga* regarding the fear and permanent scars of child soldiers is problematic.[266] Given the ICC's imperative to find the truth, here it found only the crimes committed. Consequently, the truth-seeking process failed dramatically.

Ongwen's unique case gave the ICC an enormous opportunity to create a hugely influential precedent for the world's courts. It was the first opportunity for the Court to establish the ICC's sentencing norms for former child soldiers who become perpetrators and are different from non-child soldiers. Sadly, the Trial Court's sentencing decision, confirmed by the Majority of the Appeal Court, is not ground-breaking but instead provides a Westernised continental narrow view, a mechanical check-list sentencing analysis.

The Court did not analyse proportionality, but simply repeated the term several times. Rule 145.2(a)(1) does not impose an *epiclesis* by the Court of the raised defences but a reasoned analysis of how their elements should impact sentencing considerations. Notwithstanding the gravity of the crimes, this Rule does not bend. Despite Ongwen's unique status, his moral blameworthiness was overshadowed by the LRA crimes and Kony's fandom. Conviction is not the ICC's ultimatum, and sentencing should not be a pure side effect of conviction. When the ICC tries cases of non-Western peoples, it is essential to express its understanding and respect for diversity. By addressing cultural, social, and historical aspects of the case and the offender as part of the sentencing reasoning, the ICC performs the balancing process needed for proportionality. *Ongwen* remains a disappointing opportunity for an ICC sentencing precedent.

266 The Court in *Lubanga* explicitly discussed the tremendous permanent effects conscription has on children under 15, paras 37–44, ICC-01/04-01/06-2901, 10-07-2012. Regarding consistency, as one of the fundamental principles of justice, *see* Hola, *supra* note 38, p. 3. *See also* Amicus Curiae *supra* note 97, where consistency, with reference to *Lubanga,* was emphatically mentioned, paras 13,41. *See also,* Drumbl *supra* note 77 at 242.

CHAPTER 6

Legal Traditions' Conflict Indicates the ICC's Evidence Law Avenue

1 Legal Traditions' Antagonism: Tracing the Rome Statute Negotiations

To understand the persistent antagonism between continental and common law traditions within the ICC, we must revisit the Rome Statute negotiations and preparatory works (1999–2000). My primary source, Piragoff's evidence discussions,[1] is frequently cited by ICC judges from continental backgrounds to argue that free evaluation of evidence does not necessitate admissibility rulings.[2] However, Piragoff never stated that free evaluation should be applied within the ICC in the same manner as in continental systems.

Piragoff emphasized that while strict exclusionary rules from common law were impractical for the ICC, the free evaluation of evidence, as understood in continental systems, was not fully endorsed either. In 1999, discussions on the relevance and admissibility of evidence highlighted fundamental differences between the two systems. Common law typically excludes irrelevant or unreliable evidence upfront, ensuring only relevant and reliable evidence is considered. In contrast, continental law admits all evidence and, by free evaluation, assesses its relevance, reliability, and probative value together with weight assessments.

The French proposal that all submitted evidence should be admissible, with its probative value assessed later, faced criticism from common law advocates who argued it could undermine the Rome Statute's compromise by essentially adopting a continental approach without evidence scrutiny. Some continental law proponents also criticized it for not explicitly addressing when or how evidence should be deemed admissible.

1 Donald Piragoff, "Evidence", in Roy S. Lee et al., eds., *The International Criminal Court: Elements of Crimes and Rules of Procedure and Evidence* (Ardsley, NY: Transnational Publishers, 2001) 349–401.

2 *Bemba*, ICC-01/05-01/08, November 19, 2010, at para. 17, with reference to Donald K. Piragoff. The Majority referred to the drafting history of the Rome Statute and the adoption of the civil law "flexibility" instead of the common law "technical formalities".

 | DOI:10.1163/9789004741010_007

The reformulation is encapsulated in Article 69(4). This provision allows a Chamber to freely assess all submitted evidence for relevance and admissibility per Article 64(9). By this way, it was ensured that free evaluation was not interpreted as automatic admissibility. Instead, it allowed the Chamber to either rule on the evidence's relevance before admitting it or admit it and subsequently evaluate its relevance and probative value. Piragoff said that, in both approaches, the reasoning should be "analytical" regardless of the two timeframes the Court would decide to address admissibility.[3] Both sides agreed, and the compromise happened. However, it seems that the compromise included a misunderstanding. No one secured that the continentals had fully grasped the dual mandate of evidence evaluation: one for admissibility and one for weight reasons.

This observation is underscored by the debate over the phrasing "admissibility and relevance" versus "admissibility or relevance". In *Ongwen*, we saw that Judge Tarfusser was talking about admissibility or relevance, while Judge Henderson was talking about admissibility and relevance.[4] The Piragoff records explain it.

In 1999, some continental delegations proposed using the phrase "admissibility and relevance", with admissibility to be considered first instead of "relevance and admissibility". Naturally, with the principle of free evaluation of evidence, continentals seemed eager to continue their tradition of admitting all evidence first and thinking about its relevance later. Incredibly, a genius compromise was reached (Table 6.1).

The compromise was nothing short of diplomatic wizardry: they replaced the initial conjunction "and" with "or". Then, in two cross-referenced Articles

TABLE 6.1 Article 64 para 9 *vs* Article 69 para 4

Article	Content
Article 64 par. 9	The Trial Chamber shall have, inter alia, the power on application of a party or on its own motion *to rule on the admissibility or relevance of evidence.*
Article 69 par. 4	The Court may rule on the relevance or admissibility of any evidence […].

3 Piragoff, *supra* note 1 at p. 354.

4 *Ibid* at 352–354

69(4) and 64(9), "relevance" was put either before or after "admissibility". This masterstroke of diplomacy made everyone feel like they had won. Of course, no one imagined what was lost in the translation of legal traditions or what chaos might ensue in court.

Regarding the debate over reliability, France, supported by many continental delegations, proposed that reliability issues should only be addressed while evaluating the evidence's weight. Of course, ensuring that reliability and credibility were clearly defined as two distinct legal terms in evidence evaluation was overlooked – something the common law understands but the continental system does not.[5] Unsurprisingly, no consensus was reached, and no compromise was achieved. The only acknowledgment of the reliability issue was a footnote in the Discussion Paper stating: "*Consideration needs to be given that in assessing relevance, the Court shall consider reliability*"[6] [emphasis added]. As a result, the concept of reliability remains hidden in the shadows of the Rules, much like a well-kept family secret that only the common law family seem to know.

Nothing in the evidence from the discussion papers indicates that the delegations believed or even compromised on the idea that continental professional judges possess an inherent understanding of evidence issues. This claim by professional judges that the case law repeats appears in ICTY case law and is used by the ICC.[7] But it is not only judges who serve in the ICC

5 *See also* Bertram Schmitt, "Legal diversity at the International Criminal Court: Reflections of a judge". (2021) 19: 3 *JICJ* 495: "The obligation to assess the 'relevance' of each individual piece of evidence is not easy to understand from the perspective of a civil law judge". Judge Bertram also advocates for belief and confidence in professional judges: "Even though there are practical problems in implementing the ICC Statute, it is worth *putting all professional confidence in the judges and to trust* they will faithfully interpret the ICC Statute and the Rules in light of the legislators' compromise formulae, adjusting the procedure accordingly" [emphasis added], *ibid* at 509.

6 Piragoff, *supra* note 1 at 354.

7 ICTY, *Prosecutor* v. *Jejnil Delalic and others,* Decision on the Motion of the Prosecution for the Admissibility of Evidence, January 19, 1998, at para. 20: "While the importance of the rules on admissibility in common law follows from the effect which the admission of a certain piece of evidence might have on a group of lay jurors, the trials before the International Tribunal are conducted before *professional judges, who by virtue of their training and experience are able to consider each piece of evidence which has been admitted and determine its appropriate weight*" [emphasis added]. *See also* Schmitt, *supra* note at 495: "The bench is made up of professional judges who will decide on the guilt of the accused. Because of their professional background and experience, it is not necessary to shield them from unreliable or irrelevant evidence, because they disregard such evidence automatically". *See also*, Richard May, "Evidence before the International Criminal Tribunal for the Former Yugoslavia: An Overview" (1999) 1:4 Int LF D Int at 198–199.

Chambers. According to Article 36(3) of the Rome Statute, the criteria for candidates to serve as judges at the ICC do not state or imply that only judges are eligible. Candidates must have high moral character, impartiality, and integrity and must qualify for the highest judicial offices in their home countries. They must demonstrate competence in criminal law and procedure, with experience as a judge, prosecutor, advocate, or in similar roles. Alternatively, they can have expertise in relevant areas of international law, such as international humanitarian law and human rights law, with extensive professional legal experience. Thus, if the common law judges know what to do, the continentals, by virtue of professionalism, inherit knowledge, what happens with the rest?

The historical account of what happened with the continental and common law delegations until the Rome Statute was signed does not provide solutions to the ICC evidence problems. History emphatically indicates the differences between legal traditions, a fact this book reveals and discusses. Yet, some ICC judges seem to think that merely repeating the word "compromise" and quoting Piragoff out of context will magically advance their national legal perspectives. The so-called compromise was indeed the tool that facilitated the signing of the Rome Statute. The delegations never issued an ultimatum like, "If we don't solve all evidence problems, we won't sign". Instead, they conveniently left these thorny issues for the Court to handle. Now, how the Court sometimes seems to resolve evidence problems by revisiting parts of old negotiations is nothing short of a miraculous, intuitive judicial thinking process.

2 The ICC Expert Review (2020)

An expert report for the ICC was produced in 2020.[8] The experts' task was to make "concrete, achievable and actionable recommendations aimed at enhancing the performance, efficiency and effectiveness of the Court and the Rome Statute system as a whole".[9]

The two cases discussed in this book, *Bemba* and *Gbagbo*, were referred to as "high-profile acquittals" by the Report, which gave them great attention.[10] The Report highlighted the judges' "extensive attachment" to their national

8 ICC, *Independent Expert Review of the International Criminal Court and the Rome Statute System, Final Report* (September 30, 2020), online: https://asp.icc-cpi.int/iccdocs/asp_docs/ASP19/IER-Final-Report-ENG.pdf.

9 *Ibid* at 4, para 1.

10 *Ibid* at para 616.

legal system and insistence to apply their systems within the ICC legal framework.[11] The below finding aligns with this research.

> Many of the experts' interlocutors, including Judges themselves, mentioned the *extensive "attachment" of individual Judges to their domestic legal systems*, whether common law or civil law, as one of the reasons for inconsistent practices between Chambers. The legal framework of the Court indeed is unique and contains elements from both systems, leaving at the same time a certain level of *discretion to a Judge/Chamber to decide on the conduct of the proceedings/hearings*. Rules 69, 64(8), 122(1) or 140(1) are examples where the Judge/Chamber is allowed discretion to decide about the procedural aspects of the case. There seems to be *a tendency to insist on the application of concepts or practices characteristic of or belonging to the national legal framework known to the Judges*. Understanding the hybrid nature of the legal framework and the selection of solutions it offers to best serve the scope of the proceedings, open-mindedness and readiness to learn are the characteristics that each judge should apply in their service at the Court. [emphasis added]

This Report does not reveal what might hinder the judges' understanding of each other's legal tradition regarding the distinction between procedural and evidence law. I will explain that the obstacle is purely related to conceptual misunderstandings. In the continental system, the absence of formal evidence law has made the criminal procedure akin to a "holy book" that exists but is not frequently consulted due to its generalizations. This grants judges significant discretion. Therefore, discussions on judicial discretion regarding evidence evaluation, the prosecutorial burden of proof and the presumption of innocence were never addressed in classic continental case law.

3 (Reasonable) Misunderstandings Echoing Antagonism

In this book, I examined three ICC cases that had attracted criticism. I intended to elucidate the cause of antithetic approaches to evidence evaluation by ICC judges that are prevalent in judgements. The analysis utilized the *sui generis* ICC trial model, the common law model with a focus on

---

11 *Ibid* at para 632 under section: "Conflicts Between Different Legal Systems and Best Practices".

Canada, and the classic continental model. It revealed that the root of the problem lies in the judges' familiar legal traditions and experiences. That became clear through the location of evidence law misunderstandings. However, for the continental legal tradition, the misunderstandings are reasonable. Below, I will show the findings regarding the continental misunderstandings.

3.1 *Misunderstanding One: Evidence Evaluation – How Many Times?*

In common law courts, evidence assessment occurs in two stages. The first is the evidence admission stage, where not all evidence submitted is accepted. At this stage, after the parties' objections, the court determines the relevance and reliability of the evidence, ensuring that its probative value outweighs any prejudicial impact. This is not a process that happens secretly in the judge's head. Admissibility rulings clearly state the relevant assessment.

For admissibility, each piece of evidence must likely prove a matter in issue. If an objection arises regarding an exclusionary rule, the court must determine whether the evidence is necessary and justify the reason. This involves a relevance assessment. The threshold is low and is driven by logic and common sense. Relevance focuses on evidence directly related to what needs to be proven about the crime rather than unnecessary peripheral or background information.

Next, the court assesses the probative value, measuring how likely the evidence will prove its intended point. This threshold is also low and guided by logic and common sense. The court considers the potential prejudicial effect against the accused, ensuring it does not outweigh the probative value, with a threshold driven by logic and case law.

The reliability test follows. In the common law judicial process, there are two levels of reliability. The first level, addressed during the admission stage, is threshold reliability. The second level, considered when weighing the evidence at the deliberation stage, is called ultimate reliability.

According to the adversarial perspective, evidence assessment requires a structured, step-by-step analysis for admissibility reasons. The gatekeeping role of admissibility rulings (before deliberation) is to avoid cluttering the trial record with insufficient and unreliable evidence. This meticulous process ensures that when the court considers the evidence accurately, it understands precisely what each piece of evidence is intended to prove and for what reason.[12]

---

12 *See also* Jennifer L. Mnookin, "Atomism, Holism, and the Judicial Assessment of Evidence" (2013) 60:6 UCLA L Rev 1524, where the author argues that in common law, the

In the decision stage (deliberation), the court evaluates the totality of the admitted evidence to issue a verdict. During this stage, credibility is scrutinized. The court's decision is issued after considering the whole evidence and weighing it against the prosecutorial burden of proof. If the prosecution's evidence outweighs a reasonable doubt, given the totality of the admitted evidence, conviction is the only reasonable outcome.

In classic continental courts, all submitted evidence is admitted without an admissibility assessment. This practice is not due to a preference for a holistic approach but because the principle of free evaluation of evidence has governed continental trials since the aftermath of the French Revolution. The term "holistic" was never part of the Napoleonic Criminal Procedure Code discussions.[13] Continentals avoid engaging in admissibility discussions, which suits their system. However, at the ICC, the evidence offered by the parties requires an admissibility analysis mandated by the Statute. Judges unfamiliar with this common law process struggle to apply it correctly. As seen from the Statute's negotiations and the case law discussed here, particularly in *Bemba*, free evaluation may apply to the admittance of evidence but not to its admissibility assessment whenever the courts decide to do it (either before or during the decision stage). The mistake occurs when some judges, unfamiliar with the admissibility evaluation process, incorrectly perceive the absence of such an evaluation as a holistic approach.[14] This conflation not

---

choice between holistic or atomistic approach to evidence admissibility depends on balancing power between judges and attorneys and judges and juries, and whether the assessment is a low-threshold (relevance) determination favouring admissibility or a high-threshold one like expert evidence evaluation. For a discussion on the atomistic versus holistic approach, see William Twining, *Rethinking Evidence: Exploratory Essays*, 2nd ed. (New York, NY: Cambridge University Press, 2006) 309–311.

13 "Inspired by the American Declaration of Independence in 1776 and the spirit of the Enlightenment, the Declaration of the Rights of Man and of the Citizen of 1789 marked the beginning of a new political era. Since then, it has never ceased to be a reference text. The Fifth Republic explicitly states its attachment to it, citing it in the preamble of its Constitution, and the Constitutional Council recognized its constitutional value in 1971". Elysée. fr. *Declaration of the Rights of Man and of the Citizen*: online https://www.elysee.fr/en/french-presidency/the-declaration-of-the-rights-of-man-and-of-the-citizen; Zacharie Clémence, *The Code D'Instruction Criminelle*, 1808, online: https://www.napoleon.org/en/history-of-the-two-empires/articles/the-code-dinstruction-criminelle-1808/.

14 *See also* the discussion in Yvonne McDermott's "Strengthening the Evaluation of Evidence in International Criminal Trials" (2017) 17 Int Crim Law Rev 688–689; Yvonne McDermott, "Inferential Reasoning and Proof in International Criminal Trials" (2015) 13:3 J. Int. Crim. Just. 528. McDermott argues that the danger of the holistic approach is that it might overlook deficiencies in the evidence, effectively "papering over the cracks". This is rooted in the judges' subjective belief that the defendant is guilty, resem-

only merges the two distinct stages of evidence evaluation in their decisions but also misinterprets evidence terminology, as demonstrated in *Ongwen*. While this misunderstanding might stem from inexperience, it cannot be justified as a holistic evaluation method that reflects the Statute's compromise.

3.2 *Misunderstanding Two: Exclusionary Evidence Rules and the Mastery of Professional Continental Judges*

In all three examined cases, the decisions recurringly referenced the role of common law exclusionary rules designed for jury trials. Additionally, there was a strong emphasis on professional judges in the continental system who do not need exclusionary rules to ensure a fair trial. In the continental system, professional judges are those who complete specialized judicial training after passing exams before assuming their roles.

The misunderstanding in this argument lies in the erroneous belief that exclusionary rules are solely necessary for jury trials. Continental judges need to be made aware that exclusionary rules have fostered the development of a principled (functional) approach to evidence law, which also governs judge-alone trials. They need to understand the structured admissibility process, as evidenced by the Canadian legal system, because they mistakenly believe they inherently possess the requisite knowledge for determining admissibility. In the continental legal tradition, the principle of free evaluation of evidence dictates the trial process from the admission of evidence to the determination of its weight, resulting in judges not engaging in specific admissibility rulings. Due to this principle, discussions on admissibility are not incorporated into their judicial training.

Consequently, they believe the etiology of the existence of exclusionary rules (designed for jury trials) is incompatible with their professional training. As a result, they mistakenly equate the admissibility process with the very existence of exclusionary rules. Thus, they fail to recognize the distinct functions the rules and admissibility process serve within the framework of evidence law. Additionally, they are unaware of the structured path of evidence law, which is profoundly absent from their judicial training curricula due to the predominance of the free evaluation principle.

The need for awareness is highlighted by historical developments in other legal systems. For instance, in 1970, in Canada, the first case that discussed the abandonment of formalism in evidence was a judge-alone trial (not a jury

---

bling the concept of *l'intime conviction,* where the prosecutorial standard of proof beyond a reasonable doubt does not apply.

trial) in a civil case.[15] With this case, the Canadian common law system moved to principled analysis of evidence and left behind the formalistic application of evidence preconditions defined in evidence rules.

When we read the following excerpt along with Canadian evidence case law, it is clear that the continentals' argument that "evidence rules are technical rules for jury trials" is rather stereotypic if not based on a persistent cognitive bias. Probably, it's time for the followers of the stereotype to reconsider their dated argument because:

> The new evidence law, accordingly, is a dynamic model based upon the application of the competing goals of the law of evidence, competing societal interests, and competing Charter rights and values. Gone is the static model of rigid generic rules and exceptions which Courts arbitrarily tried to apply to every fact situation. It is replaced by a set of principles and governing factors to guide the trial judge in making the appropriate ruling in context to best achieve "justice" in the broad sense of the word.[16]

3.3 *Misunderstanding Three: Prosecutorial Burden of Proof Beyond a Reasonable Doubt and Free Evaluation of Evidence, Two in One*

In the classic continental system of free evaluation of evidence, the prosecutorial burden of proof is an untold enigma. However, the Rome Statute has incorporated both the concept of free evaluation and the prosecutorial burden of proof beyond a reasonable doubt. The prosecutorial burden of proof remains steadfast from the inception to the conclusion of the trial, while the free evaluation of evidence is limited to the narrow confines of admissibility and the admittance process.

The classic continental ICC judges' misunderstanding that both principles can coexist leads to fundamental confusion when determining guilt. The continental judges must confront the stark reality, which has been evident since the Statute's negotiations: the prosecutorial burden of proof, which demands unwavering adherence throughout the trial and rigorous analysis for the determination of guilt or innocence, cannot coexist with the uncertainty of the free evaluation of evidence. This is the harsh realization imposed by the Rome Statute.

15 *Ayres v. Venner*, 1970 SCR 608.

16 Sidney N. Lederman, Alan W. Bryant, & Michelle K. Fuerst, *The Law of Evidence in Canada*, 4th ed. (Toronto: LexisNexis Canada, 2014) 97.

3.4 *Misunderstanding Four: Holistic, Atomistic, a Poisoned Chalice, and the Greater Likelihood Standard of Proof*

This perplexing title about evidence quality involves the prosecutorial standard of proof beyond a reasonable doubt and the cost of acquittals. Evidence quality is crucial to securing convictions. In carefully reading the judgments and the interlocutory decisions in the cases of *Bemba and Gbagbo and Blé Goudé*, the evidence was insufficient to support the necessary inference of guilt. If the free evaluation of evidence had been applied in these cases and the prosecutorial burden of proof ignored, the "greater likelihood" standard of proof, suggested by Nancy Combs in her work *Fact-Finding without Facts*, might have led to convictions.[17] However, would this be legally correct according to the Rome Statute?

Nancy Combs challenged the usefulness of the ad hoc tribunals for Rwanda (ICTR) and Sierra Leone (SCSL) in determining "who did what to whom during a mass atrocity".[18] She focused on direct evidence, specifically eyewitness testimonies, and discussed their frailties and the reasons for inconsistencies. She examined the adequacy of inferences regarding evidence quality. Her findings showed a low likelihood of obtaining reliable and objective evidence. However, later in her research, she became more optimistic, suggesting that mechanisms, such as the International, Independent, and Impartial Mechanism (IIIM),[19] could improve evidence quality over time.[20]

Her research is particularly relevant when examining the acquittals by the ICC because it is closely tied to the poor quality of evidence. However, the evidence was predominantly circumstantial in both *Bemba* and *Gbagbo and*

---

17 Nancy A. Combs, *Fact-Finding Without Facts: The Uncertain Evidentiary Foundations of International Criminal Convictions* (Cambridge: Cambridge University Press, 2010).

18 *Ibid* at p. 4.

19 Regarding the IIIM: "On 21 December 2016, the United Nations General Assembly adopted resolution A/71/248, establishing the International, Impartial and Independent Mechanism to assist in the investigation and prosecution of persons responsible for the most serious crimes under International Law committed in the Syrian Arab Republic since March 2011. It is more commonly referred to as 'the Mechanism', or 'the IIIM'." https://iiim.un.org/.

20 With reference to the International, Independent, and Impartial Mechanism (IIIM), along with the Independent Investigative Mechanism for Myanmar (IIIM), Combs said that they show a commitment to quality investigations. Nancy A. Combs, "Evidentiary Deficiencies in International Criminal Law: Tracing the Trajectory from Ignored to Integral to Irrelevant" (2021) 22: 5–6 *ICLR* 845–846. In 2017, Combs criticized the ICC judges for having quite stringent standards for prosecutorial evidence, Nancy A. Combs, "Grave Crimes and Weak Evidence: A Fact-Finding Evolution in International Criminal Law" (2017) 58: 47 Harv Int L J 124.

Ble Goudé acquittals. This is significant because, in circumstantial evidence, the inference of guilt must be the only reasonable inference without other possible alternative inferences. In both cases, even if the facts could be established, the required *mens rea* of the accused should still be proven beyond a reasonable doubt under the Rome Statute.

Combs found the reasonable doubt standard too stringent in the context of mass atrocities, where evidence is often massive with frailties. She questioned whether it is worse to acquit a guilty person than to convict an innocent one, suggesting that it is equally, if not more, serious to let a guilty person escape justice.[21] Consequently, she proposed that the standard of proof should consider the "greater likelihood" that the accused committed atrocities rather than adhering strictly to the "certainty" of the reasonable doubt standard. However, Combs asserted that she did not advocate either for a lower standard of reasonable doubt or speculative convictions.

Similar concerns regarding the acquittal of guilty persons were highlighted in Darryl Robinson's "Another Poisoned Chalice" in *Gbagbo and Ble Goudé*. Robinson criticized the analysis of circumstantial evidence of the no-case-to-answer decision as overly atomistic and advocated for a holistic approach, criticizing the acquittal as unorthodox.[22]

Combs's and Robinson's perspectives present significant issues from an evidence law standpoint. In a criminal trial for atrocities, proving the required *mens rea* ("guilty mind") is essential for securing a conviction, in addition to establishing the *actus reus* ("criminal act"). If the standard of proof beyond a reasonable doubt is diluted to a vague standard (the greater likelihood standard), or if the prosecutorial burden of proof vanishes by adopting a holistic approach resembling the free evaluation of evidence, the integrity of the Rome Statute and the guarantee of a fair trial are at risk. In 2025, can we afford such a legal deconstruction for the sake of achieving a few more convictions?

---

21 Combs, *supra* note 17 at 345, 358. Combs stated that "international acquittals" affect victims and damage the reputation of criminal justice. However, Judge Meron argued that it is incorrect to assess acquittals based on victims' expectations as a measure of international criminal justice's failure to deliver justice. *See* Theodor Meron, *Standing Up for Justice: The Challenges of Trying Atrocity Crimes* (Oxford: Oxford University Press, 2021) 36–37.

22 Darryl Robinson, "The Other Poisoned Chalice: Unprecedented Evidentiary Standards in the Gbagbo Case?" (Part 1), Ejitalk.org, online https://www.ejiltalk.org/the-other-poisoned-chalice-unprecedented-evidentiary-standards-in-the-gbagbo-case-part-1/, November 5, 2019; "The Other Poisoned Chalice: Unprecedented Evidentiary Standards in the Gbagbo Case?" (Part 2), November 6, 2019; "The Other Poisoned Chalice: Unprecedented Evidentiary Standards in the Gbagbo Case? (Part 3)", November 6, 2019.

Will our legal civilization be able to justify the loss of the beyond-a-reasonable-doubt standard in criminal trials in exchange for potentially unsafe convictions?

In light of similar concerns, Judge Eboe-Osuji criticized using conviction counts as a measure of ICC success, arguing that it pressures the Court towards unjust "show trials".[23] He emphasized that acquittals are equally vital for justice, echoing Robert H. Jackson's sentiment at Nuremberg that a fair trial means acquittal if guilt isn't proven beyond doubt. He stated:[24]

> It is wrong to put the Court under pressure to produce convictions in every case, lest the Court is seen as "not performing". As a judge of this Court, I have felt that pressure. It is disappointing. The attitude needs to stop.

Judge Theodor Meron said that the criticism of acquittals is painful. However, they do not resemble the failure of international criminal justice. He emphatically said:[25]

> A true failure of international criminal justice would be if international courts were to convict an individual where there is an inadequate evidentiary or legal basis to do so.

Interestingly, Combs referenced Laudan and the historical context in which the reasonable doubt standard was established, mainly due to the only available penalty of death for felonies. Laury Laudan has questioned whether a single standard like beyond a reasonable doubt is suitable for all crimes since varied punishments apply, suggesting that uniform application of the reasonable doubt standard may not be suitable.[26] However, despite death penalties in continental countries, the beyond-a-reasonable doubt standard never took root in the classic continental tradition. The common law prosecutorial burden of proof has effectively existed for centuries, and evidence law

23 ICC-02/11-01/15-1400-Anx1-Corr-Red 09-04-2021, Appeal Judgment –March 31, 2021 – Separate Concurring Opinion – Judge Eboe-Osuji, at para 44.

24 Judge Chile Eboe-Osuji, *President International Criminal Court, Valedictory Statement and End of Mandate Overview. Submitted to the 19th Session of the Assembly of States Parties to the Rome Statute*, December 14, 2020, online https://www.icc-cpi.int/sites/default/files/itemsDocuments/201214-icc-president-speech-asp.pdf, at p. 13.

25 Theodor Meron, *supra* note 21 at p. 25.

26 Larry Laudan, *Truth, Error, and Criminal Law: An Essay in Legal Epistemology* (Cambridge: Cambridge University Press, 2006) 55.

has evolved to safeguard the presumption of innocence, our remaining "golden thread".[27] Removing or even selectively applying the beyond-a-reasonable doubt standard in criminal trials is attacking the presumption of innocence, deliriously demolishing the backbone of our legal civilization.

The misunderstanding of holistic evidence evaluation lies in two things: First, the concept of holistic evidence evaluation is not recognized legally in the terminology of evidence rules and law. Second, the proponents of free evaluation confuse the free evaluation evidence with applying a supposed holistic approach to evidence. This confusion was evident in the above analysed ICC case law . Such misinterpretations lead to the mistaken disregard of the Rome Statute's mandate for the prosecutorial standard of proof beyond a reasonable doubt.

Philosophical terms regarding evidence evaluation may not be helpful for the ICC judges. The fictitious legal distinction between atomistic and holistic approaches creates a true legal dichotomy that results in a sharp, legally unsubstantial antithesis. Both traditions evaluate the whole of evidence: the continental system without the prosecutorial standard and the common law system with it. In legal terms, it is unclear what the evaluation method – holistic or atomistic – actually provides. If it is self-evident, it is genuinely problematic for the ICC's evidence law issues. It is clear, however, that the Rome Statute left it to the Court's discretion to freely admit evidence, not to freely evaluate its admission. Instead, it provided guidelines of relevance, probative value, and prejudice. According to the Statute, during deliberation, the prosecutorial burden steers the process, while free evaluation drifts aimlessly on open seas.

4 Don't Fear, Mr Precedent, Evidence Law Is Alive and Kicking

According to Article 21(2) of the Rome Statute, the ICC may apply principles and rules of law as interpreted in its previous decisions, leading to a non-binding precedent approach. However, the ICC decisions consistently refer to ICC case law. Sometimes, they also refer to case law from ad hoc tribunals and, frequently, to case law issued by common law courts, as explicitly seen in the *Gbagbo* and *Ongwen* cases. The same approach is seen in the parties' briefs. Therefore, even if precedent is not binding, it is guiding.

---

27 *Woolmington v DPP*, [1935] AC 462.

The problem arises when interpretations about evidence issues try to advance one of the two legal cultures over the other, leading to antithetical case law, as seen in the *Bemba* and *Gbagbo* evidence discussions. While this is inherently problematic, it certainly does not help the Court's evolution. Above all, it reveals the persistence of legal traditions to monopolize at any cost.

When we talk about the prosecutorial burden of proof, the continental persistence of free evaluation of evidence is contrary to the Rome Statute. Yet, it persists. When we talk about admissibility rulings, despite the Court's ability to freely decide when to issue them, it must do so properly. Again, the persistence in the free evaluation autocracy is not permitted by the Rome Statute. Yet, some judges believe otherwise, and their need to validate their belief makes case law chaotic and inconsistent.

To truly advance the discussion on ICC evidence law, we must begin by using legal terms that resonate with all judges, parties, and participants. A mutual understanding of legal terminology is essential for consistently applying and interpreting the Rules. Imagine a framework enriched with explanations and case law examples from jurisdictions that have spent years refining their approaches to similar evidence problems.

By building a robust body of case law on evidence law issues, we can effectively tackle the unique evidence difficulties arising in the wake of atrocities. Moreover, consistency will be ensured.[28] This endeavour will not only address evidence problems but also offer solutions drawn from extensive experience. Picture a legal landscape where the ICC, informed by decades of jurisprudence, develops a coherent and functional approach to evidence law, ensuring fairness.

With the Rome Statute firmly in place, achieving this today is undeniable progress. Nonetheless, the challenges range from harmonizing diverse legal traditions to ensuring uniform interpretation and application of evidence law. However, the Rome Statute's secure foundation offers a unique opportunity to build a comprehensive and sophisticated evidence law for the ICC. The ICC cannot only meet this challenge but it can also excel, fostering an evidence law paradigm for international criminal tribunals.

The 2020 Report advanced the continuing development of judges to enhance collegiality.[29] It said that the ICC's two programmes, the Induction

28 See the discussion of Judge Meron regarding the common law-trained judges who are interested in referring to solutions given by precedents and the continental trained judges who "situate their decision in a general theory of law whether international or not". Meron *supra* note 21 at 147.

29 ICC Expert Report *supra* note 8 at paras 414–421.

Programme and the Programme of Continuing Professional Development (CPD), should "inspire in the Judges a sense *that this is their Court*, to promote a spirit of mutual understanding of and respect for Judges and staff from a variety of cultures" [emphasis added]. It is crucial, though, for all judges, parties and participants to ensure mutual legal understanding of evidence law. While plurality is interesting and attractive in an international legal setting, evidence law requires concrete and standardized legal terminology to solve serious problems in a principled way. This approach will save enormous time in trials. Understanding legal terms and their application is the starting point for evidence law discussions.

Waiting for harmonization to happen on its own is hope deferred:

> A hungry jackdaw had perched on a fig tree,
> and finding that the figs were still hard was waiting for them to ripen.
> A fox who noticed that it had become a fixture there inquired the reason,
> and, on being told, said: it is a mistake to let hope engross your attention.
> Hope can only delude you; it will never fill your stomach.[30]

5 Summing Up or Growing Up?

To conclude this exploration of evidence law and the ICC, it is crucial to dispel persistent stereotypes. One misconception is that evidence rules are purely technical, leaving judges no discretion to solve evidence law problems. Another is that common law, being precedent-bound, prevents judges from making case-by-case decisions and, therefore, their discretion is limited. Another is the assumption that professional judges of the continental tradition inherently understand evidence law.

Firstly, evidence is not synonymous with evidence law. Secondly, evidence rules are not the entirety of evidence law. Thirdly, evidence law terms cannot be reduced to sociological or common-sense daily interpretations. In continental legal systems where evidence law is not formally studied and evolved, judges must rely on personal understandings, contrasting sharply with the structured approach of common law judges.

In this book, I am not advocating for transplanting any national legal tradition into the ICC. Instead, I propose the development of a bespoke ICC evi-

30 Aesop, Fables of Aesop (London: Penguin Classics, 1964) 73.

dence law. This will address the ICC's specific evidentiary problems, which have historically led to contradictions, deepening the divide between common law and continental law traditions.

In matters as serious as those handled by the ICC, there is no room for divisive views driven by stubbornness and ego. The ICC's survival and efficacy depend on bridging these gaps through cooperation and understanding. Whether we, the continentals, like it or not, common law systems have made enormous strides to safeguard a principled approach to evidence law. Uninformed hostility towards evolved legal systems reflects voluntary blindness. Informed hostility is unintelligence.

Continental legal traditions have thrived in countries where philosophy and great ideas have shaped global thinking. Our philosophical heritage empowers us to embrace and learn from the common law principled approach to evidence law. This will contribute to the ICC's effective sustainability and ensure justice is done and seen. By developing a system of evidence law tailored to the ICC's needs, our Court will mature.

> No organic law can ever be framed with a provision specifically applicable to every question which may occur in practical administration. No foresight can anticipate nor any document of reasonable length contain express provisions for all possible questions.[31]

Olympian Zeus spoke among the immortals and said:

> Look you now, how ready mortals are to blame the gods. It is from us; they say that evils come, but they, even of themselves, through their own blind folly, have sorrows beyond that which is ordained.
>
> HOMER, *ODYSSEY* 1, 35

---

31 First Inaugural Address of President Lincoln, March 4, 1861 (Gilder Lehrman Collection) 6: online https://www.gilderlehrman.org/sites/default/files/inline-pdfs/01264_0.pdf.

Bibliography

International Materials

Directive (EU) 2016/343, 2016.
Paris Declaration on the Effectiveness of International Criminal Justice | ENM, 2017.
Rome Statute of the International Criminal Court, 1998.
Rules of Procedure and Evidence | International Criminal Court.
Treaty on the Functioning of the European Union.

Secondary Sources: Books

Alfaro, Ricardo J. "Continental Principles of International Intercourse", in *Proceedings of the American Society of International Law at Its Annual Meeting (1921–1969)*, vol 35, 1941, Cambridge University Press, 1–8.

Allen, Tim, *Trial Justice: The International Criminal Court and the Lord's Resistance Army* (London, New York: Zed Books, 2006).

Allen, Tim & Koen Vlassenroot, eds, *The Lord's Resistance Army. Myth and Reality*, (London, New York: Zed Books, 2010).

Ambos, Kai et al., *Core Concepts in Criminal Law and Criminal Justice: Anglo-German Dialogues* (Cambridge: Cambridge University Press, 2020).

Atkinson, Ronald R, *The Roots of Ethnicity: The Origins of the Acholi of Uganda Before 1800* (Philadelphia: University of Pennsylvania Press, 1994).

Baetens, Freya, *Identity and Diversity on the International Bench: Who is the Judge?*, first edition. ed, International courts and tribunals series (Oxford: Oxford University Press, 2020).

Baines, Erin, *Buried in the Heart: Women, Complex Victimhood and the War in Northern Uganda*, Cambridge Studies in Law and Society (Cambridge: Cambridge University Press, 2016).

Baker, John, *Introduction to English Legal History*, 5th ed (Oxford, New York: Oxford University Press, 2019).

Bassiouni, M Cherif, *The Statute of the International Criminal Court: A Documentary History* (Leiden: Brill Nijhoff, 1999).

Bassiouni, M Cherif & William A Schabas, *The Legislative History of the International Criminal Court* (*2 vols.*) 2nd revised ed. (Leiden: Brill, 2016).

Bassiouni, M Cherif & William A Schabas, *The Legislative History of the International Criminal Court: Introduction, Analysis, and Integrated Text* (*3 vols*) (Leiden: Brill, 2021).

Behrend, Heike, *Alice Lakwena and the Holy Spirits: War in Northern Uganda, 1985–97* (Athens: Ohio University Press, 2000).

Bergsmo, Morten, Wui Ling Cheah, Antonio Angotti, *Old Evidence and Core International Crimes: Second Edition*, 2nd ed (Brussels: Torkel Opsahl Academic Epublisher, 2024).

Boas, Gideon, *International Criminal Law: Developments in the Case Law of the ICTY* (Leiden: Martinus Nijhoff Publishers, 2003).

Brady, Helen, "The System of Evidence in the Statute of the International Criminal Court", in Flavia Lattanzi & William S. Schabas, eds, *Essays on the Rome Statute of the International Criminal Court*, Vol.1 (Ripa Fagnamo Alto: Editrice Il Sirente,1999) 279–302.

Branch, Adam, "Exploring the Roots of LRA Violence: Political Crisis and Ethnic Politics in Acholiland", in Tim Allen & Koen Vlassenroot, eds, *The Lord's Resistance Army: myth and reality* (New York: Zed Books, 2010).

Broun, Kenneth S et al, eds, *McCormick on Evidence*, 5th ed (St. Paul Minnesota: West Group, 1999).

Bouwknegt, Thijs B, "The International Criminal Trial Record as Historical Source", in Nanci Adler, ed, *Understanding the Age of Transitional Justice* (New Brunswick, NJ, US: Rutgers University Press, 2018).

Carter, Linda & Fausto Pocar, *International Criminal Procedure: The Interface of Civil Law and Common Law Legal Systems* (Cheltenham, Gloucestershire: Edward Elgar Publishing, 2013).

Cassese, Antonio, *Cassese's International Criminal Law* (Oxford: Oxford University Press, 2013).

Cassese, Antonio, *Realizing Utopia: The Future of International Law* (OUP Oxford, 2012).

Cassese, Antonio, *The Human Dimension of International Law: Selected Papers of Antonio Cassese* (OUP Oxford, 2008).

Clooney, Amal & Philippa Webb, *The Right to a Fair Trial in International Law* (New York: Oxford University Press, 2021).

Coleman, Michelle, *The Presumption of Innocence in International Human Rights and Criminal Law*, 1st ed (Milton Park, Abingdon, Oxon ; New York, NY: Routledge, 2021).

Combs, Nancy A, *Fact-Finding without Facts: The Uncertain Evidentiary Foundations of International Criminal Convictions* (Cambridge: Cambridge University Press, 2010).

Cook, Nicolas, *Côte d'Ivoire Post-Gbagbo: Crisis Recovery* (Washington, D.C.: Congressional Research Service, 2011).

Cross, Ruper, *Evidence*, 5th ed (London: Butterworth, 1958).

Cryer, Robert, *An Introduction to International Criminal Law and Procedure*, 4th ed (Cambridge: Cambridge University Press, 2019).

Cunliffe, Emma, "A new Canadian Paradigm? Judicial Gatekeeping and the Reliability of Expert Evidence", in Paul Roberts & Michael Stockdale, eds., *Forensic Science*

Evidence and Expert Witness Testimony (Cheltenham: Edward Elgar Publishing, 2018) 310–332.

Daddieh, Cyril K, *Historical Dictionary of Cote d'Ivoire* (*The Ivory Coast*), 3rd ed (Lanham, MD, USA: Rowman & Littlefield, 2016).

Damaška, Mirjan, *Evaluation of Evidence: Pre-Modern and Modern Approaches* (Cambridge: Cambridge University Press, 2018).

Damaška, Mirjan, *The Faces of Justice and State Authority* (New Haven: Yale University Press, 1986).

Damaška, Mirjan R et al., eds, *Crime, Procedure and Evidence in a Comparative and International Context: Essays in Honour of Professor Mirjan Damaška* (Oxford; Portland, Or: Hart Publishers, 2008).

Damaška, Mirjan, *Evidence Law Adrift* (New Haven: Yale University Press, 1997).

Damaška, Mirjan, *The Faces of Justice and State Authority: a Comparative Approach to the Legal Process* (New Haven: Yale University Press, 1986).

D'Ascoli, Silvia, *Sentencing in International Criminal Law: The UN Ad Hoc Tribunals and Future Perspectives for the ICC*, Studies in international and comparative criminal law ; vol 6 (Oxford: Hart, 2011).

DeGuzman, Margaret M. "Is the ICC Targeting Africa Inappropriately? A Moral, Legal, and Sociological Assessment" Contemporary Issues Facing the International (Leiden, the Netherlands: Brill) 333-337.

Delisle, Ronald Joseph et al, *Evidence: Principles and Problems* (Toronto: Carswell, 1989).

Delmas-Marty, Mireille & John R Spencer, *European Criminal Procedures* (Cambridge: Cambridge University Press, 2002).

Descartes, René, *Discourse on the Method of Rightly Conducting One's Reason and of Seeking Truth in the Sciences*, translated by John Veitch (1993).

Dolan, Chris, *Social Torture: The Case of Northern Uganda, 1986–2006* (New York, NY: Berghahm Books, 2009).

Donovan, James M, *Juries and the Transformation of Criminal Justice in France in the Nineteenth and Twentieth Centuries* (Chapel Hill: University of North Carolina Press, 2010).

Drumbl, Mark A, *Atrocity, Punishment, and International Law* (Cambridge: Cambridge University Press, 2007).

Drumbl, Mark A, *Reimagining Child Soldiers in International Law and Policy* (New York: Oxford University Press, USA, 2012).

Drumbl, Mark A, *Reimagining Child Soldiers in International Law and Policy* (Oxford: Oxford University Press, 2012).

Drumbl, Mark A & Jastine C Barrett, *Research Handbook on Child Soldiers* (Cheltham: Edward Elgar Publishing, 2019).

Engdahl, Ola & Pål Wrange, eds, *Law at War: The Law as it Was and the Law as it Should Be.* (Leiden: Brill Nijhoff, 2009).

Esmein, Adhémar, *A History of Continental Criminal Procedure: With Special Reference to France* (Clark, NJ: The Lawbook Exchange, 2000).

Ferencz, Benjamin, "The Experience of Nuremberg", in Dina Shelton, ed, *International Crimes, Peace, and Human Rights: The Role of the International Criminal Court* (Leiden: Brill Nijhoff, 2000) 3.

Frase, Richard S., "Prior-Conviction Sentencing Enhancements: Rationales and Limits Based on Retributive and Utilitarian Proportionality Principles and Social Equality Goals", in J. Roberts & A von Hirsch, eds, *Previous Convictions at Sentencing: Theoretical and Applied Perspectives* (Oxford: Hart Publishing, 2010) 117.

Frase, Richard S, "Sentencing and Comparative Theory", (3 June 2010) in John Jackson, Máximo Langer & Peter Tillers, eds., Crime, Procedure and Evidence in a Comparative and International Context: Essays in Honour of Professor Mirjan Damaska (Oxford: Hart Publishing, 2008), Minnesota Legal Studies Research Paper No. 10–32, Available at SSRN: https://ssrn.com/abstract=1619926.

Fraser, Julie, Brianne McGonigle Leyh, & Edward Elgar Publishing, *Intersections of law and culture at the international criminal court* (Northampton: Edward Elgar Publishing, 2020).

Friedman, Lawrence M, *American Law in the Twentieth Century* (Yale University Press, 2002).

Friman, Håkan, "International Criminal Procedures: Trials and Appeals Procedures", in William A. Schabas & Nadia Bernaz, eds, 279 *Routledge Handbook of International Criminal Law* (Abingdon, Oxon: Routledge, 2011) 279.

Frindéthié, K Martial, *From Lumumba to Gbagbo: Africa in the Eddy of the Euro-American Quest for Exceptionalism* (Jefferson, NC: McFarland, 2016).

Glanert, Simone, *Comparative Law-Engaging Translation* (Abingdon, Oxon: Routledge, 2014).

Glenn, Patrick H, *Legal Traditions of the World: Sustainable Diversity in Law.* (New York, NY: Oxford University Press, 2014).

Gless, Sabine & Thomas Richter, eds, *Do Exclusionary Rules Ensure a Fair Trial?: A Comparative Perspective on Evidentiary Rules* (Chams: Springer Open, 2019).

Gnaka, Lagoke, *Laurent Gbagbo's Trial and the Indictment of the International Criminal Court* (Wilmington: Vernon Press, 2024).

Green, Thomas A, *Verdict According to Conscience: Perspectives on the English criminal trial jury 1200–1800* (Chicago: University of Chicago Press, 1985).

Grover, Sonja C, *Child Soldier Victims of Genocidal Forcible Transfer: Exonerating Child Soldiers Charged With Grave Conflict-related International Crimes* (Cham: Springer Science & Business Media, 2012).

Gunn, John & Paul Mevis, "Adversarial Versus Inquisitorial Systems of Trial and Investigation in Criminal Procedure", in Kris Goethals, ed, *Forensic Psychiatry and Psychology in Europe: A Cross-Border Study Guide 1* (Cham: Sprinter, 2018) 3–17.

Hafetz, Jonathan, *Punishing Atrocities Through a Fair Trial: International Criminal Law from Nuremberg to the Age of Global Terrorism* (Cambridge: Cambridge University Press, 2018).

Hampel, George, "Dealing with Expert Evidence", in Elizabeth King et al, eds, *Victim Advocacy before the International Criminal Court* (Cham: Springer International Publishing, 2022) 141.

Hara, Fabienne & Gilles Yabi, "Côte D'ivoire, 2002–2011", in Jane Boulden, *Responding to Conflict in Africa: The United Nations and Regional Organizations* (New York, NY: Palgrave Macmillan, 2013) 145–175.

Harhoff, Frederik, "Sense and Sensibility in Sentencing-Taking stock of international criminal punishment", in Ola Engdahl & Pal Wrange, eds, *Law at War: The Law as it Was and the Law as it Should Be* (Leiden, Brill Nijhoff) 133–152.

Heller, Kevin et al, eds, *The Oxford Handbook of International Criminal Law*, 1st ed (Oxford: Oxford University Press, 2020).

Heller, Kevin Jon & Markus Dubber, *The Handbook of Comparative Criminal Law* (Redwood City: Stanford University Press, 2020).

Hirschl, Ran, *Comparative matters: the renaissance of comparative constitutional law* (Oxford: Oxford University Press, 2014).

Ho, Hock Lai, *A Philosophy of Evidence Law: Justice in the Search for Truth* (New York: Oxford University Press, 2008).

Hogue, Arthur R, *Origins of the Common Law* (Indianapolis: Liberty Fund, 1986).

Holá, Barbora & Thijs B Bouwknegt, "Child Soldiers in International Courtrooms: Unqualified Perpetrators, erratic Witnesses and Irreparable Victims?", in Mark A Drumbl & Jastine C Barrett (eds), *Research Handbook on Child Soldiers* (Edward Elgar Publishing, 2019) 350–373.

Honwana, Alcinda, *Child Soldiers in Africa* (Philadelphia: University of Pennsylvania Press. 2011).

Hudson, John, *The Formation of the English Common Law: Law and Society in England from King Alfred to Magna Carta*, 2nd edition ed (Abingdon, Oxon ; New York, NY: Routledge, 2017).

Hughes, Edel, Ramesh Thakur & William A Schabas, *Atrocities and International Accountability* (UN Publications, 2007).

Human Rights Watch, *World Report 2005* (New York, NY: Human Rights Watch, 2005).

Karton, Joshua, "Lessons from International Uniform Law", in Jean E. Kalicki & Anna Joubin-Bret, *Reshaping the Investor-State Dispute Settlement System* (Leiden: Brill Nijhoff, 2015) 48–90.

Kaushik, Nikila & Steven Freeland, "Crimes Committed by Child Soldiers: an Argument for Coherence", in Mark Drumbl & Jastine C. Barrett, eds, *Research Handbook on Child Soldiers* (Chelteham, Edward Elgar Publishing, 2019).

Kersten, Mark, *Justice in Conflict: The Effects of the International Criminal Court's Interventions on Ending Wars and Building Peace* (Oxford: Oxford University Press, 2016).

Kersten, Mark, *The Life and Trials of Dominic Ongwen: A JiC Symposium* (Toronto: Newstex, 2021).

Khan, Karim A A, Caroline Buisman & Christopher Gosnell, eds, *Principles of Evidence in International Criminal Justice* (Oxford ; New York: Oxford University Press, 2010).

Klamberg, Mark, *Evidence in International Criminal Trials: Confronting Legal Gaps and the Reconstruction of Disputed Events* (Leiden: Martinus Nijhoff Publishers, 2013).

Kyemba, Henry, *State of Blood: The Inside Story of Idi Amin*, 1st ed (New York, NY: Putnam Pub Group, 1977).

Lagoké, Gnaka, *Laurent Gbagbo's Trial and the Indictment of the International Criminal Court: A Pan-African Victory* (Wilmington, DE: Vernon Press, 2023).

Langbein, John H, *The Origins of Adversary Criminal Trial* (Oxford: Oxford University Press, 2003).

Langbein, John H, *Torture and the Law of Proof: Europe and England in the Ancien Régime* (Chicago: University of Chicago Press, 2012).

Langbein, John H, Renee Lettow Lerner & Bruce P Smith, *History of the Common Law: The Development of Anglo-American Legal Institutions*, 2nd ed (Austin : New York, NY: Aspen Publishers, 2009).

Langer, Máximo, "The Long Shadow of the Adversarial and Inquisitorial Categories", in Markus D. Dubber & Tatiana Höernle, eds, *Oxford Handbook of International Law* (Oxford: Oxford University Press, 2014).

Laudan, Larry, *Truth, Error, and Criminal law: An Essay in Legal Epistemology*, Cambridge Studies in Philosophy and Law (Cambridge: Cambridge University Press, 2006).

Lederman, Sidney N, *The Law of Evidence in Canada*, 4th ed (Markham, Ont: LexisNexis, 2014).

Lederman, Sidney N, Michelle K Fuerst & Hamish Stewart, *Sopinka, Lederman & Bryant: The Law of Evidence in Canada* (Markham, Ont: LexisNexis Canada, 2022).

Lee, Roy S, Project on International Courts and Tribunals, & United Nations Institute for Training and Research, *The International Criminal Court: the making of the Rome Statute–issues, negotiations, results* (The Hague; Boston: Kluwer Law International, 1999).

Lee, Roy S. K. & Håkan Friman, eds, *The International Criminal Court: Elements of Crimes and Rules of Procedure and Evidence* (Ardsley, NY: Transnational Publishers, 2001).

Legrand, Pierre, *Negative Comparative Law: A Strong Programme for Weak Thought* (Cambridge: Cambridge University Press, 2022).

Legrand, Pierre & Roderick Munday, *Comparative Legal Studies: Traditions and Transitions* (Cambridge: Cambridge University Press, 2003).

Manson, Allan et al, *Sentencing and Penal Policy in Canada: Cases, Materials, and Commentary*, 3rd ed (Toronto: Emond Publishing, 2016).

Manson, Allan et al., *The Law of Sentencing* (Toronto: Irvin Law, 2001).

Mayerfeld, Jamie, *Suffering and Moral Responsibility*, Oxford Ethics Series (New York, NY: Oxford University Press, USA, 2002).

McDermott, Yvonne, *Fairness in International Criminal Trials* (Oxford: Oxford University Press, 2016).

McDermott, Yvonne, "Rights in Reverse: A Critical Analysis of Fair Trial Rights Under International Criminal Law", in William A. Schabas, Yvonne McDermott & Niamh Hayes, eds., *The Ashgate Research Companion to International Criminal Law: Critical Perspectives*, (Aldershot: Ashgate, 2012).

Minow, Martha & Todd Rakoff, "Is the 'Reasonable Person' a Reasonable Standard in a Multicultural World?", in Austin Sarat et al, eds, *Everyday Practices and Trouble Cases* Fundamental Series in Law and Society Research (Illinois: Northwestern University Press and The American Bar Association, 1998) 40.

Meron, Theodor, *Standing Up for Justice: The Challenges of Trying Atrocity Crimes* (Oxford: Oxford University Press, 2021).

Mosler, Hermann, *The International Society as a Legal Community* (Leiden: Brill, 1980).

Mousourakis, George, *Comparative Law and Legal Traditions* (Cham: Springer, 2019).

Murphy, Peter, ed, *Evidence, Proof, and Facts: A Book of Sources* (Oxford ; New York: Oxford University Press, 2003).

Mwenda, Andrew, "Uganda's politics of foreign aid and violent conflict: the political uses of the LRA rebellion", in Tim Allen & Koen Vlassenroot, eds, *The Lord's Resistance Army. Myth and Reality*, (London, New York: Zed Books, 2010) 45.

Nelken, David & Johannes Feest, *Adapting Legal Cultures* (London: Bloomsbury Publishing, 2001).

Nistor, Adina-Loredana, Andrew Merrylees, & Barbora Holá, "Spellbound at the ICC: the intersection of spirituality and international criminal law", in Julie Fraser & Brianne McGonigle Leyh ed, *Intersections of Law and Culture at the International Criminal Court* (Cheltenham: Edward Elgar Publishing, 2020).

Nortje, Windell & Noëlle Quénivet, *Child Soldiers and the Defence of Duress under International Criminal Law* (Cham: Palgrave Macmillan, 2021), online: <http://repository.uwc.ac.za/xmlui/handle/10566/6214>.

Nortje, Windell & Noëlle Quénivet, "Limits of, and Exclusions from, the Defence of Duress", in *Child Soldiers and the Defence of Duress under International Criminal Law* (Cham: Springer, 2020) 87.

Nortje, Windell & Noëlle Quénivet, "The Application of the Requirements of Duress to Child Soldiers", in *Child Soldiers and the Defence of Duress under International Criminal Law* (Cham: Springer, 2020) 49.

Ohlin, Jens, "Proportional Sentences at the ICTY", in Bert Swart et al., ed, *The Legacy of the International Criminal Tribunal for the Former Yugoslavia* (Oxford: Oxford University Press, 2011).

Okello, Lucima, ed, *Protracted Conflict, Elusive Peace: Initiatives to End the Violence in Northern Uganda* (London: Conciliation Resources, 2002).

Oloya, Opiyo, *Child to Soldier: Stories from Joseph Kony's Lord's Resistance Army* (Toronto: University of Toronto Press, 2013).

Orie, Alphons, "Accusatorial V. Inquisitorial Approach in International Criminal Proceedings Prior to the Establishment of the ICC and in the Proceedings Before the ICC", in Antonio Cassese, Paola Gaeta & RWD John Jones, eds, *The Rome Statute of the International Criminal Court: a commentary* (Oxford: Oxford University Press, 2002) 1439.

Paciocco, David M, Palma Paciocco & Lee Stuesser, *The Law of Evidence*, 8th ed (Toronto: Irwin Law Inc., 2020).

Peat, Daniel, *Comparative Reasoning in International Courts and Tribunals*, Cambridge Studies in International and Comparative Law (Cambridge: Cambridge University Press, 2019).

Piragoff Donald, "Evidence", in Richard S. K. Lee & Håkan Friman, *The International Criminal Court : Elements of Crimes and Rules of Procedure and Evidence* (Ardsley, NY: Transnational Publishers, 2001) 349–401.

Posner, Richard A, *How Judges Think* (Cambridge, MA: Harvard University Press, 2010).

Posner, Richard A, *Law, Pragmatism, and Democracy* (Cambridge, MA: Harvard University Press, 2009).

Posner, Richard A, *Overcoming Law* (Cambridge, MA: Harvard University Press, 1995).

Reid, Richard J, *A History of Modern Uganda* (Cambridge: Cambridge University Press, 2017).

Reid, Richard J, *Frontiers of Violence in North-East Africa: Genealogies of Conflict since c.1800*, Zones of Violence (Oxford: Oxford University Press, 2011).

Roberts, Julian V, *Mitigation and Aggravation at Sentencing* (Cambridge: Cambridge University Press, 2011).

Roberts, Paul & Adrian Zuckerman, *Roberts & Zuckerman's Criminal Evidence* (Oxford: Oxford University Press, 2022).

Robinson, Darryl, *Justice in Extreme Cases: Criminal Law Theory Meets International Criminal Law* (Cambridge: Cambridge University Press, 2020).

Roht-Arriaza, Naomi & Javier Mariezcurrena, *Transitional Justice in the Twenty-First Century: Beyond Truth versus Justice* (Cambridge: Cambridge University Press, 2006).

Roht-Arriaza, Naomi & Javier Mariezcurrena, eds, *Transitional Justice in the Twenty-First Century: Beyond Truth versus Justice* (Cambridge: Cambridge University Press, 2006).

Roumier, William, *L'Avenir Du Jury Criminel* (Paris: LGDJ, 2003).

Ryberg, Jesper, Julian V Roberts & Jan Willem de Keijser, *Sentencing Multiple Crimes* (Oxford: Oxford University Press, 2018).

Schabas, William, *Unimaginable Atrocities: Justice, Politics, and Rights at the War Crimes Tribunals* (Oxford: Oxford University Press, 2012).

Schabas, William A, *An Introduction to the International Criminal Court* (Cambridge: Cambridge University Press, 2011).

Schabas, William A, *The UN International Criminal Tribunals: The Former Yugoslavia, Rwanda and Sierra Leone* (Cambridge: Cambridge University Press, 2006).

Shapiro, Barbara J, *A culture of Fact: England, 1550–1720* (Ithaca: Cornell University Press, 2000).

Sluiter, G et al, *International Criminal Procedure: Principles and Rules* (Oxford: Oxford University Press, 2013).

Stahn, Carsten, *A Critical Introduction to International Criminal Law* (Cambridge: Cambridge University Press, 2019).

Stahn, Carsten, *The Law and Practice of the International Criminal Court* (New York, NY: Oxford University Press, USA, 2015).

Stahn, Carsten & Göran Sluiter, eds, *The Emerging Practice of the International Criminal Court* (Leiden: Brill Nijhoff, 2008).

Steinberg, Gerald, Anne Herzberg & Jordan Berman, *Best Practices for Human Rights and Humanitarian NGO Fact-Finding* (Leiden: Brill Nijhoff, 2012).

Steinberg, Gerald, Anne Herzberg & Jordan Berman, *The Need for Standardized Fact-Finding Methodology* (Leiden: Brill Nijhoff, 2012).

Stephen, James Fitzjames, *A History of the Criminal Law of England*, Cambridge Library Collection – British and Irish History, 19th Century (Cambridge: Cambridge University Press, 2014).

Swart, A H J, Alexander Zahar & Göran Sluiter, *The Legacy of the International Criminal Tribunal for the Former Yugoslavia* (Oxford: Oxford University Press, 2011).

Thayer, James Bradley, *A Preliminary Treatise on Evidence at the Common Law* (Boston, MA: Little, Brown, and Company, 1898).

Thoolen, Hans & Berth Verstappen, *Human Rights Missions: A Study of the Fact-Finding Practice of Non-Governmental Organizations* (Dordrecht, Boston: Martinus Nijhoff, 1986).

Tonry, Michael, *Sentencing Policies and Practices in Western Countries*, Crime and Justice 45 (Chicago: University of Chicago Press, 2016).

Tonry, Michael & Richard Frase, *Sentencing and Sanctions in Western Countries* (Oxford: Oxford University Press, 2001).

Trifftener, Otto, *Commentary on the Rome Statute of the International Criminal Court* (München: C.H. Beck Hart Nomos, 2008).

Trifftener, Otto & Kai Ambos, *The Rome Statute of the International Criminal Court: A Commentary*, 3d ed (München: Beck/Hart, 2016).

Truth and Reconciliation Commission of Canada, Honouring the Truth, Reconciling for the Future: Summary of the Final Report of the Truth and Reconciliation Commission of Canada (Vancouver: The Truth and Reconciliation Commission of Canada, 2015).

Twining, William, Theories of Evidence: Bentham and Wigmore. (London: Weidenfeld and Nicolson, 1985).

Twining, William L, Rethinking evidence: Exploratory Essays, 2nd ed, Law in Context (Cambridge: Cambridge University Press, 2006).

Twining, William & David Miers, *How to Do Things with Rules: A Primer of Interpretation* (Cambridge: Cambridge University Press, 1999).

Vitkauskas, Dovydas & Grigoriy Dikov, *Protecting the right to a fair trial under the European Convention on Human Rights* (Strasbourg: Council of Europe, 2012).

Watson, Alan, *Legal Origins and Legal Change* (London: A&C Black, 1991).

Watson, Alan, *Legal Transplants: An Approach to Comparative Law* (Athens, GA: University of Georgia Press, 1993).

Weisbord, Noah, *The Crime of Aggression* (Princeton, NJ: Princeton University Press, 2019).

Weisbord, Noah & Carla Reyes, "War Crimes", in Mangai Nararayan, ed, *International Crime and Justice* (Cambridge: Cambridge University Press, 2011).

Wigmore, John Henry, *The Principles of Judicial Proof: As Given by Logic, Psychology, and General Experience, and Illustrated in Judicial Trials*, 20th-century legal treatises ; fiches 20,854–20,867 (Boston: Little, Brown, and Co, 1913).

Yabi, Gilles & Andrew Goodwin, "From Linas-Marcoussis to the Ouagadougou Political Agreement", Hany Besada, ed, *From Civil Strife to Peace Building* (Berlin: De Gruyter, 2009) 17–32.

Cases

Carter v Canada (Attorney General), [2015] 1 SCR 331.

DPP *v Boardman*, [175] AC421.

Makin v Attorney General for New South Wales, [1894] [1984] AC57.

Prosecutor v Jejnil Delalic and others, 1998 ICTY.
R v Borde, 2003 Court of Appeal for Ontario.
R v Bui, 2014 Court of Appeal for Ontario.
R v Burns, [1994] 1 SCR 656.
R v Defaveri, 2014 Court of Appeal for British Columbia.
R v Dipnarine, 2014 Court of Appeal of Alberta.
R v Ewanchuk, [1999] 1 SCR 330.
R v Gladue, [1999] 1 SCR 688.
R v Hamilton, 2004 Court of Appeal for Ontario.
R v Handy, [2002] 2 SCR 908.
R v Ipeelee, [2012] 1 SCR 433.
R v Khela, [2009] 1 SCR 104.
R v Khelawon, [2006] 2 SCR 787.
R v Lifchus, [1997] 3 SCR 320.
R v Morris, 2021 Court of Appeal for Ontario.
R v Sheppard, [2002] 1 SCR 869.
R v Steane, [1947] KB 997, (1948) 32 Cr App R 61, .
R v Villaroman, [2016] 1 SCR 1000.
R v W(D), [1991] 1 SCR 742.
Taxquet v Belgium, 2010 ECtHR [GC].
The Prosecutor v Bosco Ntaganda, International Criminal Court.
The Prosecutor v Dominic Ongwen, International Criminal Court.
The Prosecutor v Jean-Pierre Bemba Gombo, ICC.
The Prosecutor v Laurent Gbagbo and Charles Blé Goudé, International Criminal Court.
The Prosecutor v Mathieu Ngudjolo Chui, International Criminal Court.
The Prosecutor v Simone Gbagbo, International Criminal Court.
The Prosecutor v Thomas Lubanga Dyilo, International Criminal Court.
The Prosecutor v William Samoei Ruto and Joshua Arap Sang, International Criminal Court.
Victor v Nebraska, 511 US 1 (1994), [1994] 511 US 1.
Woolmington v DPP, [1935] UKHL 1 | United Kingdom House of Lords, Judgment, Law, casemine.com, [1935] [1935] UKHL 1.

Secondary Sources: Journals

Aksenova, Marina, "The Modes of Liability at the ICC: The Labels That Don't Always Stick" (2015) 15:4 Int'l Crim L Rev 629–664.

All, Jeannine Wood, "The nature of memory: Controversies about retrieved memories and the law of evidence" (1998) 26:2 The Journal of Psychiatry & Law 151–218.

Allen, Ronald J & Gerald TG Seniuk, "Two Puzzles of Juridical Proof" (1997) 76 Can B Rev 65.

Allen, Tim, "Understanding Alice: Uganda's Holy Spirit Movement in Context" (1991) 61:3 Africa: Journal of the International African Institute 370–399.

Alvarez, Jose E, "Contemporary International Law: An Empire of Law or the Law of Empire" (2008) 24:5 Am U Int'l L Rev 811–842.

Ambos, Kai, "Intime Conviction' in Germany. Conceptual Foundations, Historical Development and Current Meaning" (2023) 4 Quaestio facti Revista internacional sobre razonamiento probatorio 167–189.

Ambos, Kai, "Critical issues in the Bemba confirmation decision" (2009) 22:4 Leiden Journal of International Law 715–726.

Ambos, Kai, "International Criminal Law at the Crossroads: From Ad Hoc Imposition to a Treaty Based Universal System" (2011) Future Perspectives on International Criminal Justice 161–177.

Ambos, Kai, "International Criminal Procedure: 'Adversarial', 'Inquisitorial' or Mixed?" (2003) 3:1 International Criminal Law Review 1–37.

Ambos, Kai, "The first judgment of the International Criminal Court (Prosecutor v. Lubanga): A Comprehensive Analysis of the Legal Issues" (2012) 12:2 Int Crim Law Rev 115–153.

Ambos, Kai, "The Status, Role and Accountability of the Prosecutor of the International Criminal Court: A Comparative Overview on the basis of 33 National Reports" (2000) 8 Eur J Crime Crim L & Crim Just 89.

Ambos, Kai, "'Witness Proofing' before the International Criminal Court: A Reply to Karemaker, Taylor, and Pittman" (2008) 21:4 Leiden Journal of International Law 911–916.

Ambos, Kai & Dennis Miller, "Structure and Function of the Confirmation Procedure before the ICC from a Comparative Perspective" (2007) 7:2 & 3 Int'l Crim L Rev 335–360.

Amoore, Louise, "Risk before Justice: When the Law Contests Its Own Suspension" (2008) 21:4 LJIL 847–861.

Ashworth, Andrew, "Four Threats to the Presumption of Innocence" (2006) 123:1 S African LJ 63–97.

Atkinson, Ronald R, "The Evolution of Ethnicity among the Acholi of Uganda: The Precolonial Phase" (1989) 36:1 Ethnohistory 19–43.

Bailey, Sydney D, "Un Fact-Finding and Human Rights Complaints" (1972) 48:2 International Affairs (Royal Institute of International Affairs 1944-) 250–266.

Baines, Erin K, "Complex Political Perpetrators: Reflections on Dominic Ongwen" (2009) 47:2 The Journal of Modern African studies 163–191.

Barrett, Jastine C, "Child Soldiers and the Defence of Duress under International Criminal Law" (2020) 38:4 Nordic Journal of Human Rights 341–344.

Basedow, Jürgen, "Comparative Law and Its Clients" (2014) 62:4 The American Journal of Comparative Law 821–857.

Bassiouni, M Cherif, "A Functional Approach to General Principles of International Law" (1989) 11:3 Mich J Int'l L 768–818.

Bassiouni, M Cherif, "Appraising UN Justice-Related Fact-Finding Missions The Institute for Global Legal Studies Inagural Colloquium: The UN and the Protection of Human Rights" (2001) 5 Wash U JL & Pol'y 35–50.

Bassiouni, M Cherif, "From Versailles to Rwanda in Seventy-Five Years: The Need to Establish a Permanent International Criminal Court" (1997) 10 Harv Hum Rts J 11–62.

Bassiouni, M Cherif, "Human Rights in the Context of Criminal Justice: Identifying International Procedural Protections and Equivalent Protections in National Constitutions" (1992) 3:2 Duke J Comp & Int'l L 235–298.

Bassiouni, M Cherif, "International Crimes: 'Jus Cogens' and 'Obligatio Erga Omnes'" (1996) 59:4 Law and Contemporary Problems 63–74.

Bassiouni, M Cherif, "International Recognition of Victims' Rights" (2006) 6:2 Human Rights Law Review 203–279.

Bassiouni, M Cherif, "Justice and Peace: The Importance of Choosing Accountability over Realpolitik War Crimes Research Symposium: The Role of Justice in Building Peace" (2003) 35:2 Case W Res J Int'l L 191–204.

Bassiouni, M Cherif, "Searching for Peace and Achieving Justice: The Need for Accountability Accountability for International Crime and Serious Violations of Fundamental Human Rights" (1996) 59:4 Law & Contemp Probs 9–28.

Bassiouni, M Cherif, "The ICC – Quo Vadis?" (2006) 4:3 Journal of International Criminal Justice 421–427.

Bassiouni, M Cherif, "The Time Has Come for an International Criminal Court" (1991) 1 Ind Int'l & Comp L Rev 1–44.

Bassiouni, M Cherif, "Universal Jurisdiction for International Crimes: Historical Perspectives and Contemporary Practice" (2002) Post-Conflict Justice 945–1001.

Bassiouni, M Cherif, "World War I: The War to End All Wars and the Birth of a Handicapped International Criminal Justice System" (2001) 30:3 Denv J Int'l L & Pol'y 244–291.

Bassiouni, M Cherif & Christopher L Blakesley, "The Need for an International Criminal Court in the New International World Order" (1992) 25:2 Vand J Transnat'l L 151–182.

Bassiouni, M & Peter Manikas, "The law of the International Criminal Tribunal for the Former Yugoslavia" (1996) College of Law Faculty 1092.

Beaumont, Paul R, "The jurisprudence of the European Court of Human Rights and the European Court of Justice on the Hague Convention on International Child Abduction" (2008) 335 Recueil des cours 9–104.

Beltran Montoliu, Ana, "Judicial Impartiality and Evidence at the International Criminal Court Dossier: Criminal Procedure Systems and Judicial Impartiality" (2018) 4:2 Rev Brasileira de Direito Processual Penal 605–644.

Bensouda, Fatou, "The ICC Statute – An Insider's Perspective on a Sui Generis System for Global Justice" (2010) 36 NCJ Int'l L & Com Reg.

Beresford, Stuart, "Unshackling the Paper Tiger – The Sentencing Practices of the Ad Hoc International Criminal Tribunals for the Former Yugoslavia and Rwanda" (2001) 1:1 and 2 Int'l Crim L Rev 33–90.

Berkowitz, Daniel, Katharina Pistor, Jean-Francois Richard, "The Transplant Effect" (2003) 51 Am J Comp L 163.

Boas, Gideon, "Creating Laws of Evidence for International Criminal Law: The ICTY and the Principle of Flexibility" (2001) 12:1 Criminal Law Forum 41–90.

Boas, Gideon John, "A Code of Evidence and Procedure for International Criminal Law? The Rules of the ICTY" (2004) International Criminal Law Developments in the Case Law of the ICTY 1–33.

Bocchese, Marco, "Gbagbo's Lost Bet: When Inviting External Judicial Scrutiny Backfires" (2019) 23:10 The International Journal of Human Rights 1648–1672.

Bradley, M M, "Determining the Intensity Threshold in a Mosaic of Non-International Armed Conflicts from Lubanga to Ongwen: The Contribution of the International Criminal Court to a Cumulative Assessment Approach" (2021) 84:2 THRHR 199–217.

Branch, Adam, "Dominic Ongwen on trial: The ICC's African dilemmas" (2017) 11:1 30–49.

Caianiello, M, "First Decisions on the Admission of Evidence at ICC Trials: A Blending of Accusatorial and Inquisitorial Models?" (2011) 9:2 Journal of International Criminal Justice 385–410.

Caianiello, Michele, "Law of Evidence at the International Criminal Court: Blending Accusatorial and Inquisitorial Models" (2011) 36:2 NCJ Int'l L & Com Reg 287–318.

Carcano, Andrea, "Sentencing and the Gravity of the Offence in International Criminal Law" (2002) 51:3 Int Comp Law Q 583–609.

Carter, Kim, "Proof Beyond a Reasonable Doubt?: Collecting Evidence for the International Criminal Tribunal for the Former Yugoslavia" (1994) 31 Canadian Yearbook of International Law/Annuaire canadien de droit international 235–263.

Cassese, Antonio, "Reflections on International Criminal Justice" (1998) 61:1 MLR 1–10.

Chen-Wishart, Mindy, "Legal Transplant and undue Influence: Lost in Translation or a Working Misunderstanding?" (2013) 62:1 International & Comparative Law Quarterly 1–30.

Chifflet, Pascale & Ian Freckelton, "The Mental Incapacity Defence in International Criminal Law: Ramifications from the Ongwen Trial Judgment" (2022) 1:aop International Criminal Law Review 1–29.

Clermont, Kevin M & Emily Sherwin, "A Comparative View of Standards of Proof" (2002) 50:2 Am J Comp L 243–275.

Cogan, Jacob Katz, "The Problem of Obtaining Evidence for International Criminal Courts" (2000) 22:2 Hum Rts Q 404–427.

Cohen, Moshe, "The Burden of Proof in Comparative and International Human Rights Law: Civil and Common Law Approaches with Special Reference to the American and German Legal Systems" (1999) 93:2 AJIL 556–559.

Cole, Tony, "Review: Larry Laudan: Truth, Error, and Criminal Law: An Essay in Legal Epistemology" (2007) 27:6 Philosophy in Review (Edmonton) 286–288.

Combs, Nancy Amoury, "Evidentiary Deficiencies in International Criminal Law: Tracing the Trajectory from Ignored to Integral to Irrelevant" (2022) 22:5–6 ICLR 835–846.

Combs, Nancy Amoury, "Grave Crimes and Weak Evidence: A Fact-Finding Evolution in International Criminal Law" (2017) 58:1 Harv Int'l LJ 47–126.

Corda, Alessandro, "Sentencing and Penal Policies in Italy, 1985 to 2015: The Tale of a Troubled Country" (2016) 45 Sentencing Policies and Practices in Western Countries 108.

Coundouriotis, Eleni, "The Child Soldier Narrative and the Problem of Arrested Historicization" (2010) 9:2 J Hum Rights 191–206.

Coutts, J A, "No Case to Answer: A Postscript" (1963) 27 J Crim L 68.

Cras, Steven & Anže Erbežnik, "The Directive on the Presumption of Innocence and the Right to Be Present at Trial" (2016) Eucrim, online: <https://doi.org/10.30709/eucrim-2016-002>.

Crenshaw, Mariah, "Innocence Lost: From Child to Perpetrator of International Crimes Literary Review" (2018) 10:1 Amsterdam LF 23–26.

Cross, Jane E, "A Summary of Legal System Amalgamation: An Introduction to Judge Patrick L. Robinson's Observations on the Hybrid Nature of the Rules of Procedure and Evidence of the International Criminal Tribunal for the Former Yugoslavia Articles & Essays" (2009) 16:1 ILSA J Int'l & Comp L 1–4.

Cryer, Robert, "Witness Evidence before the International Criminal Tribunals" (2003) 2:3 Law & Prac Int'l Cts & Tribunals 411–440.

Dalaman, Zeynep Banu & Türkan Melis Parlak, "Child Soldier Reality in Uganda: International Law and Reintegration" (2020) 10:2 Border Crossing 189–202.

Damaška, Mirjan, "Evidentiary Barriers to Conviction and two Models of Criminal Procedure: A Comparative Study" (1973) 121:3 University of Pennsylvania Law Review 506–589.

Damaška, Mirjan, "The Competing Visions of Fairness: The Basic Choice for International Criminal Tribunals" (2010) 36 NCJ Int'l L & Com Reg 365.

Damaška, Mirjan, "Truth in Adjudication" (1997) 49 Hastings LJ 289.

Damaška, Mirjan R, "A Continental Lawyer in an American Law School: Trials and Tribulations of Adjustment" (1968) 116:8 U Pa L Rev 1363 17.

Damaška, Mirjan R, "Epistemology and Legal Regulation of Proof" (2003) 2:2 Law, Probability and Risk 117–130.

Damaška, Mirjan R, "Free Proof and Its Detractors" (1995) 43:3 The American Journal of Comparative Law 343–357.

Damaška, Mirjan R, "Of Hearsay and Its Analogues: The Hearsay Reform Conference" (1991) 76:3 Minn L Rev 425–458.

Damaška, Mirjan R, "Presentation of Evidence and Factfinding Precision" (1974) 123 U Pa L Rev 1083.

Dana, Shahram, "Revisiting the Blaskic Sentence: Some Reflections on the Sentencing Jurisprudence of the ICTY Comments" (2004) 4:3 Int'l Crim L Rev 321–348.

Davern Wright, R J, "Practice: Submission of No Case to Answer: Election Not to Call Evidence Notes and Comments" (1948) 4:1 Res Judicatae 49–52.

DeFrancia, Cristian, "Due Process in International Criminal Courts: Why Procedure Matters" (2001) 87:7 Virginia Law Review 1381–1439.

Delmas-Marty, Mireille, "The Contribution of Comparative Law to a Pluralist Conception of International Criminal Law" (2003) 1:1 Journal of International Criminal Justice 13–25.

Denov, Myriam & Anaïs Cadieux Van Vliet, "Children born of Wartime Rape on Fatherhood: Grappling with Violence, Accountability, and Forgiveness in Postwar Northern Uganda" (2020) Peace and Conflict: Journal of Peace Psychology.

Derham, Roger, Nicole Derham, "From Ad hoc to Hybrid: The Rules and Regulations Governing Reception of Expert Evidence at the International Criminal Court" (2010) 14:1 Int'l J Evidence & Proof 25–56.

Dickson-Gõmez, Julia, "Growing up in Guerrilla Camp: The Long-Term Impact of Being a Child Soldier in El Salvador's Civil War" (2002) 30:4 Ethos 327–356.

Djalovski, Inbal, "Prosecutor v. Laurent Koudou Gbagbo: Judgment on the Appeal Against the Decision of Pre-Trial Chamber I on Jurisdiction and Stay of the Proceedings (Int'l. Crim. CT.)" (2014) 53:3 International Legal Materials 477–501.

Doherty, Joseph W & Richard H Steinberg, "Punishment and Policy in International Criminal Sentencing: An Empirical Study" (2016) 110:1 AJIL 49–81.

Doherty, Justice T A, "Evidence in International Criminal Tribunals: Contrast between Domestic and International Trials" (2013) 26:4 LJIL 937–945.

Dolidze, Anna, "Bridging Comparative and International Law: Amicus Curiae Participation as a Vertical Legal Transplant" (2015) 26:4 EJIL 851–880.

Drumbl, Mark A, "A Former Child Soldier in The Hague, as an Accused" (2016) 1 African Yearbook on International Humanitarian Law.

Drumbl, Mark A, "Child Soldiers and Clicktivism: Justice, Myths, and Prevention" (2012) 4:3 Journal of Human Rights Practice 481–485.

Drumbl, Mark A, "Children, Armed Violence and Transition: Challenges for International Law & Policy Children and International Criminal Justice Conference" (2014) 43:3 Ga J Int'l & Comp L 623–628.

Drumbl, Mark A, "Restorative Justice and Collective Responsibility: Lessons for and from the Rwandan Genocide" (2002) 5:1 Contemporary Justice Review 5–22.

Drumbl, Mark A, "Sclerosis: Retributive Justice and the Rwandan Genocide" (2000) 2:3 Punishment & Society 287–307.

Drumbl, Mark A, "The Effects of the Lubanga Case on Understanding and Preventing Child Soldiering" (2012) 15 Yearbook of International Humanitarian Law 87–116.

Drumbl, Mark A, "Victims who Victimise" (2016) 4:2 London Rev Int Law 217–246.

Drumbl, Mark A & Kenneth S Gallant, "Sentencing Policies and Practices in the International Criminal Tribunals" (2002) 15 Fed Sent R 140.

Dubinsky, Andrew, "An Examination of International Sentencing Guidelines and a Proposal for Amendments to the International Criminal Court's Sentencing Structure Note" (2007) 33:2 New Eng J on Crim & Civ Confinement 609–638.

Dufraimont, Lisa, "Limited Admissibility and Its Limitations" (2013) 46 UBCL Rev 241.

Dufraimont, Lisa, "Realizing the Potential of the Principled Approach to Evidence in Memory of Ron Delisle" (2013) 39:1 Queen's LJ 11–40.

Edwards, Harry T, "Comments on Mirjan Damaska's of Evidentiary Transplants Symposium: Civil Procedure Reform in Comparative Context" (1997) 45:4 Am J Comp L 853–860.

Evensen, Jens, "Evidence before International Courts" (1955) 25 Nordisk Tidsskrift Int'l Ret 44–62.

Ewing, Benjamin & Lisa Kerr, "Reconstructing Gladue" (2024) 74:2 University of Toronto Law Journal 156–197.

Ezennia, Celestine Nchekwube, "The Modus Operandi of the International Criminal Court System: An Impartial or a Selective Justice Regime" (2016) 16:3 Int'l Crim L Rev 448–479.

Fairlie, Megan, "The Marriage of Common and Continental Law at the ICTY and Its Progeny, Due Process Deficit" (2004) 4:3 Int'l Crim L Rev 243–320.

Fassassi, Idris, "Understanding the ICC Prosecutor through the Game of Chess" (2014) 36:1 Loy LA Int'l & Comp L Rev 35–64.

Faulkner, Frank, "Kindergarten Killers: Morality, Murder and the Child Soldier Problem" (2001) 22:4 Third World Quarterly 491–504.

Ferencz, Benjamin B, "International Criminal Code and Court: Where They Stand and Where They're Going" (1992) 30 Colum J Transnat'l L 375.

Ferencz, Benjamin B, "International Criminal Courts: The Legacy of Nuremberg" (1998) 10 Pace Int'l L Rev 203.

Findlay, Mark, "International Criminal Trial and Access to Justice" (2002) 2:3 Int'l Crim L Rev 237–260.

Findlay, Mark, "Synthesis in Trial Procedures: The Experience of International Criminal Tribunals" (2001) 50:1 Int'l & Comp LQ 26–53.

Findlay, Mark & Julia Grix, "Challenging Forensic Evidence: Observations on the Use of DNA in Certain Criminal Trials" (2002) 14:3 Current Issues Crim Just 269–282.

Findley, Keith A, "Adversarial Inquisitions: Rethinking the Search for the Truth" (2011) 56 NYL Sch L Rev 911.

Fisher, Adrian S, "Outlawry of War and Disarmament" Recueil des cours t 133 (1971-II) 389–412.

Fitzmaurice, G G, "The Juridical Clauses of the Peace Treaties" Recueil des cours t 73 (1948-II) 255–367.

Fitzmaurice, Gerald, "The Contribution of the Institute of International Law to the Development of International Law" Recueil des cours t 138 (1973-I) 203–260.

Fitzmaurice, Gerald, "The General Principles of International Law Considered from the Standpoint of the Rule of Law" Recueil des cours t 92 (1957-*II*) 1–227.

Ford, Stuart, "Can the International Criminal Court Succeed? An Analysis of the Empirical Evidence of Violence Prevention" (2019) 43:2 Loy LA Int'l & Comp L Rev 101–124.

Franck, Thomas M, "Fairness in the International Legal and Institutional System: General Course on Public International Law" Recueil des cours t 240 (1993) 9–498.

Frase, Richard S, "Comparative Criminal Justice as a Guide to American Law Reform: How Do the French Do It, How Can We Find Out, and Why Should We Care" (1990) 78 Calif L Rev 539.

Frase, Richard S, "Historical and Comparative Perspectives on the Exceptional Severity of Sentencing in the United States" (2004) 36:1 The George Washington International Law Review 227.

Frase, Richard S, "Main-Streaming Comparative Criminal Justice: How to Incorporate Comparative and International Concepts and Materials into Basic Criminal Law and Procedure Courses Comparative Law Symposium: Is There a European Advantage in Criminal Procedure" (1997) 100:4 W Va L Rev 773–798.

Frase, Richard S, "Sentencing Principles in Theory and Practice" (1997) 22 Crime and Justice 363–433.

Frase, Richard S, "The Search for the Whole Truth about American and European Criminal Justice" (2000) 3:2 Buffalo Criminal Law Review 785–849.

Frase, Richard S & Thomas Weigend, "German Criminal Justice as a Guide to American Law Reform: Similar Problems, Better Solutions" (1995) 18:2 B C Int'l & Comp L Rev 317–360.

Freeland, Steven & Pernille Walther, "Reimagining the Unimaginable? Reflections on Mark A. Drumbl's Vision of Child Soldiers" (2017) 11:1 Criminal Law and Philosophy 37–48.

Freeman, Lindsay & Raquel Vazquez Llorente, "Finding the Signal in the Noise" (2021) 19:1 JICJ 163–188.

Fresnedo De Aguirre, Cecilia, "Public Policy: Common Principles in the American States (Volume 379)" Recueil des cours t 379 (2016) (Recueil des cours).

Friedman, Richard D, "A Presumption of Innocence, Not of Even Odds Commentary" (1999) 52:4 Stan L Rev 873–888.

Friman, Håkan, "Inspiration from the International Criminal Tribunals When Developing Law on Evidence for the International Criminal Court" (2003) 2:3 Law & Prac Int'l Cts & Tribunals 373–400.

Friman, Håkan, "The International Criminal Court: Investigations Into Crimes Committed in the DRC and Uganda. What Is Next?" (2004) 13:4 African Security Studies 19–27.

Gacka, Patryk, "Can Duress Exclude Criminal Responsibility of Former Child Soldiers? The Case of Dominic Ongwen Before the International Criminal Court" (2020) 82 Studia Iuridica 78–100.

Gaja, Giorgio, "The Protection of General interests in the International Community. General Course on Public International Law (2011)" Recueil des cours t 364 (2012) (Recueil des cours) 9–185.

Garcia-Amador, Francisco V, "State Responsibility: Some New Problems" Recueil des cours t 94 (1958-*II*) 365–491.

Gavrilović Nilsson, Mirjana, "Julie Fraser and Brianne McGonigle Leyh (eds), *Intersections of Law and Culture at the International Criminal Court*" (2022) Journal of International Criminal Justice mqab077.

Ghareh Baghi, Venus, "Critical Study on Mental Incapacity in International Criminal Court" (2011) 2011:2 Acta U Danubius Jur 78–86.

Goldbach, Toby S, "Why Legal Transplants?" (2019) 15:1 Annual Review of Law and Social Science 583–601.

Goudkamp, James, "Bad Character Evidence and Reprehensible Behaviour" (2008) 12:2 Int'l J Evidence & Proof 116–140.

Gray, Kevin R, "Introduction: Papers Presented at the British Institute of International and Comparative Law Conference on Evidence before International Criminal Tribunals" (2003) 2:3 Law Pract Int Courts Trib 369–372.

Green, L C, "Comparative Law as a Source of International Law" (1967) 42:1 Tul L Rev 52–66.

Gurmendi, Silvia A Fernández de & Håkan Friman, "The Rules of Procedure and Evidence of the International Criminal Court" (2000) 3 Yearbook of International Humanitarian Law 289–336.

Hamilton, Rebecca J, "The ICC's Exit Problem" (2014) 47:1 NYU J Int'l L & Pol 1–58.

Hamilton, Tomas, "Case Admissibility at the International Criminal Court" (2015) 14:2 Law & Prac Int'l Cts & Tribunals 305–317.

Hammash, Abdelsalam A & Ahmad M AL Louzi, "The Rules of Procedure and Evidence in Front of International Criminal Courts: A System Sui Generis" (2014) 24 JL Pol'y & Globalization [i]–53.

Hampton, Jean, "Correction Harms versus Righting Wrongs: The Goal of Retribution" (1991) 39:6 UCLA L Rev 1659–1702.

Hans, Valerie P, "Trial by Jury: Story of a Legal Transplant" (2017) 51:3 Law & Society Review 471–499.

Harder, Justin, "Future Perspective on the Disposition of the Insane and the Unfit to Stand Trial in the International Criminal Court, A Articles and Commentaries" (2010) 8 NZ YB Int'l L 145–166.

Hassan-Morlai, Patrick Matthew, "Evidence in International Criminal Trials: Lessons and Contributions from the Special Court for Sierra Leone" (2009) 3:1 Afr J Legal Stud 96–118.

Hammash, Abdelsalam A & Ahmad M AL Louzi, "The Rules of Procedure and Evidence in Front of International Criminal Courts: A System Sui Generis" (2014) 24 JL Pol'y & Globalization [i]–53.

Hampton, Jean, "Correction Harms versus Righting Wrongs: The Goal of Retribution" (1991) 39:6 UCLA L Rev 1659–1702.

Hans, Valerie P, "Trial by Jury: Story of a Legal Transplant" (2017) 51:3 Law & Society Review 471–499.

Harder, Justin, "Future Perspective on the Disposition of the Insane and the Unfit to Stand Trial in the International Criminal Court, A Articles and Commentaries" (2010) 8 NZ YB Int'l L 145–166.

Hassan-Morlai, Patrick Matthew, "Evidence in International Criminal Trials: Lessons and Contributions from the Special Court for Sierra Leone" (2009) 3:1 Afr J Legal Stud 96–118.

Hassellind, Filip Strandberg, "The International Criminal Trial as a Site for Contesting Historical and Political Narratives: The Case of Dominic Ongwen" (2021) 30:5 Social & Legal Studies 790–809.

Heller, Kevin Jon, "Radical complementarity" (2016) 14:3 Journal of International Criminal Justice 637–665.

Henham, Ralph, "Procedural Justice and Human Rights in International Sentencing" (2004) 4:2 Int'l Crim L Rev 185–210.

Henham, Ralph, "Sentencing Theory, Proportionality and Pragmatism" (2000) 28:3 International Journal of the Sociology of Law 239–263.

Henham, Ralph, "Some Issues for Sentencing in the International Criminal Court" (2003) 52:1 Int Comp Law Q 81–114.

Henham, Ralph, "Theory and Contextual Analysis in Sentencing" (2001) 29:3 International Journal of the Sociology of Law 253–276.

Henham, Ralph, "Theory, Rights and Sentencing Policy" (1999) 27:2 International Journal of the Sociology of Law 167–183.

Henham, Ralph & Mark Findlay, "Criminal Justice Modelling and the Comparative Contextual Analysis of Trial Process" (2002) 2 International Journal of Comparative Criminology 162.

Henham, Ralph & Grazla Mannozzi, "Victim Participation and Sentencing in England and Italy: a Legal and Policy Analysis" (2003) 11 Eur J Crime Crim L & Crim Just 278.

Ho, Hock Lai, "Comparative Observations on the Burden of Proof for Criminal Defences" (2011) 9:2 Int'l Comment on Evidence [i]–25.

Hodgson, Jacqueline, "Conceptions of the Trial in Inquisitorial and Adversarial Procedure" (2006) Judgment and Calling to Account, A Duff, L Farmer, S Marshall and V Tadros, eds 223–42.

Hodgson, Jacqueline, "Hierarchy, Bureaucracy, and Ideology in French Criminal Justice: Some Empirical Observations" (2002) 29:2 Journal of Law and Society 227–257.

Hole, Adrian, "The Sentencing Provisions of the International Criminal Court" (2005) 1:1 IJPS 37–69.

Huxley, Andrew, "Jeremy Bentham on Legal Transplants" (2007) 2 J Comp L 177.

Ipinyomi, Foluke, "Is Cote d'Lvoire a Test Case for R2P: Democratization as Fulfillment of the International Community's Responsibility to Prevent" (2012) 56:2 J Afr L 151–174.

Issa, Layal, "Avoiding the Third Tragedy: Evaluating Criminal Responsibility of Child Soldiers under International Law" (2019) 34:1 Temp Int'l & Comp LJ 61–93.

Jackson, John, "Finding the Best Epistemic Fit for International Criminal Tribunals: Beyond the Adversarial–Inquisitorial Dichotomy" (2009) 7:1 J Int Crim Justice 17–39.

Jackson, John & Yassin M'Boge, "The Effect of Legal Culture on the Development of International Evidentiary Practice: From the Robbing Room to the Melting Pot Hague International Tribunals: International Criminal Courts and Tribunals: Symposium: Expertise, Uncertainty, and International Law" (2013) 26:4 LJIL 947–970.

Jackson, Robert H, "The Rule of Law Among Nations" (1945) 31:6 American Bar Association Journal 290–294.

Jakšić, Milena, "Looking for the Child Soldier: The Judicial Investigation in the case of Thomas Lubanga Dyilo" (2020) 4:1 Journal of Legal Anthropology 46–70.

Janssen, Sander, "Mental Condition Defences in Supranational Criminal Law" (2004) 4:1 Int'l Crim L Rev 83–98.

Kabano, Jacques, "The Criminal Responsibility of Child Soldier Under International Criminal Law, Case Study: Northern Uganda and Democratic Republic of Congo (DRC)" (2017) 2:2 E-Journal of Law 15–29.

Kan, Gamaliel, “The Prosecution of a Child Victim and a Brutal Warlord: The Competing Narrative of Dominic Ongwen” (2018) 70–82.

Karemaker, Ruben, B Don Taylor & Thomas Wayde Pittman, “Witness Proofing in International Criminal Tribunals: Response to Ambos” (2008) 21:4 LJIL 917–923.

Karemaker, Ruben, B Don Taylor & Thomas Wayde Pittman, “Lost in Translation: International Criminal Tribunals and the Legal Implications of Interpreted Testimony” (2008) 41:1 Vanderbilt Journal of Transnational Law, online: <https://papers.ssrn.com/abstract=1511946>.

Katzman, Rachel, “The Non-Disclosure of Confidentiality Exculpatory Evidence and the Lubanga Proceedings: How the ICC Defense System Affects the Accused’s Right to a Fair Trial” (2009) 8:1 Nw U J Int’l Hum Rts 77–101.

Kawano, Mariko, “The Role of Judicial Procedures in the Process of the Pacific Settlement of International Disputes” Recueil des cours t 346 (2009) (Recueil des cours) .

Keen, Peter Carmichael, “Tempered Adversariality: The Judicial Role and Trial Theory in the International Criminal Tribunals” (2004) 17:4 LJIL 767–814.

Keïta, Xavier-Jean, “Disclosure of Evidence in the Law and Practice of the ICC” (2016) 16:6 Int Crim Law Rev 1018–1047.

Kerr, Lisa, “The Legitimate Scope of Criminal Law: A Question for Legal History?” (2017) 4 Critical Analysis L 11.

Kersten, Mark, “The ICC and the Road to Juba” in *Justice in Conflict* (Oxford: Oxford University Press, 2016).

Kielsgard, Mark, “Sentencing Insights in the International Crimes Court of Cambodia” (2011) 3:1 City U HK L Rev 43–64.

Kielsgard, Mark D, “The Legality Principle in Sentencing at the ECCC: Making Up Law as It Goes Along?” (2012) 2:1 Asian Journal of International Law 119–136.

Kirabira, Tonny Raymond & Leila Delphine Choukroune, “Dominic Ongwen: ICC Conviction of Former Child Soldier Establishes ‘Forced Pregnancy’ as a War Crime” (2021).

Kirabira, Tonny Raymond & Mugero Jesse, “Dominic Ongwen Conviction: A Move towards Gender Sensitive International Criminal Justice” (2021) Women, Peace and Security.

Kirsch, Stefan, “The Trial Proceedings before the ICC” (2006) 6 Int Crim Law Rev 275–292.

Kiyala, Jean Chrysostome K, “Responding to Epistemic Injustice against Child Soldiers” (2021) 29:3 The International Journal of Children’s Rights 662–700.

Klamberg, Mark, “Fact-Finding in International Criminal Procedure: How Collection of Evidence May Contribute to Testing of Alternative Hypotheses” (2011) SSRN Journal, online: <http://www.ssrn.com/abstract=1847710>.

Klamberg, Mark, "The Alternative Hypothesis Approach, Robustness and International Criminal Justice: A Plea for a 'Combined Approach' to Evaluation of Evidence" (2015) 13:3 J Int Criminal Justice 535–553.

Klamberg, Mark, "What Are the Objectives of International Criminal Procedure: Reflections on the Fragmentation of a Legal Regime" (2010) 79:2 Nordic J Int'l L 279–302.

Kress, Claus, "The Procedural Law of the International Criminal Court in Outline: Anatomy of a Unique Compromise" (2003) 1:3 JICJ 603–617.

Krug, Peter, "The Emerging Mental Incapacity Defense in International Criminal Law: Some Initial Questions of Implementation" (2000) 94:2 AJIL 317–335.

Krzan, Bartlomiej, "Admissibility of Evidence and International Criminal Justice Admissibility of Evidence in Criminal Process. Between the Establishing of the Truth, Human Rights and the Efficiency of Proceedings" (2021) 7:1 Rev Brasileira de Direito Processual Penal 161–188.

Ladd, Mason, "The Relationship of the Principles of Exclusionary Rules of Evidence to the Problem of Proof" (1933) 18 Minn L Rev 506.

Langbein, John H, "Historical Foundations of the Law of Evidence: A View from the Ryder Sources" (1996) 96 Colum L Rev 1168.

Langbein, John H, "The Criminal Trial before Lawyers" (1978) 45:2 The University of Chicago Law Review 263–316.

Langbein, John H, "The Origins of Public Prosecution at Common Law" (1973) 17 Am J Legal Hist 313.

Langbein, John H, "Trashing the German Advantage" (1987) 82 Nw UL Rev 763.

Langbein, John H & Lloyd L Weinreb, "Continental Criminal Procedure: Myth and Reality" (1977) 87 Yale LJ 1549.

Langert, Mfximo & Joseph W Dohertyft, "Managerial Judging Goes International, but Its Promise Remains Unfulfilled: An Empirical Assessment of the ICTY Reforms" (2011) 36:2 Yale J Int'l L 241–306.

Lanz, David, "The ICC's Intervention in Northern Uganda: Beyond the Simplicity of Peace vs. Justice" (2007) The Fletcher School of Law and Diplomacy.

Larson, Carlton FW, "The Origins of Adversary Criminal Trial in America" (2023) 57 UC Davis L Rev 1.

Piragoff Donald, in Lee, R. S. K.; Friman, H. The International Criminal Court : Elements of Crimes and Rules of Procedure and Evidence; Transnational Publishers: Ardsley, NY, 2001, pp. 349–401 in 349.

Legate, Barbara L, "The Admissibility of Demonstrative Evidence in Jury Trials: Applying the Principled Approach to the Law of Evidence" (2006) 31 Advoc Q 316.

Legrand, Pierre, "European Legal Systems are not Converging" (1996) 45:1 ICLQ 52–81.

Legrand, Pierre, "The Impossibility of 'Legal Transplants'" (1997) 4:2 MJ 111–124.

Lemmings, David, "Criminal Trial Procedure in Eighteenth-Century England: The Impact of Lawyers" (2005) 26:1 The Journal of Legal History 73–82.

Levi, Ron, John Hagan & Sara Dezalay, "International Courts in Atypical Political Environments: The Interplay of Prosecutorial Strategy, Evidence, and Court Authority in International Criminal Law – The Variable Authority of International Courts" (2016) 79:1 Law & Contemp Probs [i]–314.

Levin, Anthony, "Making the Invisible Visible: Photographic Trials in Neil Abramson's Soldier Child" (2013) 44:2 Research in African Literatures 105–124.

Lundqvist, Ulf S, "Admitting and Evaluating Evidence in the International Criminal Tribunal for the Former Yugoslavia Appeals Chamber Proceedings. A Few Remarks HAGUE INTERNATIONAL TRIBUNALS: International Criminal Tribunal for the Former Yugoslavia" (2002) 15:3 LJIL 641–666.

Lyons, Beth S, "Enough is Enough: the Illegitimacy of International Criminal Convictions: A Review Essay of *Fact-Finding Without Facts, The Uncertain Evidentiary Foundations of International Criminal Convictions* by Nancy Amoury Combs" (2011) 13:3 Journal of Genocide Research 287–312.

Mackey, Allison, "Troubling Humanitarian Consumption: Reframing Relationality in African Child Soldier Narratives" (2013) 44:4 Research in African Literatures 99–122.

Malu, Linus Nnabuike, "The International Criminal Court and the Complex Road to Peace in Cote d'Ivoire" (2016) 16:5 Int'l Crim L Rev 826–855.

Mann, Howard, "International Law and the Child Soldier" (1987) 36:1 Int'l & Comp LQ 32–57.

Marchesi, Diletta, "Intercepted Communications in the Ongwen Case: Lessons to Learn on Documentary Evidence at the ICC" (2021) 1:aop Int Crim Law Rev 1–21.

Mariniello, Triestino, "Questioning the Standard of Proof Symposium: Proof in International Criminal Trials" (2015) 13:3 J Int'l Crim Just 579–600.

Mason, J K, "Expert Evidence in the Adversarial System of Criminal Justice" (1986) 26:1 Med Sci & L 8–12.

Mastey, David, "Child Soldier Stories and Their Fictions" (2016) 18:1 Interventions 143–158.

May, "Evidence before the International Criminal Tribunal for the Former Yugoslavia: An Overview" (1999) 1:4 International law forum (Hague, Netherlands) 197–201.

May, Richard & Marieke Wierda, "Trends in International Criminal Evidence: Nuremberg, Tokyo, The Hague, and Arusha Essays on the Laws of War and War Crimes Tribunals in Honor of Teleford Taylor" (1998) 37:3 Colum J Transnat'l L 725–766.

Mayans-Hermida, Beatriz E., & Barbora Holá, "Punishing Atrocity Crimes in Transitional Contexts: Advancing Discussions on Adequacy of Alternative Criminal Sanctions Using the Case of Colombia" (2023) 43:1 Oxford Journal of Legal Studies 1-31

Mbakwe, Tom, "Côte d'Ivoire: The Laurent Gbagbo Saga – The Story behind the Story", online: <https://newafricanmagazine.com/17893/>.

McClelland, Gregory A, "A Non-adversary Approach to International Criminal Tribunals" (2002) 26:1 Suffolk Transnat'l L Rev 1–38.

McCormick, Mark, "Scientific Evidence: Defining a New Approach to Admissibility" (1981) 67 Iowa L Rev 879.

McDermott, Yvonne, "Inferential Reasoning and Proof in International Criminal Trials: The Potentials of Wigmorean Analysis" (2015) 13:3 JICJ 507–533.

McDermott, Yvonne, "Strengthening the Evaluation of Evidence in International Criminal Trials" (2017) 17 Int C L R 682–702.

McDermott, Yvonne & Colin Aitken, "Analysis of Evidence in International Criminal Trials Using Bayesian Belief Networks" (2017) 16:2–3 Law, Prob & Risk 111–130.

Mcdermott, Yvonne & John D Jackson, "Evidence and Proof in the Practice of the International Criminal Tribunal for Rwanda" (2015) 26:3–4 Criminal Law Forum 347–349.

McQueen, Ally, "Falling Through the Gap: The Culpability of Child Soldiers Under International Criminal Law" (2018) 94 Notre Dame L Rev Online 91.

Megret, Frederic, "Beyond Fairness: Understanding the Determinants of International Criminal Procedure" (2009) 14:1 UCLA J Int'l L Foreign Aff 37–76.

Meintjes-Van der Walt, Lirieka, "Decision-Makers' Dilemma: Evaluating Expert Evidence" (2000) 13:3 S Afr J Crim Just 319–343.

Meron, Theodor, "From Nuremberg to the Hague Nuremberg and the Rule of Law: A Fifty-Year Verdict" (1995) 149 Mil L Rev 107–112.

Meron, Theodor, "International Criminalization of Internal Atrocities" (1995) 89:3 AJIL 554–577.

Meron, Theodor, "International Law in the Age of Human Rights: General Course on Public International Law" Recueil des cours t 301 (2003) 9–489.

Meron, Theodor, "Is International Law Moving towards Criminalization?" (1998) 9:1 EJIL 18–31.

Meron, Theodor, "Procedural Evolution in the ICTY" (2004) 2 J Int'l Crim Just 520.

Meron, Theodor, "Rape as a Crime under International Humanitarian Law" (1993) 87:3 AJIL 424–428.

Minkova, Liana Georgieva, "Expressing What? The Stigmatization of the Defendant and the ICC's Institutional Interests in the Ongwen Case" (2021) 34:1 LJIL 223–245.

Miraglia, Michela, "Admissibility of Evidence, Standard of Proof, and Nature of the Decision in the ICC Confirmation of Charges in Lubanga Symposia: Lubanga Before the ICC" (2008) 6:3 J Int'l Crim Just 489–504.

Miraglia, Michela, "First Decision of the ICC Pre-Trial Chamber Notes and Comments" (2006) 4:1 J Int'l Crim Just 188–195.

Mnookin, Jennifer L, "Atomism, Holism, and the Judicial Assessment of Evidence" (2013) 60:6 UCLA Law Review 1524-.

Moffett, Luke, "Reparations for 'Guilty Victims': Navigating Complex Identities of Victim–Perpetrators in Reparation Mechanisms" (2016) 10:1 International Journal of Transitional Justice 146–167.

Mohamed, Saira, "Of Monsters and Men: Perpetrator Trauma and Mass Atrocity" (2015) 115:5 Colum L Rev 1157–1216.

Mouctar Bah, Thierno, "Addressing Cote d'Ivoire's Deeper Crisis" (2012) 19:3 Africa Security Brief, online: <https://apps.dtic.mil/sti/citations/ADA559233>.

Mousourakis, George, "Legal Transplants and Legal Development: A Jurisprudential and Comparative Law Approach" (2013) 54:3 Acta Juridica Hungarica 219–236.

Mousourakis, George, "Transplanting Legal Models Across Culturally Diverse Societies: A Comparative Law Perspective" (2010) 57 Osaka University Law Review 87–106.

Mundis, Daryl A, "From 'Common Law' Towards 'Civil Law': The Evolution of the ICTY Rules of Procedure and Evidence" (2001) 14:2 Leiden Journal of International Law 367–382.

Mundis, Daryl A, "The Legal Character and Status of the Rules of Procedure and Evidence of the ad hoc International Criminal Tribunals" (2001) 1:3 and 4 Int'l Crim L Rev 191–240.

Murphy, Peter, "Excluding Justice or Facilitating Justice – International Criminal Law Would Benefit from Rules of Evidence" (2008) 12:1 Int'l J Evidence & Proof 1–31.

Murphy, Peter, "No Free Lunch, No Free Proof : The Role of Defence in International Criminal Trials" (2010) 8:2 J Int'l Crim Just 539–574.

Murphy, Peter & Lina Baddour, "International Criminal Law: Celebrating Its Achievements, Fearing for Its Future" (2013) 55:2 S Tex L Rev 307–338.

Nerlich, Volker, "The Confirmation of Charges Procedure at the International Criminal Court: Advance or Failure Tribute Issue: Antonio Cassese's International Criminal Justice: IV. Institutions and Procedures" (2012) 10:5 J Int'l Crim Just 1339–1356.

Newton, Michael, "The Chameleon Court: The Changing Face of the ICC Critical Assessments of International Criminal Courts" (2009) 27:1 Law Context: A Socio-Legal J 5–32.

Newton, Michael, "The Complementarity Conundrum: Are We Watching Evolution or Evisceration?" (2010) 8 Santa Clara Journal of International Law 115.

Ngane, Sylvia Ntube, "Witnesses before the International Criminal Court" (2009) 8:3 Law & Prac Int'l Cts & Tribunals 431–458.

Niv, Ady, "The Schizophrenia of the No Case to Answer Test in International Criminal Tribunals" (2016) 14:5 J Int'l Crim Just 1121–1138.

Nortje, Windell, "Victim or Villain: Exploring the Possible Bases of a Defence in the Ongwen Case at the International Criminal Court" (2016) 17:1 Int'l Crim L Rev 186–207.

Nyamutata, Conrad, "Young Terrorists or Child Soldiers? ISIS Children, International Law and Victimhood" (2020) 25:2 Journal of Conflict and Security Law 237–261.

Nyeko, Oryem & Harriet Aloyocan, "Community Perceptions on Dominic Ongwen" (2015) Justice and Reconciliation Project Situational Brief, online: <www.justiceandreconciliation.com>.

O'Brian, William E Jr, "Court Scrutiny of Expert Evidence: Recent Decisions Highlight the Tensions" (2003) 7:3 Int'l J Evidence & Proof 172–184.

Okafor, Obiora C, "International Human Rights Fact-Finding Praxis in Its Living Forms: A Twail Perspective" (2014) 1 Transnat'l Hum Rts Rev 59–105.

Okonkwo, C O, "The Submission of No Case to Answer in Criminal Proceedings" (1972) 6 Nigerian LJ 1–15.

Olasolo, Hector, "The Prosecutor of the ICC before the Initiation of Investigations: A Quasi-Judicial or a Political Body" (2003) 3:2 Int'l Crim L Rev 87–150.

Omeri, Sheryn, "Guilty Pleas and Plea Bargaining at the ICC: Prosecutor v. Ongwen and Beyond" (2016) 16:3 Int Crim Law Rev 480–502.

Oosterveld, Valerie, "The International Criminal Court and the Closure of the Time-Limited International and Hybrid Criminal Tribunals" (2010) 8:1 Loy U Chi Int'l L Rev 13–32.

Paciocco, David M, "Context, Culture and the Law of Expert Evidence" (2001) 24 Advoc Q 42.

Paciocco, David M, "Coping with Expert Evidence about Human Behaviour" (1999) 25 Queen's LJ 305.

Pananjung, Dino Panji & Sigar Aji Poerana, "Former Child Soldiers: Product of Armed Conflicts and How the International Criminal Court Fails so See Its Significance" (2019) 3:2 Padjadjaran Journal of International Law 181–201.

Pananjung, Mochammad Dino Panji & Resha Roshana Putri, "A Former Child Soldier Perpetrator: The Application of Article 31 (1)(a) of Rome Statute" 3:5 AJHSSR 31–40.

Pangalangan, Raphael Lorenzo Aguiling, "Dominic Ongwen and the Rotten Social Background Defense: The Criminal Culpability of Child Soldiers Turned War Criminals" (2017) 33 Am U Int'l L Rev 605.

Parlopiano, Brandon T, "The Burden of Proving Insanity in the Medieval Lus Commune" (2012) 72:2 Jurist 515–543.

Paulsson, J, "Issues arising from Findings of Denial of Justice" (2020) The Hague Academy Collected Courses Online / Recueil des cours de l'Académie de La Haye en ligne (Collected Courses of the Hague Academy of International Law) .

Piccolino, Giulia, "David against Goliath in Côte d'Ivoire? Laurent Gbagbo's war against global governance" (2012) 111:442 African Affairs 1–23.

Piccolino, Giulia, "One Step Forward, Two Steps Back? Côte d'Ivoire's 2015 Presidential Polls" (2016) 51:1 Africa Spectrum 97–110.

Pickard, Daniel B, "Proposed Sentencing Guidelines for the International Criminal Court" (1997) 20:1 Loy LA Int'l & Comp LJ 123–164.

Piragoff, Donald K, "Evidence", in Otto Trifftener, ed, *Commentary on the Rome Statute of the International Criminal Court* (München: C.H. Beck Hart Nomos, 2008).

Pizzi, William, "Overcoming Logistical and Structural Barriers to Fair Trials at International Tribunals" (2007) 4:1 Int'l Comment on Evidence [i], online: <https://www.degruyter.com/document/doi/10.2202/1554-4567.1051/html>.

Pizzi, William T & Mariangela Montagna, "The Battle to Establish an Adversarial Trial System in Italy" (2003) 25 Mich J Int'l L 429.

Plachta, Michael & Afrah Tahir, "International Criminal Court and Ad Hoc Courts Section I" (2020) 36:8 IELR 293–297.

Plender, Richard, "Procedure in the European Courts: Comparisons and Proposals" Recueil des cours t 267 (1997) 9–343.

Politi, Mauro & Federica Gioia, "The Criminal Procedure before the International Criminal Court: Main Features Special Issue: Papers Presented at the Symposium: New International Tribunals and New International Proceedings, Organized by the University LUISS Guido Carli of Rome in Collaboration with the IILA (Istituto Italo-latinoamericano) and the Italian Ministry of Education, University and Research" (2006) 5:1 Law & Prac Int'l Cts & Tribunals 103–124.

Posner, Richard A, "An Economic Approach to the Law of Evidence" (1998) 51 Stan L Rev 1477.

Posner, Richard A, "Statutory Interpretation: In the Classroom and in the Courtroom" (1983) 50:2 The University of Chicago law review 800–822.

Posner, Richard A, "What Do Judges and Justices Maximize? (The Same Thing Everybody Else Does)" (1993) 3 Supreme Court Economic Review 1–41.

Powles, Steven, "International Criminal Courts: Practice, Procedure and Problems Relating to Evidence – Privilege from Testimony at the ICTY and the ICTR" (2003) 2:3 Law & Prac Int'l Cts & Tribunals 467–478.

Qing, Tian, "On Two Approaches to Communication of Evidence to the Pre-trial Chamber" (2016) 67 (FICHL Policy Brief Series) 4.

Ramos, Carse, "Dominic Ongwen on Trial: Problematizing Definitional Boundaries and Exploring the Possibilities of Socialization" in *Research Handbook on Child Soldiers* (Edward Elgar Publishing, 2019).

Rasmussen, Mary Ann, "Rules of Evidence for the International Criminal Court" (1995) 64:2 Nordic J Int'l L 275–292.

Redmayne, Mike, "Expert Evidence and Scientific Disagreement Symposium: International Perspectives on Scientific Evidence" (1996) 30:4 UC Davis L Rev 1027–1080.

Risacher, Benjamin J, "No Excuse: The Failure of the ICC's Article 31 Duress Definition Note" (2013) 89:3 Notre Dame L Rev 1403–1426.

Roben, Volker, "Procedure of the ICC: Status and Function of the Prosecutor, The Focus: ICC and International Criminal Law" (2003) 7 Max Planck YB UN L 513–552.

Robinson, D, "International Criminal Law as Justice" (2013) 11:3 Journal of international criminal justice 699–711.

Robinson, Darryl, "Inescapable Dyads: Why the International Criminal Court Cannot Win" (2015) 28, no.2 Leiden Journal of International Law 323–347.

Robinson, Patrick L, "Rough Edges in the Alignment of Legal Systems in the Proceedings at the ICTY" (2005) 3:5 JICJ 1037–1058.

Rodman, Kenneth A & Petie Booth, "Manipulated Commitments: The International Criminal Court in Uganda" (2013) 35:2 Human Rights Quarterly 271–303.

Roht-Arriaza, Naomi, "The New Landscape of Transitional Justice – Transitional Justice in the Twenty-First Century" in *Transitional Justice in the Twenty-First Century: Beyond Truth versus Justice* (Cambridge University Press, 2006) 1.

Roodt, Christa, "A Historical Perspective on the Accusatory and Inquisitorial Systems" (2004) 2004:10 Fundamina: A Journal of Legal History 137–158.

Rothe, Dawn L & Angela Overton, "The International Criminal Court and the External Non-Witness Expert(s), Problematic Concerns: An Exploratory Endeavor" (2010) 10:3 Int'l Crim L Rev 345–364.

Roht-Arriaza, Naomi, "The New Landscape of Transitional Justice: Transitional Justice in the Twenty-First Century" in *Transitional Justice in the Twenty-First Century: Beyond Truth versus Justice* (Cambridge University Press, 2006) 1.

Roodt, Christa, "A Historical Perspective on the Accusatory and Inquisitorial Systems" (2004) 2004:10 Fundamina: A Journal of Legal History 137–158.

Rothe, Dawn L & Angela Overton, "The International Criminal Court and the External Non-Witness Expert(s), Problematic Concerns: An Exploratory Endeavor" (2010) 10:3 Int'l Crim L Rev 345–364.

Rudstein, David S, "Retrying the Acquitted in England Part III: Prosecution Appeals against Judges' Rulings of No Case to Answer" (2011) 13:1 San Diego Int'l LJ 5–128.

Sánchez, Sofía Campos et al, "Procedural Issues Concerning ICC Trial Chamber Is No Case To Answer Decision in the Gbagbo and Blé Goudé Case".

Sander, Barrie, "History on Trial: Historical Narrative Pluralism within and beyond International Criminal Courts" (2018) 67:3 ICLQ 547–576.

Scaliotti, Massimo, "Defences before the International Criminal Court: Substantive Grounds for Excluding Criminal Responsibility – Part 2" (2002) 2:1 Int'l Crim L Rev 1–46.

Schabas, William, "Sentencing by International Tribunals: A Human Rights Approach" (1997) 7:2 Duke Journal of Comparative & International Law 461–518.

Schabas, William A, "Complementarity in Practice': Some Uncomplimentary Thoughts" (2008) 19:1 Criminal law forum 5–33.

Schabas, William A, "Relationships Between International Criminal Law and Other Branches of International Law" (2021) The Hague Academy Collected Courses Online / Recueil des cours de l'Académie de La Haye en ligne (Collected Courses of the Hague Academy of International Law).

Schabas, William A, "Sentencing by International Tribunals: A Human Rights Approach Symposium: Justice in Cataclysm Criminal Trials in the Wake of Mass Violence" (1996) 7:2 Duke J Comp & Int'l L 461–518.

Schabas, William A, "The Banality of International Justice" (2013) 11:3 Journal of International Criminal Justice 545–551.

Schabas, William A, "The International Criminal Court at Ten" (2011) 22:4 Criminal Law Forum 493–509.

Schabas, William A, "Victor's Justice: Selecting Situations at the International Criminal Court" (2009) 43 J Marshall L Rev 535.

Schabas, William A & Yvonne McDermott, "Article 66: Presumption of Innocence" (2015) Ambos, KO The Rome Statute of the International Criminal Court: A Commentary Baden-Baden: Nomos Verlagsgesellschaft mbH & Co KG 1635–1649.

Schlesinger, Rudolf B, "Comparative Criminal Procedure: A Plea for Utilizing Foreign Experience" (1976) 26 Buff L Rev 361.

Schmitt, Bertram, "Legal Diversity at the International Criminal Court: Reflections of a Judge" (2021) 19:3 Journal of International Criminal Justice 485–510.

Schuon, Christine, "The Appeals Decision in the ICC's Jean-Pierre Bemba Gombo Case on the Trial Chamber's Decision on the Admission into Evidence of Materials Contained in the Prosecution's List of Evidence Hague International Tribunals: International Criminal Courts and Tribunals" (2012) 25:2 LJIL 511–520.

Schwebel, Stephen M, "Aggression, Intervention and Self-Defence in Modern International Law" Recueil des cours t 136 (1972-*II*) 411–497.

Schweizer, Mark, "Comparing Holistic and Atomistic Evaluation of Evidence" (2014) 13:1 Law, Probability and Risk 65–89.

Schwöbel, Christine E J, "The Comfort of International Criminal Law" (2013) 24:2 Law Critique 169–191.

Silva Santaularia, Natalia, "Mental Insanity at the International Criminal Court: Proposal for a New Regulation" (2014) Available at SSRN 2533743.

Skilbeck, Rupert, "Frankenstein's Monster: Creating a New International Procedure" (2010) 8:2 JICJ 451–462.

Sluiter, Göran, "I Beg You, Please Come Testify – The Problems Absence of Subpoena Powers at the ICC" (2009) 12:4 New Crim L Rev 590–608.

Sluiter, Göran, "Obtaining Evidence for the International Criminal Tribunal for the Former Yugoslavia: An Overview and Assessment of Domestic Implementing Legislation" (1998) 45:1 Netherlands international law review 87–113.

Sluiter, Göran, "The Law of International Criminal Procedure and Domestic War Crimes Trials" (2006) 6:4 JICJ 605–635.

Sorvatzioti, Demetra Fr, "Free Evaluation of Evidence: Does the ICC Need a Law of Evidence?" (2021), 22(5–6), International Criminal Law Review, 895–919.

Sorvatzioti, Demetra Fr, "Proportionality and Moral Blameworthiness in Ongwen's ICC Sentencing Decision" (2023) 23:5–6 International Criminal Law Review 755–781.

Sorvatzioti, Demetra & Allan Manson, "Burden of Proof and L'intime Conviction: Is the Continental Criminal Trial Moving to the Common Law?" (2019) 23 CCLR 107–129.

Souris, Renée Nicole, "Virtue Ethics, Criminal Responsibility, and Dominic Ongwen" (2019) 19:3 International Criminal Law Review 475–504.

Souris, Renée Nicole, "What Is so Wrong with Using Child Soldiers?" (2021) The International Journal of Human Rights 1–26.

Spencer, John R, "Adversarial vs Inquisitorial Systems: Is There Still such a Difference?" (2016) 20:5 The International Journal of Human Rights 601–616.

Stapleton, Sara, "Ensuring a Fair Trial in the International Criminal Court: Statutory Interpretation and the Impermissibility of Derogation" (1998) 31 NYUJ Int'l L & Pol 535.

Stauffer, Jill, "How to Be the Crux of a Diachronic Plot: Levinas, Questions and Answers, and Child Soldiering in International Law, in Four Acts" (2021) 14 Levinas Studies 151–164.

Stauffer, Jill, "Law, Politics, the Age of Responsibility, and the Problem of Child Soldiers" (2020) 16:1 Law, Culture and the Humanities 42–52.

Steffen, Thomas L, "Truth as Second Fiddle: Reevaluating the Place of Truth in the Adversarial Trial Ensemble" (1988) Utah L Rev 799.

Stewart, Hamish, "Justice Frank Iacobucci and the Revolution in the Common Law of Evidence" (2007) 57:2 The University of Toronto Law Journal 479–497.

Stockdale, Michael & Adam Jackson, "Expert Evidence in Criminal Proceedings: Current Challenges and Opportunities Special Issue: Expert Evidence" (2016) 80:5 J Crim L 344–363.

Sungi, Simeon P & George R Kakoti, "Abducted, inducted, and indicted. The case of Dominic Ongwen in the International Criminal Court" in *The Routledge Handbook of African Law* (Routledge) 528.

Swart, B, "Damaska and the Faces of International Criminal Justice" (2008) 6:1 JICJ 87–114.

T Rosenberg, Sophie, "The International Criminal Court in Côte d'Ivoire: Impartiality at Stake?" (2017) 15:3 Journal of International Criminal Justice 471–490.
T Rosenberg, Sophie, "The International Criminal Court in Côte d'Ivoire: Impartiality at Stake?" (2017) 15:3 Journal of International Criminal Justice 471–490.
Taruffo, Michele, "Rethinking the Standards of Proof" (2003) 51:3 The American Journal of Comparative Law 659–677.

Thorburn, Malcolm & Allan Manson, "The Sentencing Theory Debate: Convergence in Outcomes, Divergence in Reasoning" (2007) 10:2 New Criminal Law Review: An International and Interdisciplinary Journal 278–310.
Thorburn, Malcolm & Allan Manson, "The Sentencing Theory Debate: Convergence in Outcomes, Divergence in Reasoning" (2007) 10:2 New Criminal Law Review: An International and Interdisciplinary Journal 278–310.
Tobin, John, "The Psychiatric Defence and International Criminal Law" (2007) 23:2 Medicine, Conflict and Survival 111–124.

Tochilovsky, Vladimir, "International Criminal Justice: 'Strangers in the Foreign System'" (2004) 15:3 Criminal Law Forum 319–344.

Tochilovsky, Vladimir, "Trial in International Criminal Jurisdictions: Battle or Scrutiny" (1998) 6:1 Eur J Crime Crim L & Crim Just 55–59.

Trindade, Antônio Augusto Cançado, "Co-existence and Co-ordination of Mechanisms of International Protection of Human Rights: At Global and Regional Levels" Recueil des cours t 202 (1987) 9–435.

Turner, Jenia Iontcheva, "Limits on the Search for Truth in Criminal Procedure: A Comparative View" in *Comparative Criminal Procedure* (Edward Elgar Publishing, 2016) 35.

Vagias, Michail & Janos Ferencz, "Burden and Standard of Proof in Defence Challenges to the Jurisdiction of the International Criminal Court Hague International Tribunals: International Criminal Courts and Tribunals" (2015) 28:1 LJIL 133–156.

Van Den Berg, Stephanie & Amedee Mwarabu, "Congolese Ex-Vice President Bemba Acquitted of War Crimes on Appeal | Reuters", 8 June 2018, online: <https://www.reuters.com/article/world/icc-overturns-war-crimes-conviction-of-congolese-politician-bemba-idUSKCN1J4267/>.

Van Koppen, Peter J & Steven D Penrod, "Adversarial or Inquisitorial: Comparing Systems" in *Adversarial versus Inquisitorial Justice: Psychological Perspectives on Criminal Justice Systems* (New York, NY: Plenum, 2003) 2–20.

Van Wallendael, Kacper, "Legal transplants: Profitable Borrowing or Harmful Dependency? The Use of the Legal Transplant Framework for the Adoption of EU Law: The Case of Croatia", in Agnieszka et al., eds, *Evolving Dependency Relations: Old and New Approaches* (Poznań: Revolutions Research Center, 2014) 75–98.

Vogler, Richard, "Reform Trends in Criminal Justice: Spain, France and England & (and) Wales" (2005) 4 Wash U Global Stud L Rev 631.

Volkmann-Schluck, Thomas, "Continental European Criminal Procedures: True or Illusive Model" (1981) 9 Am J Crim L 1.

Vos, Christian M De, "Investigating from Afar: The ICC's Evidence Problem" (2013) 26:4 LJIL 1009–1024.

Wald, Patricia M, "CTY Judicial Proceedings: An Appraisal from Within" (2004) 2:2 JICJ 466–473.

Wallach, Evan J, "The Procedural and Evidentiary Rules of the Post-World War II Crimes Trials: Did They Provide an Outline for International Legal Procedure Essays on the Laws of War and War Crimes Tribunals in Honor of Teleford Taylor" (1998) 37:3 Colum J Transnat'l L 851–884.

Ward, Kevin, "'The Armies of the Lord': Christianity, Rebels and the State in Northern Uganda, 1986-1999" (2001) 31:2 Journal of Religion in Africa 187–221.

Watson, Alan, "Comparative Law and Legal Change" (1978) 37:2 The Cambridge Law Journal 313–336.

Watson, Alan, "From Legal Transplants to Legal Formants" (1995) 43 Am J Comp L 469.

Watson, Alan, "Legal Change: Sources of Law and Legal Culture" (1982) 131 U Pa L Rev 1121.

Weigend, Thomas, "Assuming that the Defendant Is Not Guilty: The Presumption of Innocence in the German System of Criminal Justice" (2014) 8:2 Criminal Law, Philosophy 285–299.

Weigend, Thomas, "Is the Criminal Process about Truth: A German Perspective Law and Truth" (2003) 26:1 Harv J L & Pub Pol'y 157–174.

Weigend, Thomas, "Should We Search for the Truth, and Who Should Do It" (2010) 36:2 NCJ Int'l L & Com Reg 389–416.

Wierda, Marieke, "International Criminal Evidence: New Directions" (2003) 2:3 Law & Prac Int'l Cts & Tribunals 401–410.

Xavier, Isabelle, "The Incongruity of the Rome Statute Insanity Defence and International Crime" (2016) 14:4 J Int'l Crim Just 793–814.

Zaldivar-Giuffredi, Alessandra M, "Simone Gbagbo: First Lady of Cote D'Ivoire, First Woman Indicted by the International Criminal Court, One Among Many Female Perpetrators of Crimes Against Humanity" (2018) 25 ILSA J Int'l & Comp L 1.

Zilic, Lejla & Semir Mujezinovic, "Admissibility of Illegally Obtained Evidence before the International Criminal Court-Hypothetical Case Professional Papers" (2019) 24 Annals Fac LU Zenica 191–204.

Zounmemou, David, "Côte d'Ivoire's Post-Conflict Challenges" (2011) 2011:4 Conflict Trends 28–37.

Zounmemou, David & Abdul Rahman Lamin, "Côte D'Ivoire's Post-electoral Crisis: Ouattara Rules But Can He Govern? | EISA" (2011) 10:2 Journal of African Elections 8–9.

Zounmenou, David, "Côte d'Ivoire's Post-Electoral Conflict: What Is at Stake?" (2011) 20:1 African Security Review 48–55.

Secondary Sources: Internet Sites

"ICC a Bunch of Useless People – Museveni", *New Vision* (12 May 2016), online: <https://www.ewvision.co.ug/articledetails/1424384>.

"Joseph Kony Is Still at Large. Here's Why the U.S. and Uganda Were Willing to Give Up the Hunt". The Washington Post (22 April 2017), online: <https://www.washingtonpost.com/news/worldviews/wp/2017/04/22/joseph-kony-is-still-at-large-heres-why-the-u-s-and-uganda-were-willing-to-give-up-the-hunt/>.

"LRA Rebel Dominic Ongwen Surrenders to US Forces in CAR – BBC News" (7 January 2015), online: <https://www.bbc.com/news/world-africa-30705649>.

"'They Killed Them Like It Was Nothing'" (2011) Human Rights Watch, online: <https://www.hrw.org/report/2011/10/05/they-killed-them-it-was-nothing/need-justice-cote-divoires-post-election-crimes>.

"US Offers up to $5m for Leads on Uganda warlord Kony", *BBC News* (3 April 2013), online: <https://www.bbc.com/news/world-africa-22017853>.

"Zambia : Museveni Praises South Africa's Decision to Leave ICC as He Arrives in Zambia for Uhuru celebrations", (23 October 2016), online: <https://www.lusakatimes.com/2016/10/23/museveni-praises-south-africas-decision-leave-icc-arrives-zambia-uhuru-celebrations/>.

Amnesty International, *Cote d'Ivoire: The Victors' Law: The Human Rights Situation Two Years after the Post-Electoral Crisis*, by Amnesty International, AFR 31/001/2013 (2013).

Arnould, Valerie, "The Limits of International Criminal Justice: Lessons from the Ongwen Case", (27 January 2015), online: *Egmont Institute* <http://www.egmontinstitute.be/the-limits-of-international-criminal-justice-lessons-from-the-ongwen-case/>.

Atingo, Jackline, "Watching the ICC Judgement of LRA commander Dominic Ongwen with Ugandan Victims of Enforced Marriage" (February 17 2021) Africa at LSE. Online: https://blogs.lse.ac.uk/africaatlse/2021/02/17/watching-icc-judgement-lra-commander-dominic-ongwen-uganda-victims-rape-marriage/.

Bohórquez Murcia, Daniela et al, *Sentencing Process in Cases Involving Former Child Soldiers at the ICC*, workingPaper, by Daniela Bohórquez Murcia et al, repository.urosario.edu.co, workingPaper (Universidad del Rosario, 2020).

Bradley, Craig M, *The Convergence of the Continental and the Common Law Model of Criminal Procedure* (Springer, 1996).

Buitrago, Lina et al, *The Practice of Abduction and Its Application to the Ongwen's case*, workingPaper, repository.urosario.edu.co, Working Paper (Universidad del Rosario, 2017).

Bouwknegt, Thijs B & Barbora Holá, "Dominic Ongwen: The ICC's Poster and Problem Child" (2020), JusticeInfo, online: <https://www.justiceinfo.net/en/44014-dominic-ongwen-icc-poster-and-problem-child.html>.

Daft, Shireen, *Whither Justice for Former Child Soldiers?* (Australia, Canberra, 2017).

Ferencz, Benjamin, "Ferencz Closes Lubanga Case for ICC Prosecution", (August 2011), online: *Benjamin B Ferencz* <https://benferencz.org/articles/2010-present/ferencz-closes-lubanga-case-for-icc-prosecution/>.

FRANET, "Presumption of Innocence: procedural rights in criminal proceedings – Country research", (31 March 2021), online: *European Union Agency for Fundamental Rights* <https://fra.europa.eu/en/country-data/2021/presumption-innocence-procedural-rights-criminal-proceedings-country-research>.

Gersony, Robert, *The Anguish of Northern Uganda – Section 1 – Uganda* (Government of United States of America, 1997).

Gordon, Gregory S, *Toward an International Criminal Procedure: Due Process Aspirations and Limitations*, SSRN Scholarly Paper, by Gregory S Gordon, papers.ssrn.com, SSRN Scholarly Paper ID 928908 (Rochester, NY: Social Science Research Network, 2006).

Heller, Kevin Jon, "Poor ICC Outreach — Uganda Edition", (22 September 2015), online: *Opinio Juris* <http://opiniojuris.org/2015/09/22/poor-icc-outreach-uganda-edition/>.

Human Rights Watch, *World Report 2014: Côte d'Ivoire*, by Human Rights Watch, Human Rights Watch (2014).

International Federation of Human Rights (FIDH), *Jean-Pierre Bemba Gombo Before the Judges, Report of the FIDH Legal Action Group (LAG)*, by International Federation of Human Rights (FIDH), July 2008-N°502a (1–24).

Heller, Kevin Jon, "The Bemba Case: Heavily criticised, the ICC must maintain victims' legal representation as the establishment of assistance programmes for victims is awaited", (1 October 2018), online: *International Federation for Human Rights* <https://www.fidh.org/en/region/Africa/central-african-republic/the-bemba-case-heavily-criticised-the-icc-must-maintain-victims-legal>.

JusticeInfoNet, Ephrem Rugiririza, "The Rise and Fall of Ivorian Ex-First Lady Simone Gbagbo", (9 March 2017), online: *JusticeInfo.net* <https://www.justiceinfo.net/en/32412-the-rise-and-fall-of-ivorian-ex-first-lady-simone-gbagbo.html>.

Kersten, Mark, "Beyond the Ongwen Verdict: Justice for Government Atrocities in Uganda", (9 February 2021), online: *Justice in Conflict* [*BLOG*] <http://www.proquest.com/docview/2487356402/citation/FC4FD6FAE664483APQ/1>.

Kersten, Mark, "Dominic Ongwen: 'It is very difficult to Balance all that'", (2 February 2021), online: *Justice in Conflict* [*BLOG*] <http://www.proquest.com/docview/2484885618/citation/4B35EDCE37FF4DEDPQ/1>.

Kersten, Mark, "The Dominic Ongwen Trial and the Prosecution of Child Soldiers – A JiC Symposium", (11 April 2016), online: *Justice in Conflict* <https://justiceinconflict.org/2016/04/11/the-dominic-ongwen-trial-and-the-prosecution-of-child-soldiers-a-jic-symposium/>.

Kersten, Mark, "The Life and Trials of Dominic Ongwen: A JiC Symposium", (1 February 2021), online: *Justice in Conflict* [*BLOG*] <http://www.proquest.com/docview/2484288266/citation/832B99EAB6E74C7DPQ/1>.

Kersten, Mark, "'These Conflicts will be Resolved by Law or War.' An Interview with former ICC Judge Howard Morrison", (28 April 2021), online: *Justice in Conflict* <https://justiceinconflict.org/2021/04/28/these-conflicts-will-be-resolved-by-law-or-war-an-interview-with-former-icc-judge-howard-morrison/>.

Kersten, Mark, "Why the ICC Won't Prosecute Museveni", (17 March 2015), online: *Justice Hub* <https://justicehub.org/article/why-the-icc-wont-prosecute-museveni/>.

Kersten, Mark, "Yeah, Right … ICC Officials Say There's No Evidence Against Ugandan Military", (5 May 2016), online: *Justice in Conflict* <https://justiceinconflict.org/2016/05/05/yeah-right-icc-officials-say-theres-no-evidence-against-ugandan-military/>.

Kouassi, Abraham, "After Gbagbo's Return, Traditional Leaders Speak on Reconciliation", (22 June 2021), online: *JusticeInfo.net* <https://www.justiceinfo.net/en/78981-after-gbagbo-return-traditional-leaders-speak-on-reconciliation.html>.

Marinelli, Stefano, "Great Expectations: The International Criminal Court after Gbagbo's Acquittal", (11 February 2019), online: *International Law Blog* <https://internationallaw.blog/2019/02/11/great-expectations-the-international-criminal-court-after-gbagbos-acquittal/>.

Manoba, Joseph A & Anushka Sehmi, "What the Dominic Ongwen Trial Could Mean for Traditional Justice Mechanisms in the ICC" Africa at LSE. LSE Research (26 July 2021), online: https://blogs.lse.ac.uk/africaatlse/2021/07/26/dominic-ongwen-trial-traditional-justice-mechanisms-uganda-international-criminal-court-icc/

Moorehead, Alex & Jemera Rone, *Uprooted and Forgotten Impunity and Human Rights Abuses in Northern Uganda*, by Alex Moorehead & Jemera Rone, Vol.17 No 12 (A) (Human Rights Watch, 2005).

Mugero, Jese, "Transitional Justice in Uganda: The Dilemma of Children Born of War", (24 July 2020), online: *International Law Blog* <https://internationallaw.blog/2020/07/24/transitional-justice-in-uganda-the-dilemma-of-children-born-of-war/>.

Open Society Justice Initiative, *The Trial of Laurent Gbagbo and Charles Blé Goudé at the ICC*.

Otunnu, Olara A, "The Secret Genocide", (October 2009), online: *Foreign Policy* <https://foreignpolicy.com/2009/10/19/the-secret-genocide/>.

Peniguet, Maxence, "Why the ICC acquitted Laurent Gbagbo and Charles Blé Goudé", (17 September 2019), online: *JusticeInfo.net* <https://www.justiceinfo.net/en/42384-why-icc-acquitted-laurent-gbagbo-charles-ble-goude.html>.

Pieter, Nini Els & Tony Raymond Kirabina, "The Ongwen Judgement at the ICC: A Missed Opportunity for Former Child Soldiers?", (22 June 2021), online: *International Law Blog* <https://internationallaw.blog/2021/06/22/the-ongwen-judgement-at-the-icc-a-missed-opportunity-for-former-child-soldiers/>.

Robinson, Darryl, "The Identity Crisis of International Criminal Law", (2008), online: <https://www.cambridge.org/core/journals/leiden-journal-of-international-law/article/identity-crisis-of-international-criminal-law/47836B8BE0B803C6DE8B79306A3906F6>.

Robinson, Darryl, "The Other Poisoned Chalice: Unprecedented Evidentiary Standards in the Gbagbo Case? (Part 1)" (5 November 2019), online: *EJIL: Talk!* <https://www.ejiltalk.org/the-other-poisoned-chalice-unprecedented-evidentiary-standards-in-the-gbagbo-case-part-1/>.

Robinson, Darryl, "The Other Poisoned Chalice: Unprecedented Evidentiary Standards in the Gbagbo Case? (Part 1)", (5 November 2019), online: *EJIL: Talk!* <https://www.ejiltalk.org/the-other-poisoned-chalice-unprecedented-evidentiary-standards-in-the-gbagbo-case-part-1/>.

Robinson, Darryl, "The Other Poisoned Chalice: Unprecedented Evidentiary Standards in the Gbagbo Case? (Part 2)", (6 November 2019), online: *EJIL: Talk!* <https://www.ejiltalk.org/the-other-poisoned-chalice-unprecedented-evidentiary-standards-in-the-gbagbo-case-part-2/>.

Robinson, Darryl, "The Other Poisoned Chalice: Unprecedented Evidentiary Standards in the Gbagbo Case? (Part 3)", (6 November 2019), online: *EJIL: Talk!* <https://www.ejiltalk.org/17618-2/>.

Sander, Barrie, "Why Is Museveni Allowing Dominic Ongwen to be Sent to the ICC?", (15 January 2015), online: *Justice in Conflict* <https://justiceinconflict.org/2015/01/15/why-is-museveni-allowing-dominic-ongwen-to-be-sent-to-the-icc/>.

Sorvatzioti, Demetra, *Why Sentencing Needs a Separate Trial in the Continental System* (Nomos Verlagsgesellschaft mbH & Co. KG, 2020).

Sterio, Milena, "Ongwen Blog Symposium: Precedent on the Prosecution of Juvenile Offenders for International Crimes", (12 April 2021), online: *Armed Groups and International Law* <https://armedgroups-internationallaw.org/2021/04/12/ongwen-blog-symposium-precedent-on-the-prosecution-of-juvenile-offenders-for-international-crimes/>.

Street, Farnam, "The Feynman Technique: Master the Art of Learning", (26 April 2012), online: *Farnam Street* <https://fs.blog/feynman-technique/>.

Vale, Christian, "A Feminist Critique on the Charging of Male Sexual Violence in International Law", (1 July 2021), online: *International Law Blog* <https://internatio

nallaw.blog/2021/07/01/a-feminist-critique-on-the-charging-of-male-sexual-violence-in-international-law/>.

Abducted and Abused: Renewed War in Northern Uganda, Human Rights Watch (Human Rights Watch, 2003).

"Alassane Ouattara", online: *World Bank Live* <https://live.worldbank.org/en/experts/a/alassane-ouattara>.

"An Extremely Rare Interview with Joseph Kony (2006) – YouTube", online: <https://www.youtube.com/watch?v=scMHLWzGOdo>.

Canada's Chief Justice Calls Treatment of First Nations an Attempt at "Cultural Genocide", Beverley McLachlin (2015).

"Coercion and Intimidation of Child Soldiers to Participate in Violence", (16 April 2008), online: *Human Rights Watch* <https://www.hrw.org/news/2008/04/16/coercion-and-intimidation-child-soldiers-participate-violence>.

"Combating Holocaust Denial: Evidence of the Holocaust presented at Nuremberg" in *Holocaust Encyclopedia*.

"Côte d'Ivoire: Impartial Justice Poses Test for Ouattara | Human Rights Watch", (6 October 2011), online: <https://www.hrw.org/news/2011/10/06/cote-divoire-impartial-justice-poses-test-ouattara>.

"Cote d'Ivoire: Silencing the Opposition – 77 Prisoners of Conscience Convicted", online: *Amnesty International* <https://www.amnesty.org/en/documents/afr31/008/1992/en/>.

"Crisis Tracker", online: <https://crisistracker.org/incidents/377274>.

"Eichmann's Mistake: The Problem of Thoughtlessness in International Criminal Law | Canadian Journal of Law & Jurisprudence | Cambridge Core", online: <https://www.cambridge.org/core/journals/canadian-journal-of-law-and-jurisprudence/article/eichmanns-mistake-the-problem-of-thoughtlessness-in-international-criminal-law/56BC8DC684B1C4BAACFDEAF53509E137>.

Hostile to Democracy (Human Rights Watch, 1999).

How to Hold a Former Child Soldier Accountable?: Dominic Ongwen, Kidnapped by the LRA at Age 10, to Face ICC Judgment, Human Rights Watch (Human Rights Watch, 2021).

"ICC: Investigate All Sides in Uganda", (4 February 2004), online: *Human Rights Watch* <https://www.hrw.org/news/2004/02/04/icc-investigate-all-sides-uganda>.

"ICC: Investigate All Sides in Uganda | Human Rights Watch", (4 February 2004), online: <https://www.hrw.org/news/2004/02/04/icc-investigate-all-sides-uganda>.

"ICC-20040129-44, ICC – President of Uganda Refers Situation Concerning the Lord's Resistance Army (LRA) to the ICC", (24 January 2004), online: *International Criminal Court* <http://www.icc-cpi.int/news/icc-president-uganda-refers-situation-concerning-lords-resistance-army-lra-icc>.

"ICC-OTP-20051014-109, Statement by the Chief Prosecutor Luis Moreno–Ocampo on the Uganda Arrest Warrants.Press Conference on the Uganda Arrest Warrants", (14 October 2005), online: *International Criminal Court* <http://www.icc-cpi.int/news/press-conference-uganda-arrest-warrants>.

"Inferential Reasoning and Proof in International Criminal Trials | Journal of International Criminal Justice | Oxford Academic", online: <https://academic.oup.com/jicj/article-abstract/13/3/507/890730>.

"Inferential Reasoning and Proof in International Criminal Trials | Journal of International Criminal Justice | Oxford Academic", online: <https://academic.oup.com/jicj/article/13/3/507/890730?login=true>.

"Is the ICC Targeting Africa Inappropriately? A Moral, Legal, and Sociological Assessment – Queen's University", online: <https://ocul-qu.primo.exlibrisgroup.com/discovery/fulldisplay?docid=cdi_scopus_primary_2_s2_0_84978766038&context=PC&vid=01OCUL_QU:QU_DEFAULT&lang=en&search_scope=OCULDiscoveryNetwork&adaptor=Primo%20Central&tab=OCULDiscoveryNetwork&query=any,contains,Margaret%20M.%20deGuzman,&offset=0&pcAvailability=true>.

"Ivory Coast's Laurent Gbagbo: A Political Fighter Who Won't Quit", (17 June 2021), online: *France 24* <https://www.france24.com/en/africa/20210617-ivory-coast-s-laurent-gbagbo-a-political-fighter-who-won-t-quit>.

"LRA Rebel Dominic Ongwen Surrenders to US Forces in CAR – BBC News", online: <https://www.bbc.com/news/world-africa-30705649>.

"Manipulated Commitments: The International Criminal Court in Uganda on JSTOR", online: <https://www-jstor-org.proxy.queensu.ca/stable/24518017>.

"Mixed Messages: The Sentencing Legacies of the Ad HOC Tribunals – Queen's University", online: <https://ocul-qu.primo.exlibrisgroup.com/discovery/fulldisplay/cdi_scopus_primary_2_s2_0_85098017153/01OCUL_QU:QU_DEFAULT>.

"Northern Uganda | Conciliation Resources", online: <https://www.c-r.org/accord/northern-uganda>.

"Presidential Elections. UNOCI Resources – United Nations Operation in Côte d'Ivoire", online: <https://peacekeeping.un.org/en/mission/past/unoci/elections.shtml>.

"Press Conference on the Uganda Arrest Warrants", online: *International Criminal Court* <http://www.icc-cpi.int/news/press-conference-uganda-arrest-warrants>.

"Prohibition of torture: landmark judgments – The European Convention on Human Rights – www.coe.int", online: *The European Convention on Human Rights* <https://www.coe.int/en/web/human-rights-convention/torture1>.

"Proportional Sentences at the ICTY – Queen's University", online: <https://ocul-qu.primo.exlibrisgroup.com/discovery/fulldisplay/cdi_scopus_primary_2_s2_0_79955418942/01OCUL_QU:QU_DEFAULT>.

"Protracted Conflict, Elusive Peace: Initiatives to End the Violence in Northern Uganda", online: *GSDRC* <https://gsdrc.org/document-library/protracted-conflict-elusive-peace-initiatives-to-end-the-violence-in-northern-uganda/>.

"R. v. Khelawon – SCC Cases", online: <https://decisions.scc-csc.ca/scc-csc/scc-csc/en/item/2332/index.do?q=khelawon>.

"Release From Imprisonment: The Law of Sentencing, Parole and Judicial Review | Office of Justice Programs", online: <https://www.ojp.gov/ncjrs/virtual-library/abstracts/release-imprisonment-law-sentencing-parole-and-judicial-review-0>.

Review of the International Criminal Court and the Rome Statute system | International Criminal Court, Final Report, Final Report (2020).

"Sudan-Uganda: Bashir Says Support for LRA Rebels Has Ceased", (August 2001), online: *ReliefWeb* <https://reliefweb.int/report/sudan/sudan-uganda-bashir-says-support-lra-rebels-has-ceased>.

"The Latest Crisis of the ICC: The Acquittal of Laurent Gbagbo", (28 March 2019), online: *Opinio Juris* <http://opiniojuris.org/2019/03/28/the-latest-crisis-of-the-icc-the-acquittal-of-laurent-gbagbo/>.

The Scars of Death: Children Abducted by the Lord's Resistance Army in Uganda, Human Rights Watch (Human Rights Watch, 1997).

Uganda: UNDHA IRIN Humanitarian Situation Report, 12/4/96 (United Nations, 1996).

Uprooted and Forgotten: Impunity and Human Rights Abuses in Northern Uganda, ocul-qu.primo.exlibrisgroup.com (Human Rights Watch, 2005).

"With Gbagbo and Blé Goudé Acquitted, What Is Next for Victims in Côte d'Ivoire? | International Center for Transitional Justice", online: <https://www.ictj.org/news/gbagbo-and-bl%C3%A9-goud%C3%A9-acquitted-what-next-victims-c%C3%B4te-d%E2%80%99ivoire>.

Index

www.ingramcontent.com/pod-product-compliance
Lightning Source LLC
Chambersburg PA
CBHW051358240926
51852CB00001B/56
9789004741003